Study Guide for

Kalat's

Biological Psychology
Seventh Edition

Elaine M. Hull
State University of New York at Buffalo

WADSWORTH

THOMSON LEARNING

Australia • Canada • Mexico • Singapore • Spain • United Kingdom • United States

For more information, contact
Wadsworth/Thomson Learning
10 Davis Drive
Belmont, CA 94002-3098
USA

For more information about our products, contact us:
Thomson Learning Academic Resource Center
1-800-423-0563
http://www.wadsworth.com

International Headquarters
Thomson Learning
International Division
290 Harbor Drive, 2nd Floor
Stamford, CT 06902-7477
USA

UK/Europe/Middle East/South Africa
Thomson Learning
Berkshire House
168-173 High Holborn
London WC1V 7AA
United Kingdom

Asia
Thomson Learning
60 Albert Complex, #15-01
Singapore 189969

Canada
Nelson Thomson Learning
1120 Birchmount Road
Toronto, Ontario M1K 5G4
Canada

ISBN 0-534-51401-4

PREFACE

When a book is as well written as Kalat's *Biological Psychology*, everything fits together logically and "makes sense." It is easy to acquire a feeling of understanding. However, the sense of security produced by passive understanding is frequently shattered by an exam that requires recall and active reconstruction of the material. One of the earliest psychological principles of learning is that recognition is easier than recall and that passively following an argument is easier than actively reconstructing it. Unfortunately, passively understood material does not become part of us in the same way that actively manipulated material does.

The role of this study guide is to stimulate your active assimilation of the material in Kalat's textbook. Each chapter of the text has its own introductory and concluding summaries and a number of review and discussion questions. Thus the initial reading and review of each chapter is directed by the text itself. The study guide is designed for more comprehensive, in-depth review. The Introduction provides a brief review of each chapter to refresh your memory at the beginning of a study session. Key Terms and Concepts provide a quick overview of the material in outline form. Make sure that each term is familiar, and note its relationship to the overall structure of the chapter. Short-Answer Questions are designed to help you organize information pertinent to specific problems. These questions are listed under headings that refer to the main divisions of the chapter. If you have difficulty answering a question fully, refer to the appropriate section of the text to find the answer. The Multiple-Choice Questions check your knowledge of detail and emphasize points that are easy to get confused. Some may seem picky, but it is better to encounter the confusing detail here rather than on an exam. Answers are listed at the end of the section. A number of chapters have graphics to be labeled or to be used in answering accompanying questions. Each graphic is adapted from or taken directly from the text; you can refer to the appropriate drawing in the text if you have difficulty labeling it. Some chapters have Helpful Hints that suggest analogies or mnemonic devices to help you understand or remember factual information. Finally, there are eight crossword puzzles, each covering one or two chapters. I hope that these provide an enjoyable way to solidify and test your knowledge of the information. The answers are given at the end of the Study Guide.

Biological psychology is full of detailed experimental knowledge and also of contradictions and perplexities. It has important general concepts and broad philosophical implications. A student once asked how anyone could stand to teach a course in which so much is unknown. However, the body does not work in a simple, stereotyped way. There is considerable orderliness about the body, but there is also a great deal of adaptability that gives rise to unresolved questions. The study of brain and behavior may well be the most exciting frontier of knowledge. In contrast to the dismay of the student who wanted knowledge handed out in tidy packets, many others have found that their biological psychology course did more to challenge and enrich their basic philosophy of life than did any other course. I hope that this text and study guide will help make your experiences with biological psychology more like those of the latter students than those of the former.

Thanks to James Kalat, author of *Biological Psychology*, to Victoria Knight, Psychology Publisher for Wadsworth Publishing, and Jennifer Wilkinson, Senior Assistant Editor for the Study Guide. My special thanks go to my husband, Richard T. Hull, a veteran crossword puzzle fan, for his help with the puzzles and many other aspects of this project.

Elaine M. Hull

CONTENTS

1

THE MAJOR ISSUES

INTRODUCTION

Biological psychology is the study of the physiological, ontogenetic (developmental), evolutionary, and functional explanations of behavior. Bird song provides an example of the four types of explanation. Increased testosterone levels during mating season cause a brain area that is important for singing to increase in size, providing a physiological mechanism for singing. Ontogenetic explanations focus both on the genes that prepare for a behavior and on experience during a sensitive period, when a bird must hear the appropriate song. Evolutionary explanations discuss the selection of traits in terms of their adaptive value to the organism. Similar behavior patterns in two different species suggests that those species evolved from a common ancestor. Functional explanations describe the advantages conferred by each trait. For example, a male bird's song attracts a female and deters competition from other males.

Human behavior is also subject to biological explanation. There are a number of theories about the relationship of the mind to the brain. According to the dualist position, the mind and the brain exist independently, but somehow interact. However, that "somehow" causes a problem. Monism holds that there is only one kind of substance, though various theorists differ as to whether that substance is mental, physical, or some combination of the two. The materialist position (a form of monism) holds that everything that exists is material (physical). Mentalism suggests that only the mind really exists. The identity position (another form of monism) proposes that mental processes are the same thing as brain activity but are described in different terms.

David Chalmers proposed that there are "easy problems" concerning the specific application of the term consciousness to wakefulness vs. sleep, or to the focusing of attention, for example. However, the "hard problem" is how *any* kind of brain activity is associated with consciousness. He suggests that consciousness is a fundamental property of matter. On the other hand, Daniel Dennett argues that, once we understand all the easy problems, the hard problem will go away. Finally, Patricia Churchland suggests that it is too soon to know which problems are really the hardest. A major difficulty in studying consciousness is that it is not directly observable. This has led some to a solipsist position: I alone am conscious. However, while few people doubt that other people are conscious, they do question whether other animals, plants, or inanimate objects, including robots, are conscious. Neuroscience cannot resolve the issues of the essence and functional significance of the mind or of its relationship to the brain, but it can contribute relevant data.

Genes are the units of heredity; they maintain their structural identity from one generation to another. Chromosomes and the genes they contain come in pairs, one from each parent. An individual with identical genes of a given pair is said to be homozygous for that gene; an individual with an unmatched pair of genes is heterozygous for that gene. Genes may be dominant or recessive; dominant genes have strong effects in either homozygous or heterozygous individuals, whereas recessive genes have effects only in the homozygous condition. When chromosomes pair up during reproduction, they sometimes break apart and one part attaches to the other chromosome; this is called "crossing over." If two genes are close together on a chromosome, they are less likely to be separated by crossing over than if they are far apart. Sex-linked genes are usually found on the X chromosome; any characteristic produced by a recessive X-linked gene will be observed primarily in males, who do not have a second X chromosome to overrule the recessive gene. Genetic variation is produced by recombination of genes during sexual reproduction and by random mutations. Most

1

mutations are maladaptive and produce recessive genes. Such mutations are not likely to produce harmful effects unless both parents have the same mutant genes.

Heritability is a correlation coefficient that describes the extent to which variations in a characteristic are due to genetic, as opposed to environmental, variations. It is determined either by comparing the resemblance between monozygotic (identical) twins with that between dizygotic (fraternal) twins or by comparing the resemblance of adopted children to their adoptive vs. biological parents. Even traits with high heritability in "standard" conditions may be influenced by environmental interventions. For example, phenylketonuria (PKU) results from a recessive gene that prevents metabolism of the amino acid phenylalanine. The resulting high levels of phenylalanine lead to brain malformations and mental retardation. However, a diet low in phenylalanine can greatly reduce the abnormalities.

DNA (deoxyribonucleic acid, the substance of genes) serves as a template for the synthesis of messenger RNA (ribonucleic acid), which in turn provides a template for the production of structural proteins and enzymes. Genetic influences on behavior may be either relatively direct, via control of brain chemicals, or indirect, by affecting height or physical activity, for example.

Evolution is a change over generations in the frequencies of various genes in a population. Genes that confer a reproductive advantage will become more prevalent in later generations. Neither use nor disuse of a given structure or behavior can cause an evolutionary increase or decrease in that feature, contrary to the theory of Lamarckian evolution. Furthermore, humans have not stopped evolving; medical treatments and welfare programs may increase survival, but may not enhance an individual's reproductive success. Evolution does not necessarily imply improvement, since previous success does not guarantee future success in a changing world. Evolution is based on the benefit for genes, not for individuals or species. Genes for altruistic behavior, for example, may be favored by reciprocal altruism or by kin selection. Sociobiology seeks functional explanations for the evolution of social behaviors. However, these explanations are often speculative. Furthermore, even if genes do predispose us towards certain behavior patterns, we still have flexibility in acting on those predispositions.

The issue of animal experimentation has become controversial. The usefulness of animal research rests both on the similarity across species of many biological functions and on the difficulty or impossibility of conducting such research on humans. In addition, we are interested in animals, both for their own sake and for the light they can shed on human evolution. Some animal rights activists, the "abolitionists", believe that all animals have the same rights as humans and should never be used by humans for any purpose. "Minimalists" agree that some animal research is necessary, but believe that it should be minimized. Valuable clinical treatments of human disorders have been gleaned from animal experiments. However, even though experimenters attempt to minimize pain, and even though animal care committees (which include veterinarians and community members as well as scientists) oversee the research, a certain amount of distress accompanies much animal experimentation. In this case, as in many other ethical issues, it is difficult to gain resolution of the competing values.

KEY TERMS AND CONCEPTS

Module 1.1 The Mind-Brain Relationship
1. Biological explanations of behavior
    No need for organism to understand function

Physiological explanation
    Reduces a behavior to activity of the brain and other organ
    Testosterone and bird song: increase in size of a brain area
Ontogenetic explanation
    Describes the development of a structure or behavior
    Song development: requires both genes and hearing song during early sensitive period
Evolutionary explanation
    Examines a structure or behavior in terms of evolutionary history
    Common ancestor
Functional explanation
    Describes why a structure or behavior evolved as it did
    Male sings to attract mate and defend territory

2. The brain and conscious experience: mind-body or mind-brain problem
    Dualism: mind and body—different kinds of substance; exist independently but interact
        Rene Descartes
            Pineal gland
        Conflict: law of conservation of matter and energy
    Monism: only one kind of existence
        Materialism
        Mentalism
        Identity
            Mental and brain processes described in different terms
    David Chalmers
        Easy problems: difference between wakefulness and sleep; mechanisms that focus
            attention
        Hard problem: how any brain activity is associated with consciousness
        Consciousness as unexplainable fundamental
    Daniel Dennett
        Hard problem = a lot of easy problems
    Patricia Churchland
        Too soon to give up on physical explanation for consciousness
    Solipsism: I alone exist.
        Problem of other minds
        Other mammals?
        Insects?
        Computers or robots?

Module 1.2 Nature and Nurture
1. The genetics of behavior
    Mendelian genetics
        Genes: units of heredity that maintain structural identity from one generation to another
        Chromosomes
        Deoxyribonucleic acid (DNA)
            Template for ribonucleic acid (RNA)
        Translation of mRNA
            Structural proteins or enzymes
        Location of genes on chromosomes
        Homozygous vs. heterozygous

          Dominant vs. recessive
          Chromosomes and crossing over
          Sex-linked and sex-limited genes
              Autosomal genes
              X and Y chromosomes
          Sources of variation
              Recombination
              Mutation
       Heritability
          Monozygotic (identical) twins
          Dizygotic (fraternal) twins
          Elevated plus maze
          Phenylketonuria (PKU)
              Inability to metabolize phenylalanine
              Brain malformations, mental retardation, irritablity
              Modified by low phenylalanine diet
   How genes affect behavior
       Increasing production of a protein
       Indirect effects
       Change in one behavior due to change in another behavior

2.   The evolution of behavior
   Evolutionary tree
   Genes associated with reproductive success
   Artificial selection
   Common misunderstandings about evolution
       Does use or disuse cause evolutionary change in that feature?
          Lamarckian evolution
       Have humans stopped evolving?
       Does evolution mean improvement?
       Does evolution benefit individual or species?
          Altruistic behavior
          Group selection
          Reciprocal altruism
          Kin selection
   Sociobiology
       Functional explanations
       Criticisms
          Explanations often speculative
          The way things are is not necessarily the way they should be

Module 1.3 The Use of Animals in Research

1.   Reasons for animal research
   Similar mechanisms of behavior
   Curiosity about animals
   Clues to human evolution
   Can't experiment on humans

2. The ethical debate
   Animal research → useful discoveries
   Minimalists vs. abolitionists
   Institutional Animal Care and Use Committees
   National laws and professional organization guidelines
   Difficulty of resolving moral issues

Module 1.4 Prospects for Further Study
1. Research
   Behavioral neuroscientist
   Neuroscientist
   Neurophysiologist
   Psychophysiologist
   Comparative psychologist
   Sociobiologist
2. Medicine
   Neurologist
   Neurosurgeon
   Psychiatrist

SHORT-ANSWER QUESTIONS

Module 1.1 The Mind-Brain Relationship
1. *Biological explanations of behavior*
   a. What are the four major types of explanation of behavior sought by biological psychologists?

   b. Discuss the singing of birds from each of these perspectives.

   c. What is the effect of testosterone on the brain of male songbirds?

d. What is an ontogenetic explanation?

e. What is an evolutionary explanation?

f. What are the two functions of the male bird's song?

g. What should we infer about an animal's or human's understanding of his or her behavior?

2. *The brain and conscious experience*
    a. What are the two major positions regarding the mind-brain relationship? List the main variants of these major positions.

    b. Give a strength and a weakness of each of these positions.

c. According to David Chalmers, what kinds of issues do "easy problems" deal with?

d. What is the main "hard problem"?

e. According to Daniel Dennett, what is the relationship of the "hard problem" to the "easy problems"?

f. What is Patricia Churchland's position on "hard" and "easy" problems?

g. What is the problem of other minds? How does solipsism deal with that problem?

h. How do non-solipsists deal with the problem of other minds in humans? In animals?

Module 1.2 Nature and Nurture
1. *The genetics of behavior*
    a. Briefly, what is a gene?

    b. What is the relationship between DNA and RNA?   Between one type of RNA and protein molecules?

    c. What are two major functions of protein molecules?

    d. What does it mean for an individual to be homozygous for a particular gene? Heterozygous?

    e. What is a dominant gene? When can the effects of a recessive gene be seen?

f.   What is "crossing over"?

g.   On which chromosome are almost all sex-linked genes?

h.   What is a sex-limited gene? On which chromosomes may it occur? Why are its effects usually limited to one sex?

i.   What are two sources of genetic variation?

j.   How is heritability of a trait determined?

k.   What is phenylketonuria (PKU)? How can its effects be modified?

1.   What are some of the ways in which genes may influence behavior?

2.   *The evolution of behavior*
     a.   What is evolution?

     b.   What is artificial selection?

     c.   Does the use or disuse of a structure or behavior cause an evolutionary increase or decrease in that feature? What is Lamarckian evolution?

     d.   Have humans stopped evolving?

     e.   Does evolution always imply improvement? Why or why not?

f. How can a gene that promotes altruistic behavior be maintained in evolution, if it places its possessor in danger?

g. What kinds of issues do sociobiologists seek to explain? What are two criticisms of sociobiological explanations?

Module 1.3 The Use of Animals in Research
1. *Reasons for animal research*
   a. What are four reasons biological psychologists study nonhuman animals?

2. *The ethical debate*
   a. Compare the positions of the "minimalists" and the "abolitionists" with regard to the conduct of animal research.

   b. What is the role of Laboratory Animal Care Committees? What groups are represented in their membership?

Module 1.4 Prospects for Further Study
1. *Research*
   a. Describe the main issues studied by neuroscientists, and specifically, behavioral neuroscientists?

   b. What is a neuropsychologist? Where do they usually work?

   c. What does a psychophysiologist study?

   d. Compare the main issues studied by comparative psychologists with those studied by sociobiologists.

2. *Medicine*
   a. Distinguish among neurologists, neurosurgeons, and psychiatrists.

POSTTEST

Multiple-Choice Questions

1. Which of the following is not a major category of biological explanation?
    a. physiological explanations
    b. ontogenetic explanations
    c. evolutionary explanations
    d. mental explanations

2. Most adult male songbirds
    a. sing throughout the year and throughout wide territories.
    b. sing when testosterone levels are high enough to increase the size and activity of a brain area that is critical for singing.
    c. sing because they are consciously aware that their songs will attract females and deter male competitors.
    d. sing the correct song, even if they have never heard the song.

3. The dualist position
    a. is problematic because it does not fit with our commonsense notion of the mind.
    b. proposes that the mind is the same thing as brain activity.
    c. cannot explain how, if the mind is not a type of matter or energy, it could possibly alter the electrical and chemical activities of the brain.
    d. proposes that mind is just an illusion.

4. The view that everything that exists is physical, and that mental events either don't exist or can be explained in purely physical terms, is characteristic of which position?
    a. materialism
    b. dualism
    c. mentalism
    d. the identity position

5. David Chalmers proposed that the "hard problem" concerning consciousness
    a. is how neural mechanisms differentiate between wakefulness and sleep and allow us to focus our attention.
    b. is why and how *any* kind of brain activity is associated with consciousness.
    c. really consists of an enormous number of easy problems.
    d. is impossible to answer, under any circumstances.

6. A solipsist
    a. assumes that other people, animals, and computers are conscious because they look and/or act much like I do.
    b. assumes that other people are conscious, but animals and computers are not.
    c. assumes that I alone exist, or I alone am conscious.
    d. is frequently a member of an organization called Solipsists United.

7. The order of bases on DNA
   a. determines the order of bases on RNA, which in turn determines the order of amino acids in proteins.
   b. directly determines the order of amino acids in proteins, which in turn determines the order of bases in RNA.
   c. is less important for genetic function than is the total number of particular bases.
   d. is more important for determining the shapes of carbohydrates and fats than of proteins.

8. An individual with a pair of identical genes at a given site on a pair of chromosomes
   a. is homozygous for that gene.
   b. is heterozygous for that gene.
   c. must have crossing over at that gene.
   d. must not have the ability to taste phenylthiocarbamide.

9. Crossing over refers to
   a. chickens getting to the other side of the road.
   b. heterozygous genes now becoming homozygous.
   c. homozygous genes now becoming heterozygous.
   d. the breaking apart of chromosomes during reproduction and reconnecting, with a part of one chromosome now attaching to the other chromosome.

10. Sex-linked genes are usually genes
    a. on autosomal chromosomes that are expressed only under hormonal conditions that are usually found only in one sex.
    b. on autosomal chromosomes that are expressed in both sexes.
    c. on the X chromosome, which cannot be overridden by a second X chromosome in males.
    d. that most frequently engage in crossing over.

11. Mutations
    a. result from the recombination of genes from the two parents.
    b. are random genetic changes that are usually maladaptive.
    c. are so rare that they almost never affect inheritance.
    d. are unlikely to produce harmful effects in offspring if the two parents are closely related; therefore, people should marry their close relatives.

12. Phenylketonuria (PKU)
    a. has high heritability under normal conditions.
    b. results from inability to metabolize phenylalanine, which results in high levels of that amino acid, which in turn results in brain damage and mental retardation.
    c. effects can be minimized by a low phenylalanine diet.
    d. all of the above.

13. The survival of genes for altruistic behavior can be explained by
    a. either reciprocal altruism or kin selection.
    b. the fact that altruism is only a little harmful to the individual.
    c. the fact that altruism benefits the species, though it may harm the individual.
    d. All of the above are equally good explanations.

14. Animal research
    a. yields no useful discoveries.
    b. is regulated by Institutional Animal Care and Use Committees, which are composed of veterinarians, community representatives, and scientists.
    c. depends entirely on the wisdom and good intentions of individual researchers for maintaining good care of the animals.
    d. all of the above.

15. "Abolitionist" animal advocates
    a. agree that some animal research is acceptable if an important goal can be achieved with minimal suffering.
    b. maintain that use of primates in experimentation should be abolished, but that "lower" animals may be used.
    c. maintain that all animal experimentation, as well as any other use of animals, should be totally eliminated.
    d. are also called "minimalists".

Answers to Multiple-Choice Questions

1. d	5. b	9. d	13. a
2. b	6. c	10. c	14. b
3. c	7. a	11. b	15. c
4. a	8. a	12. d	

2

NERVE CELLS AND NERVE IMPULSES

INTRODUCTION

Neurons, like all animal cells, are bounded by a fatty membrane, which restricts the flow of chemicals into and out of the cell. Animal cells also contain structures, such as a nucleus, ribosomes, mitochondria, lysosomes, and an endoplasmic reticulum, that are important for various genetic, synthetic, and metabolic functions. A neuron is composed of (1) dendrites, which receive stimulation from other cells; (2) the soma or cell body, which contains the genetic and metabolic machinery and also conducts stimulation to the axon; and (3) the axon, which carries the nerve impulse to other neurons, frequently across long distances. Sensory neurons are highly sensitive to specific external stimuli; motor neurons stimulate muscles and glands; and local neurons have either no axon or a very short one and can convey information only to adjacent neurons. One can infer a great deal about a neuron's function from its shape. For example, a neuron that integrates input from many sources has many branching dendrites. It is now clear that experience can modify the shapes of neurons. The nervous system also contains many support cells called glia, which help synchronize the activity of axons, remove waste, build myelin sheaths, and guide neurons during development and during regeneration of peripheral axons.

A blood-brain barrier prevents many substances, including most viruses and bacteria and most forms of nutrition, from entering the brain. In most parts of the brain, glucose is the only nutrient that can cross the barrier in significant amounts. Therefore, the brain is highly dependent on glucose and on thiamine, which is needed to metabolize glucose. Fat soluble molecules and small uncharged molecules can cross the barrier freely. The barrier depends on tight junctions between endothelial cells lining the capillaries.

The ability of a neuron to respond quickly to stimulation depends on the resting potential. A metabolically active sodium-potassium pump establishes concentration gradients by transporting sodium (Na^+) ions out of the cell and potassium (K^+) ions into the cell. There is a resultant negative charge inside the cell, because three sodium ions are pumped out for every two potassium ions pumped in. Selective permeability of the membrane increases this potential by allowing potassium ions to flow out, down their concentration gradient; the loss of the positive potassium ions leaves the inside of the neuron even more negative. The relative impermeability of sodium results in minimal inflow of positive ions to offset the potassium outflow. The concentration and electrical gradients exert opposing influences on potassium. The electrical gradient (the negative charge inside the cell) attracts more potassium inside the cell than would be there if the concentration gradient were the only influence. Sodium ions, however, are attracted to the inside by both the electrical and concentration gradients. Therefore, if the sodium channels were opened, there would be considerable impetus for sodium to flow into the cell.

A neuron may receive input that either hyperpolarizes it (makes the inside more negative) or depolarizes it (makes the inside less negative). If the membrane is depolarized to a threshold level, it briefly loses its ability to exclude sodium ions, and these ions rush in through voltage-activated sodium channels. They cause the inside of the neuron to become positive, at which point the membrane quickly becomes impermeable to sodium again. However, as the neuron becomes more depolarized, voltage-activated potassium channels open, resulting in even greater permeability than usual to potassium, which is repelled out of the neuron by both the positive electrical gradient and its own concentration gradient. The exit of the positively charged potassium ions returns the neuron approximately to its previous resting potential. This rapid exchange of ions is called the action

16

potential. All action potentials of a given axon are approximately equal in size, shape, and velocity, regardless of the size of the depolarization that gave rise to them. This principle is called the all-or-none law. Immediately after an action potential, a neuron is resistant to reexcitation. During the 1 millisecond absolute refractory period, no stimulus can initiate a new impulse; during the subsequent relative refractory period of about 2-4 milliseconds, slight hyperpolarization resulting from potassium outflow makes it more difficult, but possible, to produce an action potential.

Once an action potential occurs, entering sodium ions spread to adjacent portions of membrane, thereby depolarizing these areas to their threshold and allowing sodium to rush in there. Thus the action potential is regenerated at each succeeding area of the axon until it reaches the end. The regenerative flow of ions across the membrane is slower than electrical conduction within the axon. In some axons, 1-mm-long segments of myelin (a fatty insulating substance) are wrapped around the axon, with short uncovered segments (nodes of Ranvier) in between. The action potential is conducted passively with some decrement under the myelin sheath. There is still sufficient potential to depolarize the next node of Ranvier to its threshold, and the action potential is regenerated at full strength at each node. The impulse appears to "jump" from node to node. This mode of transmission is called saltatory conduction and is much faster than transmission without myelin. It forces the action potential to use the faster electrical conduction within the axon for a longer distance before engaging in the slower regenerative flow across the membrane. Very small local neurons use only graded potentials, not action potentials, because they transmit information over very short distances.

KEY TERMS AND CONCEPTS

Module 2.1 The Cells of the Nervous System
1. Neurons and glia
   The structures of an animal cell
      Membrane
         Two layers of fat molecules
         Protein channels
      Nucleus
      Mitochondria
      Ribosomes
      Endoplasmic reticulum
   Santiago Ramon y Cajal: pioneer of neuroanatomy: nerve cells are separate
   The structure of a neuron
      Motor neuron
      Sensory neuron
      Dendrites
         Synaptic receptors
         Dendritic spines
      Cell body or soma
         Nucleus, ribosomes, mitochondria
      Axon
         Myelin sheath
         Presynaptic terminal, bouton, or end bulb
            Mitochondria
         Afferent axon
         Efferent axon
      Local neuron
      Intrinsic neuron

17

Variations among neurons
    Purkinje cell of cerebellum
    Cells in retina
    Shape modified by experience
        Purvis and Hadley: dye technique
Glia
    Astrocytes
        Encircle several presynaptic terminals
        Absorb, store, and transfer chemicals
        Remove waste
    Oligodendrocytes (brain and spinal cord) and Schwann cells (periphery)
        Form myelin sheaths
    Radial glia (during development) and Schwann cells (during regeneration of
        peripheral axons)
        Guide neurons

2.   The blood-brain barrier
Why we need a blood-brain barrier
    Natural killer cells
    Virus infected cells
How the blood-brain barrier works
    Endothelial cells of capillaries
    Small uncharged molecules
    Fat-soluble molecules
    Active transport system
        Glucose
        Amino acids
        Vitamins
        Certain hormones

3.   The nourishment of vertebrate neurons
Dependence on glucose
    Due to blood-brain barrier
    During intense stimulation: metabolize lactate
Requirement for thiamine (vitamin B_1)
    Deficiency leads to Korsakoff's syndrome

4.   In closing: Neurons
Importance of communication among neurons

Module 2.2 The Nerve Impulse
1.   The resting potential of the neuron
Phospholipid membrane with embedded proteins
Polarization
Resting potential
    Negatively charged proteins inside
    Concentration gradient
        More sodium outside
        More potassium inside
    Microelectrode

The forces behind the resting potential
    Selective permeability
    Ion channels
    Sodium-potassium pump
        Active transport
    Electrical gradient vs. concentration gradient
Why a resting potential? Strong, fast response

2. The action potential
Hyperpolarization
Depolarization
Threshold of excitation
The molecular basis of an action potential
    Voltage-activated channels
    Sodium inflow
    Potassium outflow
    Drug effects
        Scorpion venom: opens sodium channels and closes potassium channels
        Local anesthetic: blocks sodium channels
        General anesthetic: opens potassium channels
The all-or-none law
The refractory period
    Absolute refractory period
    Relative refractory period

3. Propagation of the action potential
Axon hillock
Successive depolarization of adjacent areas
Regenerative ion flow slower than current spread in axon

4. The myelin sheath and saltatory conduction
Myelinated axons
Nodes of Ranvier
Saltatory conduction
    Increases speed by increasing distance current spreads within axon
    Conserves energy by decreasing sites of sodium inflow
Multiple sclerosis

5. Signaling without action potentials
Local neuron
Graded potentials
    Depolarization
    Hyperpolarization
Horizontal cell
On the growth of neurons and the growth of misconceptions
    Small neurons not just "baby" neurons

6. In closing: Neural messages
Communication based on multiple on/off messages

Module 2.1 The Cells of the Nervous System
1. *Neurons and glia*
   a. What did Ramon y Cajal demonstrate?

   b. List the major structures of animal cells and give the main function of each.

   c. What are the functional and structural differences between motor and sensory neurons?

   d. What are the main subdivisions of the neuron and the function of each?

   e. List several anatomical distinctions between dendrites and axons.

   f. What is the myelin sheath?

g.　What is the function of the presynaptic terminal or end bulb?

h.　Describe the structural and functional differences among sensory, motor, and local neurons.

i.　What do the terms afferent and efferent mean? Can an axon be both afferent and efferent? Explain.

j.　What is an intrinsic neuron?

k.　How do glia cells differ from neurons?

l.　What are four functions of glia?

m. What are two functions of astrocytes?

n. What two kinds of glia form myelin sheaths?

o. What is the function of radial glia? What related function do Schwann cells perform?

2. *The blood-brain barrier*
    a. Why do we need a blood-brain barrier? Why don't we have a similar barrier around other body organs?

    b. What happens if a virus does enter the nervous system?

    c. Describe the arrangement of the endothelial cells that form the blood-brain barrier.

d.   What types of chemicals can cross the blood-brain barrier freely?

e.   Give one reason why heroin produces stronger effects than does morphine.

f.   What is the role of the active transport system? What four types of chemicals are transported in this way?

3.   *The nourishment of vertebrate neurons*
     a.   What is the major fuel of neurons?

     b.   Why can't most parts of the adult brain use fuels other than glucose?

     c.   Why is a shortage of glucose usually not a problem?

d. Why is a diet low in thiamine a problem? What is Korsakoff's syndrome?

Module 2.2 The Nerve Impulse

1. *The resting potential*

a. What is the composition of the membrane covering the neuron? Describe its structure.

b. How is the electrical potential across the membrane measured?

c. What is meant by selective permeability of the membrane? Which chemicals can cross the membrane and which ones cannot? How do a few biologically important ions cross?

d. What is the sodium-potassium pump? How does its exchange of sodium and potassium ions lead directly to an electrical potential across the membrane?

e. How does the selective permeability of the membrane increase the electrical potential?

f. Describe the competing forces acting on potassium ions. Why don't all the potassium ions surrounding a neuron migrate inside the cell to cancel the negative charge there?

g. What is the advantage of expending energy during the "resting" state to establish concentration gradients for sodium and potassium?

2. *The action potential*
    a. What happens to the electrical potential of a cell if a negative charge is applied? What is this change called?

    b. What happens to the potential if a brief, small positive current is applied? What is this change called?

    c. What happens to the potential if a threshold depolarization is applied?

d. What does the term "voltage-activated sodium channels" mean?

e. What causes the initial rapid increase in positivity of the action potential? Why doesn't the potential stop at 0 rather than actually reversing polarity?

f. What accounts for the ensuing repolarization? Why does the neuron hyperpolarize slightly, rather than stopping at the previous resting potential?

g. What effect does scorpion venom have on the membrane?

h. What is the effect of local anesthetic drugs like Novocain and Xylocaine?

i. What is the effect of general anesthetics?

j.   What is the all-or-none law? How may a neuron signal "greater than"?

k.   What is the absolute refractory period? What causes it?

l.   What is the relative refractory period? What causes it?

3.   *Propagation of the action potential*
      a.   How does an action potential propagate down an axon?

4.   *The myelin sheath and saltatory conduction*
      a.   What is the major advantage of the myelin sheath, and how is this advantage conferred?

      b.   What is a node of Ranvier? What would happen if the axon were wrapped with one long expanse of myelin, without any nodes of Ranvier?

c. What is meant by saltatory conduction?

5. *Signaling without action potentials*
   a. In what ways is transmission by local neurons different from the usual conduction by axons? Why is this local transmission restricted to very short distances?

POSTTEST

Multiple-Choice Questions

1. The membrane of a cell consists primarily of
   a. two layers of protein molecules.
   b. two layers of fat molecules.
   c. two layers of carbohydrate molecules.
   d. one layer of fat molecules adjacent to a layer of protein molecules.

2. Which of the following is the site of protein synthesis in cells?
   a. ribosomes
   b. endoplasmic reticulum
   c. nucleus
   d. mitochondria

3. Which of the following is the site of chemical reactions that produce energy for the cell?
   a. ribosomes
   b. endoplasmic reticulum
   c. nucleus
   d. mitochondria

4. Which part of the cell consists of a network of thin tubes that transport newly synthesized proteins to other locations?
   a. ribosomes
   b. endoplasmic reticulum
   c. nucleus
   d. mitochondria

5. Which part of the cell contains the chromosomes?
   a. ribosomes
   b. endoplasmic reticulum
   c. nucleus
   d. mitochondria

6. Which part of the neuron is specialized to receive information from other neurons?
   a. dendrites
   b. soma
   c. axon
   d. end bulbs

7. Dendritic spines
   a. are structures inside the dendrite that give it rigidity.
   b. are the sites of all synapses on a neuron.
   c. increase the surface area available for synapses.
   d. are long outgrowths that stretch for several millimeters.

8. Sensory neurons
   a. are afferent to the rest of the nervous system.
   b. are highly sensitive to specific types of stimulation.
   c. sometimes have dendrites that merge directly into the axon, with the soma located on a stalk off the main trunk.
   d. all of the above.

9. Intrinsic neurons
   a. have multiple axons extending to numerous structures.
   b. have dendrites and axons confined within a structure.
   c. are afferent to a given structure.
   d. are efferent to a given structure.

10. Glia
    a. are larger as well as more numerous than neurons.
    b. are found in only a few areas of the brain.
    c. got their name because early investigators thought they glued neurons together.
    d. form synaptic connections with neurons and other glia.

11. Which of the following is not a function of glia?
    a. guiding the migration of neurons and the regeneration of peripheral axons
    b. exchanging chemicals with adjacent neurons
    c. forming myelin sheaths
    d. transmitting information over long distances to other cells

12. The blood-brain barrier
    a. allows some substances to pass freely, while others to pass poorly or not at all.
    b. is formed by Schwann cells.
    c. is completely impermeable to all substances.
    d. keeps the blood from washing away neurons.

13. Which of the following is true of the blood-brain barrier?
    a. Electrically charged molecules are the only molecules that can cross.
    b. It results from tight junctions between endothelial cells.
    c. Fat soluble molecules cannot cross at all.
    d. An active transport system pumps blood across the barrier.

14. If a virus enters the brain,
    a. it survives in the infected neuron.
    b. a particle of it is exposed through the neuron's membrane so that the infected cell can be killed.
    c. it is immediately removed by glia before it can enter a neuron.
    d. it is impossible for any virus ever to enter the brain.

15. Adult neurons
    a. are like all other cells of the body in depending heavily on glucose.
    b. depend heavily on glucose because they do not have enzymes to metabolize other nutrients.
    c. depend heavily on glucose because other nutrients cannot cross the blood-brain barrier in significant amounts.
    d. cannot use glucose because they do not receive enough oxygen or thiamine through the blood-brain barrier to metabolize it.

16. Potassium
    a. is found mostly outside the neuron.
    b. is pumped into the resting neuron by the sodium-potassium pump, but some flows out as a result of the concentration gradient.
    c. is actively pumped outside the neuron during the action potential.
    d. more than one of the above.

17. The sodium-potassium pump
    a. creates a negative potential inside the neuron by removing 3 sodium ions for every 2 potassium ions that it brings in.
    b. creates a negative potential inside the neuron by removing 2 sodium ions for every 3 potassium ions that it brings in.
    c. creates a positive potential inside the neuron by removing 3 sodium ions for every 2 potassium ions that it brings in.
    d. is basically a passive mechanism that requires no metabolic energy.

18. The resting potential
    a. prepares the neuron to respond rapidly to a stimulus.
    b. is negative inside the neuron relative to the outside.
    c. can be measured as the voltage difference between a microelectrode inside the neuron and a reference electrode outside the neuron.
    d. all of the above.

19. Sodium ions
    a. are found largely inside the neuron during the resting state because they are attracted in by the negative charge there.
    b. are found largely inside the neuron during the resting state because they are actively pumped in.
    c. are found largely outside the neuron during the resting state because they are actively pumped out, and the membrane is largely impermeable to their reentry.
    d. are actively repelled by the electrical charge of the neuron's resting potential.

20. Hyperpolarization
    a. refers to a shift in the cell's potential in a more negative direction.
    b. refers to a shift in the cell's potential in a positive direction.
    c. can trigger an action potential if it is large enough.
    d. occurs in an all-or-none fashion.

21. Depolarization of a neuron can be accomplished by having
    a. a negative ion, such as chloride (Cl-), flow into the cell.
    b. potassium (K+) ions flow out of the cell.
    c. sodium (Na+) ions flow into the cell.
    d. sodium ions flow out of the cell.

22. The all-or-none law
    a. applies only to potentials in dendrites.
    b. states that the size, shape, and velocity of the action potential are independent of the intensity of the stimulus that initiated it.
    c. makes it impossible for the nervous system to signal intensity of a stimulus.
    d. all of the above.

23. When a neuron receives a threshold depolarization
    a. an action potential occurs, the size of which reflects the size of the stimulus that gave rise to it.
    b. so much sodium comes in that it almost completely depletes the extracellular fluid of sodium.
    c. sodium flows in only until the potential across the membrane is zero.
    d. the membrane becomes highly permeable to sodium ions for a brief time.

24. The down slope of the action potential graph
    a. is largely a result of sodium ions being pumped back out again.
    b. is the result of potassium ions flowing in briefly.
    c. is the result of sodium ions flowing in briefly.
    d. usually passes the level of the resting potential, resulting in a brief hyperpolarization, due to potassium freely leaving the cell.

25. Which of the following is true?
    a. Local anesthetics block nerve transmission by blocking sodium channels.
    b. Scorpion venom also blocks sodium channels.
    c. General anesthetics keep sodium channels open and close potassium channels.
    d. All of the above are true.

26. The absolute refractory period is the time during which
    a. a stimulus must exceed the usual threshold in order to produce an action potential.
    b. a neuron is more excitable than usual.
    c. the sodium gates are firmly closed and no new action potentials can be generated.
    d. sodium and potassium ions are rapidly flowing.

27. Propagation of an action potential
    a. is analogous to the flow of electrons down a wire.
    b. is almost instantaneous.
    c. is inherently unidirectional because positive charges can flow only in one direction.
    d. depends on passive diffusion of sodium ions inside the axon, which depolarize the neighboring areas to their threshold.

28. Myelin sheaths
    a. would be much more efficient if they were not interrupted with a lot of leaky nodes.
    b. are interrupted about every 1 mm by a short unmyelinated segment.
    c. are much less effective in speeding transmission than a simple increase in axon size.
    d. are composed primarily of protein.

29. Saltatory conduction refers to
    a. the salt ions used in the action potential.
    b. sodium ions jumping into the neuron, once the sodium channels are opened.
    c. the impulse jumping from one node of Ranvier to the next.
    d. the impulse jumping from one myelin sheath to the next.

30. Myelin sheaths
    a. slow conduction of the impulse by blocking sodium's entry to the cell; their advantage lies in making the impulse all-or-none.
    b. are destroyed in multiple sclerosis.
    c. are found on dendrites.
    d. are found on cell bodies.

31. Nodes of Ranvier
    a. are interruptions of the myelin sheath at about 1 mm intervals.
    b. are sites of abundant sodium channels.
    c. are sites where an action potential is regenerated.
    d. all of the above.

32. Local neurons utilize
    a. graded potentials to convey information over short distances.
    b. graded potentials to convey information over long distances.
    c. action potentials to transmit information over long distances.
    d. action potentials to transmit information over short distances.

Answers to Multiple-Choice Questions

1. b	7. c	13. b	19. c	25. a	31. d
2. a	8. d	14. a	20. a	26. c	32. a
3. d	9. b	15. c	21. c	27. d	
4. b	10. c	16. b	22. b	28. b	
5. c	11. d	17. a	23. d	29. c	
6. a	12. a	18. d	24. d	30. b	

Helpful Hints

1. To remember the relative locations of sodium and potassium ions during the resting potential, remember that sodium (Na^+) is "Not allowed" inside the neuron and potassium (K^+) is labeled "Keep".

2. To appreciate the difference between fast electrical conduction inside the membrane and slow regenerative potentials across the membrane, think of ions simply elbowing their like-charged neighbors a short distance away inside the membrane, while sodium and potassium ions have to swim their equivalent of the length of a pool to cross the membrane.

Diagrams

1. Label the following structures on the diagram of a motor neuron below: axon, axon hillock, dendrites, myelin sheath, node of Ranvier, nucleus, soma, presynaptic terminals, muscle fiber.

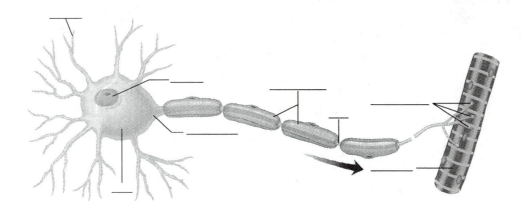

2. **In the diagram of neurons A and B below, label the directions as either afferent or efferent.**

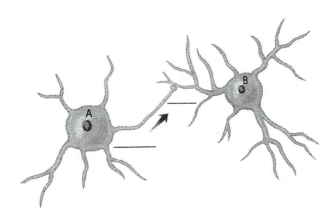

3. **Label the four types of glia cells.**

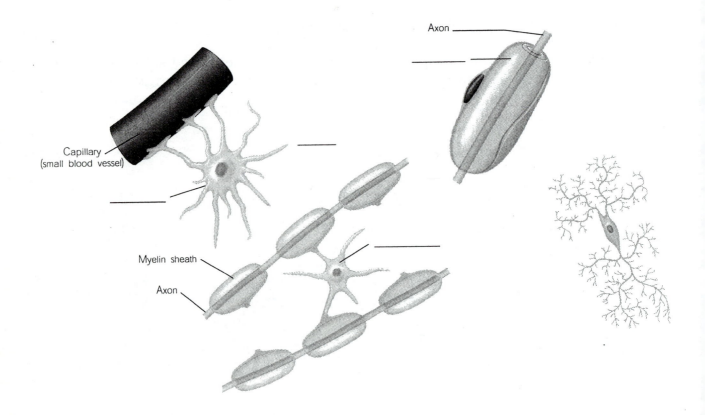

Axon

Capillary
(small blood vessel)

Myelin sheath

Axon

4. Label the blanks below as either Na+ or K+.

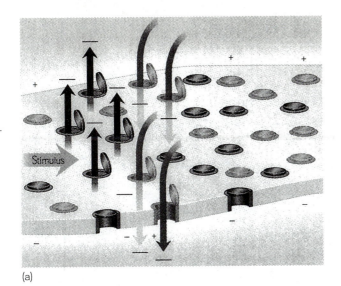

(a)

Genes, Neurons, and Behavior

Constructed by Elaine M. Hull using Crossword Weaver

11 *Theory that mental processes are the same as brain activity*

12 *Major component of membranes*

15 *_____ potential: rapid, "all-or-none" exchange of ions*

16 *Type of acid that makes up proteins*

17 *Part of dendrite that increases area for synapses*

18 *Template for protein synthesis (abbr.)*

ACROSS

3 *Direction toward a structure*

7 *Support cells*

8 *Substance of genes (abbr.)*

9 *Problem of how any kind of brain activity is associated with consciousness*

10 *Unit of heredity*

13 *Part of axon where action potentials start*

14 *Direction away from a structure*

15 *Refractory period in which no new action potential can be started*

16 *Part of neuron that conducts action potential away from soma*

17 *Main ion producing EPSPs*

19 *Fatty sheaths covering some axons*

20 *With 11 Across, segment of axon not covered by myelin*

21 *Small neuron using only graded potentials*

DOWN

1 *Refractory period in which it is more difficult, but possible, to start an action potential*

2 *Part of neuron that receives input*

4 *Type of glia that guides neurons in development*

5 *___ selection: explanation for altruistic behavior*

6 *See 23 Down*

10 *Major nutrient for brain*

3

COMMUNICATION WITHIN THE BODY:
SYNAPSES AND HORMONES

INTRODUCTION

C. S. Sherrington inferred from careful behavioral observations that neurons do not merge with each other but communicate across tiny gaps called synapses. Reflex arcs that have one or more synapses are slower than simple transmission along the same distance of unbroken axon. Sherrington also inferred that complex integration of stimuli, including spatial and temporal summation of both excitation and inhibition, occurs at synapses. Most of his inferences were later confirmed by electrophysiological recordings using microelectrodes inserted inside neurons. Inhibitory postsynaptic potentials (IPSPs) hyperpolarize the postsynaptic cell, making it more difficult to produce an action potential. Excitatory postsynaptic potentials (EPSPs) depolarize the postsynaptic neuron and may summate spatially and temporally with other EPSPs to reach triggering threshold for an action potential.

EPSPs and IPSPs result from the release of neurotransmitters from presynaptic terminals. The neurotransmitter diffuses to and combines with receptor sites on the postsynaptic neuron, giving rise to either ionotropic or metabotropic changes that produce the postsynaptic potentials. The neurotransmitter then detaches from its receptor and is either reabsorbed by the presynaptic terminal and reused or broken by enzymes into inactive components. Different neurotransmitters have different modes of inactivation, but some form of inactivation is critical to prevent the neurotransmitter from having a prolonged effect on the postsynaptic neuron, which would make it incapable of responding to new stimuli. The effect on the postsynaptic cell depends on the type and amount of neurotransmitter, the nature and number of receptors, the amount of deactivating enzyme present at the synapse, the rate of reuptake, and probably other factors. Neuromodulators are substances that alter the effects of neurotransmitters at nearby cells, frequently having no effect by themselves. Each neuron is thought to release the same neurotransmitter or combination of neurotransmitters at all of its terminals. Although each particular synapse is always excitatory or always inhibitory, each neuron receives many synapses, some of which are excitatory and some of which are inhibitory. Some synaptic mechanisms involve a brief flow of ions; others affect metabolic processes and are of slower onset and longer duration. However, all neurotransmitters must be inactivated, either by reuptake into presynaptic terminals or by enzymes. The most widely studied neurotransmitter systems are those of acetylcholine, dopamine, norepinephrine, epinephrine, serotonin, glutamate, glycine, gamma-aminobutyric acid (GABA), beta-endorphin, the enkephalins, purines (especially adenosine), and nitric oxide. Levels of some neurotransmitters can be affected by diet.

Drugs typically either impede or facilitate chemical transmission at a given type of synapse. They may either block or activate a certain type of receptor, or they may affect release, reuptake, or enzyme inactivation of the neurotransmitter. Since different neurotransmitters have different behavioral and physiological effects, we can frequently predict the effect of a drug on behavior or physiology if we know its synaptic effect. However, there are individual differences in the effectiveness and side effects of drugs, due in part to differences in the numbers and distributions of the subtypes of receptors affected by the drug.

Most abused drugs and most reinforcing activities, including electrical self-stimulation of the brain, are linked to dopamine release in the nucleus accumbens. However, dopamine in the nucleus accumbens may be more related to activational or attention-getting aspects of an event, rather than its rewarding effects. Stimulant drugs, such as amphetamine, cocaine, and methylphenidate (Ritalin), either increase the release of dopamine or block its reuptake. Nicotine acts on nicotinic receptors to increase dopamine release in the nucleus accumbens. Opiates, such as morphine and "endogenous morphines" (endorphins), increase the release of dopamine indirectly, by inhibiting inhibitory GABA neurons that would otherwise inhibit dopamine release. Low doses of MDMA ("ecstasy") increase dopamine release; higher doses increase serotonin release as well, but also destroy axons that release dopamine and serotonin.

Several drugs do not depend on dopamine synapses for their reinforcing effects. For example, some effects of opiates are not reversed by dopamine antagonists. Phencyclidine (PCP or "angel dust") produces reinforcing effects by inhibiting one type of glutamate receptors in the nucleus accumbens, rather than by stimulating dopamine synapses. Glutamate is usually excitatory; therefore, blocking its receptors would result in less excitation of postsynaptic neurons. Dopamine is usually inhibitory to the same postsynaptic neurons; therefore, drugs that stimulate dopamine synapses or that block glutamate synapses have similar behavioral effects. Marijuana and other cannabinoids mimic the effects of anandamide or 2-AG, neurotransmitters that bind to cannabinoid receptors located primarily in the hippocampus, basal ganglia, and cerebellum. Stimulation of cannabinoid receptors also inhibits activity at serotonin $5-HT_3$ synapses that produce nausea. Hallucinogenic drugs, such as LSD and mescaline, bind to serotonin receptors, especially the $5-HT_2$ subtype. Caffeine constricts blood vessels in the brain and also interferes with the inhibitory effects of adenosine on dopamine and glutamate release. Alcohol inhibits brain activity through general effects, such as decreasing sodium influx and expanding neuronal membranes, and also by decreasing serotonin activity, facilitating responses at $GABA_A$ receptors, blocking glutamate receptors, and increasing dopamine activity.

Some people with an altered form of the dopamine D_2 receptor exhibit a deficiency of reward, which increases the likelihood of a variety of unrestrained pleasure-seeking behaviors. Similarly, people with an altered form of the dopamine D_4 receptor show greater "novelty seeking" behaviors or an increased probability of schizophrenia. However, the relationships between dopamine receptors and these behaviors are not clear.

Hormones are released from various organs into the blood, which carries them throughout the body. They help to organize various organs and brain areas for a single function. There are several types of hormones. Protein and peptide hormones attach to receptors on the surface of cells, where they activate a second messenger, which in turn activates a series of enzymes. Steroid hormones attach to cytoplasmic receptors and move to the nucleus to alter gene expression. They may also have rapid effects on receptors on the cell membrane. Cortisol and corticosterone are released from the adrenal cortex during stress; they break down stored nutrients and release them for immediate use. The "sex hormones" include estrogens, progesterone, and androgens. Sex-limited genes are activated by hormones that are more abundant in one sex than in the other. High levels of anabolic steroids used by some athletes exert negative feedback effects on hormone production and may produce unwanted side effects. Additional classes of hormones include thyroid hormones, monoamines, and others that are difficult to classify. The hypothalamus controls the pituitary, which in turn controls glands throughout the body. The anterior pituitary is controlled by releasing hormones that are carried in the blood from the hypothalamus. The posterior pituitary is a neural extension of the hypothalamus.

KEY TERMS AND CONCEPTS

Module 3.1 The Concept of the Synapse
1. The properties of synapses
    Charles Sherrington's inferences

38

Reflex arc
Coordinated flexing and extending
Speed of a reflex and delayed transmission
Temporal summation
John Eccles
Microelectrode
Excitatory postsynaptic potential (EPSP)
Spatial summation
Inhibitory synapses
Inhibitory postsynaptic potential (IPSP)

2. Relationship among EPSP, IPSP, and action potential
Combination of temporal and spatial summation
Location of synapse
Spontaneous firing rate

3. In closing: The neuron as decision maker
Integration of information
Disinhibition

Module 3.2 Chemical Events at the Synapse

1. The discovery that most synaptic transmission is chemical
T. R. Elliott
Adrenalin
Sympathetic nervous system
O. Loewi
Vagus nerve
Accelerator nerve
Some electrical synapses

2. The sequence of chemical events at a synapse
Types of neurotransmitters
Amino acids
Peptides
Acetylcholine
Monoamines
Purines (including adenosine)
Gases (including nitric oxide)
Synthesis of transmitters
Role of diet
Acetylcholine
Choline
Lecithin
Catecholamines
Dopamine, norepinephrine, epinephrine
Precursors: phenylalanine, tyrosine
Serotonin
Tryptophan
Role of insulin

Transport of transmitters
    Peptides
        Times of hours or days to transport to axon terminal
    Small neurotransmitters
        Synthesized in terminals, no problem with transport
Release and diffusion of transmitters
    Vesicles
    Voltage-dependent calcium gates
    Exocytosis
    Dale's principle
        Combination of transmitters
    Ability to respond to numerous neurotransmitters, though it releases only a few
Activation of receptors of the postsynaptic cell
    Ionotropic effects (rapid, short-lived)
        Glutamate
        GABA
        Acetylcholine (nicotinic)
    Metabotropic effects and second messenger systems (slow, long-lasting)
        G-protein (coupled to guanosine triphosphate, GTP)
        Second messenger
            Cyclic AMP
    Multiple receptor subtypes
    Neuromodulators, including peptides
        Conditional effect
Inactivation and reuptake of neurotransmitters
    Acetylcholinesterase
    Reuptake
        Transporters
    Conversion to inactive chemicals
        COMT (catechol-o-methyltransferase)
        MAO (monoamine oxidase)

3.   In closing: Neurotransmitters and behavior
        Multiple receptor subtypes
        Different roles in complex behaviors

Module 3.3 Synapses, Abused Drugs, and Behavior
1.   Introduction
    Why study drugs?
        Combat drug abuse
        Develop better medications
        Understand synapses
    Why are our brains sensitive to plant chemicals?
        Plants evolved chemicals to affect animals' receptors
        Plants use the same "neurotransmitters"
2.   How drugs affect synapses
    Antagonist
    Agonist
        Mixed agonist-antagonist
    Increase or decrease synthesis

Alpha-methyl-para-tyrosine (AMPT)
DOPA
Cause leakage from vesicles
Reserpine
Increase release
Amphetamine
Decrease reuptake
Cocaine
Methylphenidate
Tricyclic antidepressants
Block enzymes that inactivate
Monoamine oxidase (MAO) inhibitors
Stimulate or block receptors
Affinity
Efficacy
Complications
Multiple receptor types

3.   Synapses, reinforcement, and drug use
Electrical self-stimulation of the brain
James Olds and Peter Milner
Self-stimulation of the brain
Nucleus accumbens
Dopamine: inhibitory transmitter
Glutamate: excitatory transmitter
Role of dopamine: pleasure vs. attention-getting
Less dopamine response to food in well-trained rat
Dopamine blocking drug: less work but food still pleasant
Unpleasant events release dopamine
Effects of stimulant drugs on dopamine synapses
Amphetamine: increases release of dopamine via reversal of transporter
Cocaine: blocks reuptake of dopamine, norepinephrine, and serotonin
Rebound "crash"
Dynorphin: counteracts reinforcing effects of cocaine
Long term disruption of brain function
Increased risk of stroke, epilepsy, and memory impairments
Methylphenidate (Ritalin): blocks reuptake of dopamine and increases serotonin release
Gradual onset and offset
Attention deficit disorder (ADD)
Dopamine effect: improved attention
Serotonin effect: calming of activity
Dopamine: mostly inhibitory, may decrease "noise"
MDMA ("ecstasy")
Low dose: stimulates dopamine release
High dose: stimulates serotonin release and destroys dopamine and serotonin axons
Nicotine (nicotinic acetylcholine receptors)
Increases dopamine release in nucleus accumbens
Long term effect: less responsive to reinforcing events
Opiates
Morphine, heroin, methadone

Endorphins (*endog*enous m*orphines*)
　　　Increase dopamine release indirectly, by inhibiting GABA release
　　　Also act independently of dopamine
Phencyclidine (PCP)
　　　Inhibits glutamate receptors (NMDA type) in nucleus accumbens
　　　Similar effect on postsynaptic cells as stimulating dopamine receptors
Marijuana (cannabinoids, related to D^9-tetrahydrocannabinol, D^9-THC)
　　　Fat soluble: slow release
　　　Anandamide in hippocampus, basal ganglia and cerebellum
　　　2-AG (sn-2 arachidonylglycerol): also binds to cannabinoid receptors
　　　Inhibits nausea by inhibiting $5\text{-}HT_3$ receptors
Hallucinogenic drugs (LSD, mescaline)
　　　$5\text{-}HT_2$ receptors
Caffeine
　　　Increases heart rate but constricts blood vessels in brain
　　　Blocks adenosine's inhibition of dopamine and acetylcholine release
Alcohol
　　　Inhibits flow of sodium and expands membrane surface
　　　Decreases serotonin activity
　　　Facilitates $GABA_A$ receptor
　　　Blocks glutamate receptors
　　　Increases dopamine activity
　　　　　Dopamine D_2 receptor deletion blocks alcohol preference
Methods 3.1: PET scans
　　　Image of brain activity made by recording radioactivity from injected chemicals
　　　Positron collides with electron
　　　Gamma rays emitted in opposite directions, detected, analyzed by computer

4.　Synapses, reinforcement, and personality
　　Reinforcement in brain, not in drug
　　Alternative form of dopamine D_2 receptor: alcoholism and reward deficiency
　　Alternative form of dopamine D_4 receptor: "novelty seeking"

Module 3.4　Hormones and Behavior
1.　Mechanisms of hormone actions
　　Classes of hormones
　　　　Protein and peptide hormones
　　　　　　Chains of amino acids
　　　　　　Glycoprotein or glycopeptide: amino acids attached to a carbohydrate
　　　　　　Membrane receptors activate second messenger
　　　　Steroid hormones
　　　　　　Four carbon rings, derived from cholesterol
　　　　　　Membrane receptors
　　　　　　Cytoplasmic receptors
　　　　　　　　Steroid-bound receptors → nucleus → affect gene expression
　　　　　　"Stress hormones"
　　　　　　　　Cortisol (humans) and corticosterone (rodents)
　　　　　　　　Adrenal cortex
　　　　　　　　Break down stored nutrients for immediate use (catabolic)
　　　　　　"Sex hormones"

Gonads and adrenal glands
Estrogens: higher levels in women
Progesterone: prepares uterus for pregnancy
Androgens: alternative form of dopamine D_2 receptor
Sex-limited genes: effects stronger in one sex
Anabolic steroids
Androstenedione
Negative feedback on pituitary
Thyroid hormones
Monoamines (including norepinephrine and dopamine)

2. Control of hormone release
Hypothalamus controls pituitary
Posterior pituitary
Neural tissue
Oxytocin and vasopressin
Anterior pituitary
Glandular tissue
Releasing hormones
Adrenocorticotropic hormone (ACTH)
Thyroid stimulating hormone (TSH)
Prolactin
Somatotropin (growth hormone, GH)
Follicle-stimulating hormone (FSH): a gonadotropin
Luteinizing hormone (LH): a gonadotropin
Negative feedback system

3. In closing: Hormones and the nervous system
Neuroimmunoendocrine system

SHORT-ANSWER QUESTIONS

Module 3.1 The Concept of the Synapse
1. *The properties of synapses*
    a. What is a reflex?

    b. What experimental evidence did Sherrington have for synaptic delay? For temporal summation?

c.   What evidence did he have for spatial summation? For coordinated excitation and inhibition?

d.   Describe John Eccles's experimental support for Sherrington's inferences.

e.   What is an EPSP, and what ionic flow is largely responsible for it?

f.   What is an IPSP, and what ionic flows can produce it?

2.   *The relationship among EPSP, IPSP, and action potential*
     a.   Why may some synapses have a greater influence than others?

     b.   What influence do EPSPs and IPSPs have on neurons with a spontaneous rate of firing?

3. *The neuron as decision maker*
    a. What factors influence a cell's "decision" whether or not to produce an action potential?

Module 3.2 Chemical Events at the Synapse

1. *The discovery that most synaptic transmission is chemical*
    a. What did T. R. Elliott propose?

    b. Describe Loewi's experiment with the two frogs' hearts.

2. *The sequence of chemical events at a synapse*
    a. What are the major events, in sequence, at a synapse?

    b. List the major neurotransmitters.

    c. How is nitric oxide unlike most other neurotransmitters?

d.   How is the synthesis of peptide neurotransmitters different from that of most other neurotransmitters?

e.   List the three catecholamines in the order of their synthesis. What is their amino acid precursor?

f.   How might one increase the amount of acetylcholine in the brain? Serotonin?

g.   How quickly can peptide neurotransmitters be transported to the terminal? Why is this not a problem for smaller neurotransmitters?

h.   Describe the process of exocytosis.

i.   What generalization can be drawn regarding the release of neurotransmitter(s) at the terminals of a given neuron?

j. Contrast ionotropic and metabotropic synaptic mechanisms. List three ionotropic neurotransmitter receptors.

k. Discuss the role of second messengers in producing the metabotropic effects of neurotransmitters. What kinds of changes can they exert?

l. What is a G-protein? What is the "first messenger"? What is one common second messenger?

m. What is a neuromodulator? How does a neuromodulator differ from most neurotransmitters?

n. How are ACh, 5-HT, and the catecholamines inactivated? Why is inactivation important?

o. Why should there be multiple receptor types for each neurotransmitter?

Module 3.3 Synapses, Abused Drugs, and Behavior
1. *How drugs affect synapses*
    a.   List six ways in which drugs may affect synaptic function.

    b.   What is an agonist? An antagonist?

    c.   How can one drug be an agonist at a given receptor, while another drug, with similar affinity for that receptor, is an antagonist?

    d.   What is the effect of the drug AMPT (alpha-methyl-para-tyrosine)? Of tricyclic antidepressants?

2. *Synapses, reinforcement and drug use*
    a.   Which brain area is especially important for reinforcement and addiction? What is the effect of dopamine on neurons there?

b.   How were the brain mechanisms of pleasure and reinforcement discovered?

c.   Is dopamine release always associated with pleasure? What evidence suggests that other processes are more closely associated with dopamine release in the nucleus accumbens?

d.   What is the effect of amphetamine on synapses?

e.   Compare the effects of cocaine with those of amphetamine. What are the similarities and differences?

f.   Why do amphetamine and cocaine users frequently report a "crash" a couple of hours after taking the drugs?

g.   How does dynorphin affect cocaine use?

h.   Why is methylphenidate (Ritalin) usually not abused?

i.-   What are the physiological effects of MDMA ("Ecstasy")?

j.   What is the basis of nicotine's reinforcing effects? Is stimulation of all types of acetylcholine receptors reinforcing?

k.   What is an endorphin? What is the derivation of its name?

l.   How do opiates increase the release of dopamine? How do we know that not all opiate effects are produced by increasing dopamine release?

m.   Which neurotransmitter has effects that are opposite those of dopamine in the nucleus accumbens? Which abused drug inhibits certain receptors for this neurotransmitter?

n. What is the main psychoactive chemical in marijuana? Why do marijuana users not experience a sudden "crash" several hours after taking the drug, as do amphetamine and cocaine users?

o. Which two brain chemicals bind to cannabinoid receptors? How might marijuana decrease nausea?

p. Where in the brain are cannabinoid receptors located? Why do large doses of marijuana not threaten breathing or heartbeat?

q. Which receptor does LSD stimulate? Can we explain the effects of LSD on behavior?

r. How does caffeine stimulate the nervous system? What is a major effect of adenosine?

s. What are two effects of alcohol on membranes? What type of receptor is made more responsive by alcohol?

t. What sorts of behaviors have been linked with alternative forms of genes for the D_2 and D_4 dopamine receptors? How strong is the association?

Module 3.4 Hormones and Behavior

1. *Mechanisms of hormone actions*

   a. Define "hormone." How clear is the distinction between hormones and neurotransmitters?

   b. What are the two major classes of hormones? What are some additional classes of hormones?

   c. By what two major mechanisms do hormones act on the nervous system?

d. What are the major differences between control mechanisms for the anterior and posterior pituitary?

e. List the hormones released from the posterior pituitary. The anterior pituitary.

f. What are releasing hormones? Where are they produced?

POSTTEST

Multiple-Choice Questions

1. C. S. Sherrington
   - a. did extensive electrophysiological recording of synaptic events.
   - b. inferred the existence and properties of synapses from behavioral experiments on reflexes in dogs.
   - c. was a student of John Eccles.
   - d. found that conduction along a single axon is slower than through a reflex arc.

2. Which of the following was **not** one of Sherrington's findings?
   - a. The speed of conduction through a reflex arc was significantly slower than the known speed of conduction along an axon.
   - b. Repeating a subthreshold pinch several times in rapid succession elicited leg flexion.
   - c. Simultaneous subthreshold pinches in different parts of the foot elicited flexion.
   - d. Reflex arcs are limited to one limb and are always excitatory.

3. Electrophysiological recording from a single neuron
   - a. utilizes a microelectrode inserted into the neuron and a reference electrode outside the neuron.
   - b. supported Sherrington's inferences.
   - c. is a field pioneered by John Eccles.
   - d. all of the above.

4. IPSPs
    a. may summate to generate an action potential.
    b. are always hyperpolarizing under natural conditions.
    c. are characterized mainly by a large influx of potassium ions.
    d. are characterized mainly by a large influx of sodium ions.

5. Which of the following is true?
    a. The size of EPSPs is the same at all excitatory synapses.
    b. The primary means of inactivation for all neurotransmitters is degradation by an enzyme.
    c. The size, duration, and direction (hyperpolarizing or depolarizing) of a postsynaptic potential are functions of the type and amount of transmitter released, the type and number of receptor sites present, the amount of deactivating enzyme present at the synapse, the rate of reuptake, and perhaps other factors.
    d. A given neuron may release either an excitatory or an inhibitory transmitter (at different times), depending on whether it was excited or inhibited by a previous neuron.

6. EPSPs and action potentials are similar in that
    a. sodium is the major ion producing a depolarization in both.
    b. sodium is the major ion producing a hyperpolarization in both.
    c. potassium is the major ion producing a depolarization in both.
    d. both decay as a function of time and space, decreasing in magnitude as they travel along the membrane.

7. EPSPs
    a. result from a flow of potassium (K^+) and chloride (Cl^-) ions.
    b. are always depolarizing in natural conditions.
    c. are always large enough to cause the postsynaptic cell to reach triggering threshold for an action potential; otherwise there would be too much uncertainty in the nervous system.
    d. are the same as action potentials.

8. EPSPs and IPSPs
    a. may alter a neuron's spontaneous firing rate.
    b. are more effective if they are located at the end of dendrites, rather than on the cell body.
    c. usually occur one at a time, so that the neuron does not get confused.
    d. all of the above.

9. T. R. Elliott discovered that
    a. adrenalin slowed a frog's heart.
    b. synaptic transmission is electrical rather than chemical.
    c. adrenalin could mimic the effects of the sympathetic nervous system.
    d. all of the above.

10. Otto Loewi discovered that a substance collected from the vagus nerve innervating one frog's heart and transferred to a second frog's heart
    a. slowed the second frog's heart.
    b. speeded the second frog's heart.
    c. either speeded or slowed the second frog's heart, depending on the quantity applied.
    d. had no effect, thereby showing that synaptic transmission is not chemically mediated.

11. The level of acetylcholine in the brain can be increased by increasing dietary intake of
    a. acetylcholine.
    b. tyrosine.
    c. choline.
    d. tryptophan.

12. The level of serotonin in the brain can be increased by eating a meal that has protein and is also high in
    a. choline.
    b. tyrosine.
    c. fat.
    d. carbohydrates.

13. The speed of transport of substances down an axon
    a. is fast enough that even the longest axons require only a few minutes for substances synthesized in the nucleus to reach the terminal.
    b. limits the availability of small neurotransmitters more than that of peptides.
    c. limits the availability of peptides more than that of small neurotransmitters.
    d. is a severe limitation on the availability of all neurotransmitters.

14. Calcium
    a. is kept outside the neuron by voltage-dependent calcium gates during the resting state.
    b. enters the terminal when an action potential opens voltage-dependent calcium gates.
    c. causes the release of neurotransmitter.
    d. all of the above.

15. Vesicles
    a. are tiny nearly-spherical packets filled with neurotransmitter.
    b. are especially important for storing nitric oxide.
    c. are the only places where transmitter is found in axon terminals.
    d. store only excitatory neurotransmitters; inhibitory neurotransmitters are never stored in vesicles.

16. Each terminal of a given axon
    a. releases a different neurotransmitter, thus providing a rich repertoire of effects.
    b. releases the same neurotransmitter or combination of neurotransmitters at every terminal of that axon.
    c. releases only one neurotransmitter, so as not to "confuse" the postsynaptic cell.
    d. releases all of the neurotransmitters known to exist in the brain.

17. Ionotropic synaptic mechanisms
    a. have slow-onset, long-lasting effects.
    b. use a cyclic AMP second messenger response.
    c. are exemplified by glutamate, GABA, and nicotinic acetylcholine receptors.
    d. frequently use hormones as transmitters.

18. Metabotropic synapses
    a. may have effects that significantly outlast the release of the transmitter.
    b. are activated when a neurotransmitter binds to its receptor site and thereby induces a change in an intracellular part of the receptor that is coupled to a G-protein.
    c. are characterized by initiation of changes in proteins by cyclic AMP, which in turn open or close ion gates or alter the structure or metabolism of the cell.
    d. all of the above.

19. Neuromodulators
    a. frequently have an effect only when the "main" neurotransmitter is present.
    b. are carried in the blood throughout the entire body.
    c. almost always produce a major effect by themselves, in addition to their modulatory effect.
    d. usually have ionotropic effects.

20. Acetylcholinesterase
    a. promotes reuptake of ACh into cholinergic terminals, thereby inactivating it.
    b. is the enzyme that produces ACh.
    c. is the enzyme that cleaves ACh into two inactive parts.
    d. blocks reuptake of choline into cholinergic terminals.

21. Reuptake of neurotransmitters
    a. is the major method of inactivation of ACh.
    b. is the major method of inactivation of serotonin and the catecholamines.
    c. is speeded up by COMT.
    d. is completely blocked by MAO.

22. An antagonist is a drug that
    a. has no affinity for a receptor.
    b. changes EPSPs into IPSPs.
    c. mimics or strengthens the effects of a neurotransmitter.
    d. blocks the effects of a neurotransmitter.

23. Reinforcement and drug addiction are frequently associated with
    a. inhibition of certain cells in the nucleus accumbens.
    b. release of dopamine in the nucleus accumbens.
    c. decreased activity of glutamate in the nucleus accumbens.
    d. all of the above.

24. Amphetamine
    a. stimulates the release of dopamine and several other neurotransmitters.
    b. stimulates nicotinic receptors.
    c. stimulates adenosine receptors.
    d. blocks the conversion of tyrosine to DOPA.

25. Cocaine
    a. blocks reuptake and enzyme degradation of glutamate, thus prolonging its effects.
    b. blocks reuptake of dopamine, norepinephrine, and serotonin, thus prolonging their effects.
    c. is absorbed into fat and released slowly, thereby preventing a "crash" a few hours later.
    d. all of the above.

26. Methylphenidate (Ritalin)
    a. is frequently abused because it acts rapidly, producing a sudden rush of excitement.
    b. inhibits certain kinds of glutamate receptors.
    c. inhibits reuptake of dopamine.
    d. is used to treat opiate addiction.

27. Nicotine
    a. stimulates nicotinic acetylcholine receptors and thereby increases dopamine release.
    b. blocks nicotinic receptors and thereby increases dopamine release.
    c. blocks dopamine receptors and thereby increases acetylcholine release.
    d. stimulates dopamine receptors directly, and thereby produces reinforcement.

28. Opiates
    a. block receptors that are stimulated by endorphins.
    b. inhibit GABA neurons and thereby increase dopamine release.
    c. inhibit dopamine neurons and thereby increase GABA release.
    d. are especially addictive when taken for medical reasons.

29. Marijuana
    a. stimulates cannabinoid receptors located primarily in the brain stem; it thereby interferes
        with breathing.
    b. blocks adenosine receptors.
    c. is very likely to produce a "crash" a couple of hours after its ingestion.
    d. mimics the effects of the endogenous neurotransmitters anandamide and 2-AG.

30. LSD
    a. stimulates the release of norepinephrine and dopamine.
    b. blocks most serotonin receptors.
    c. is an agonist at 5-HT$_2$ receptors.
    d. blocks the synthesis of serotonin.

31. Caffeine
    a. dilates blood vessels.
    b. stimulates adenosine receptors.
    c. indirectly increases the release of dopamine and acetylcholine.
    d. directly decreases the release of glutamate.

32. Alcohol
    a. inhibits the flow of sodium across the membrane.
    b. expands the surface of membranes.
    c. makes GABA$_A$ receptors more responsive.
    d. all of the above.

33. Concerning hormones, which of the following is true?
    a. All hormones bind to membrane receptors and activate second messenger systems.
    b. Steroid hormones enter the cell and bind to receptors that carry them into the nucleus,
        where they alter gene expression. They may also have rapid membrane effects.
    c. Peptide hormones enter the cell and bind to receptors that carry them into the nucleus,
        where they alter gene expression.
    d. Cortisol and corticosterone are peptide hormones that help to conserve energy.

34. Cyclic AMP
    a. is a second messenger.
    b. is a steroid hormone.
    c. is a peptide hormone.
    d. is a glycoprotein.

35. Androgens
    a. are present only in males; estrogens are present only in females.
    b. are present in both males and females but are produced in greater quantities in males.
    c. elevate blood sugar and enhance metabolism as their main effects.
    d. both b and c.

36. Sex-limited genes
    a. are present on the Y chromosomes and therefore are lacking in females.
    b. are present on the X chromosome and therefore are unopposed and dominant in males.
    c. are present in both sexes but are activated preferentially by androgens or estrogens.
    d. are the genes that code for the production of androgens and estrogens.

37. Which of the following is true?
    a. Hormone production by the anterior pituitary is controlled by releasing hormones secreted by the hypothalamus.
    b. Hormone production by the posterior pituitary is controlled by releasing hormones from the hypothalamus.
    c. FSH is a hypothalamus releasing hormone that causes the pituitary to release LH.
    d. Estrogen is secreted by the anterior pituitary.

38. Oxytocin
    a. is also known as antidiuretic hormone.
    b. is synthesized in the hypothalamus and released from the posterior pituitary, as is vasopressin.
    c. is synthesized in and released from the anterior hypothalamus, in response to releasing hormones from the hypothalamus.
    d. controls secretions of the adrenal cortex.

39. Cortisol and corticosterone
    a. are secreted by the adrenal cortex in response to stressful experiences and mobilize stored nutrients for immediate use.
    b. are secreted by the anterior pituitary and increase release of ACTH from the adrenal cortex.
    c. are especially important for storing circulating nutrients so that they will be available for later use.
    d. are secreted from the gonads and are especially potent anabolic steroids.

40. Which of the following is true?
    a. Estrogens are present only in females.
    b. Estrogens' major role is to prepare the uterus for implantation of an embryo and the maintenance of pregnancy.
    c. Progesterone's major role is to prepare the uterus for implantation of an embryo and the maintenance of pregnancy.
    d. Anabolic steroids are a safe and effective means for increasing muscle strength.

Answers to Multiple-Choice Questions

1. b	7. b	13. c	19. a	25. b	31. c	37. a
2. d	8. a	14. d	20. c	26. c	32. d	38. b
3. d	9. c	15. a	21. b	27. a	33. b	39. a
4. b	10. a	16. b	22. d	28. b	34. a	40. c
5. c	11. c	17. c	23. d	29. d	35. b	
6. a	12. d	18. d	24. a	30. c	36. c	

Diagrams

1. Label the electrical potentials shown in the graph below.

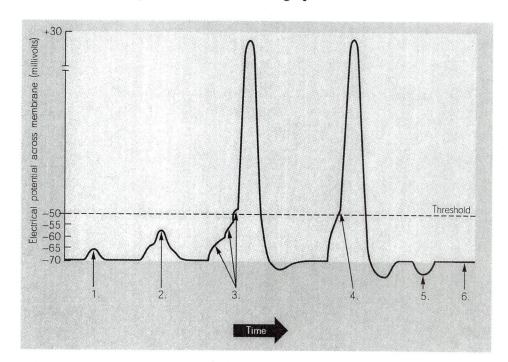

1_____ 4_____

2_____ 5_____

3_____ 6_____

2. Label the following structures of the endocrine system: hypothalamus, pituitary, pineal gland, adrenal gland, ovary, placenta, testis, pancreas, parathyroid, thyroid, thymus.

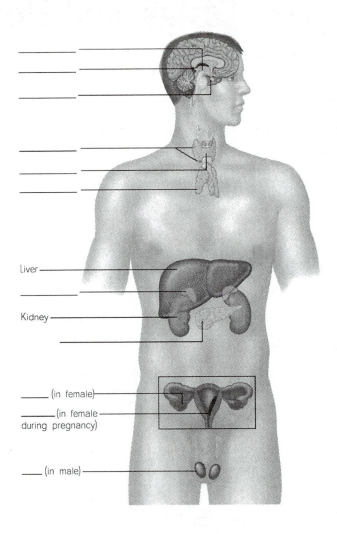

Liver

Kidney

_____ (in female)

_____ (in female during pregnancy)

_____ (in male)

Synapses, Drugs, and Hormones

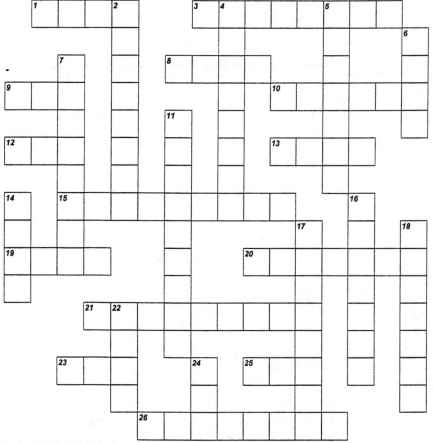

Constructed by Elaine M. Hull using Crossword Weaver

DOWN

2 *Part of pituitary controlled by releasing hormones from hypothalamus*

4 *Steroid hormone made in greater amounts in females*

5 *Drug that increases activity at a given type of synapse*

6 *Temporary depolarization (abbr.)*

7 *Adrenal steroid hormone*

11 *Excitatory transmitter*

14 *Type of receptor activated by glutamate (abbr.)*

16 *Chain of amino acids*

17 *Steroid hormone made in greater amounts by males*

18 *Effect of amphetamine on catecholamines*

22 *Discoverer of brain stimulation reward*

24 *Drug that blocks NMDA receptors (abbr.)*

ACROSS

1 *Amino acid transmitter (abbr.)*

3 *Major means of inactivating released transmitters*

8 *Anterior pituitary hormone that activates the adrenal cortex (abbr.)*

9 *Enzyme that metabolizes monoamines (abbr.)*

10 *Sex organs that produce hormones*

12 *Imaging technique using radioactive chemicals (abbr.)*

13 *Temporary hyperpolarization (abbr.)*

15 *Monoamine transmitter made from tryptophan*

19 *Person who proposed that each neuron releases the same transmitter from all of its terminals*

20 *Space between axon terminal and dendrite*

21 *Part of the pituitary that is a neural extension of the hypothalamus*

23 *Childhood disorder frequently treated with Ritalin (abbr.)*

25 *Kind of animal whose reflexes were studied by Sherrington*

26 *Transmitter important for reward or activation*

61

4

ANATOMY OF THE NERVOUS SYSTEM

INTRODUCTION

The vertebrate nervous system consists of two major divisions, the central (CNS) and the peripheral (PNS) nervous systems. The CNS is composed of the brain and the spinal cord. The PNS is divided into the somatic and the autonomic nervous systems. The somatic system consists of sensory nerves that convey information from sense organs to the spinal cord, and motor nerves carrying messages from the spinal cord to muscles and glands. A pair of sensory nerves enters (one from each side) and a pair of motor nerves exits from the spinal cord through each pair of openings in the vertebral canal. The sensory nerves enter the spinal cord from the dorsal side, and the motor axons leave from the ventral side. Cell bodies of sensory neurons lie in the dorsal root ganglia; those of the motor neurons are in the spinal cord. The autonomic nervous system also sends neurons through the vertebral openings; they synapse in ganglia outside the spinal cord. Ganglia of the sympathetic division of the autonomic nervous system are arranged in an interconnected chain along the thoracic and lumbar sections of the spinal cord. Ganglia of the parasympathetic division of the autonomic nervous system receive input from the cranial nerves and the sacral section of the cord and are located near the organs they innervate. The interconnections of the sympathetic system promote unified action by the body in a fight-or-flight situation, whereas the relative independence of the parasympathetic innervations allows for more discrete energy-saving responses. Most of the final synapses of the sympathetic nervous system use the neurotransmitter norepinephrine, while the final parasympathetic synapses use acetylcholine.

The brain is divided into the hindbrain, the midbrain, and the forebrain. The hindbrain is composed of the medulla, the pons, and the cerebellum. The medulla contains numerous nuclei that control life-preserving reflexes. The pons has many fibers that cross from right to left (and vice versa), going to the cerebellum, which is directly behind the pons. The cerebellum helps control movement and may be important for shifting attention and for timing. The reticular formation and the raphe system, which increase and decrease, respectively, the brain's readiness to respond to stimuli, have diffusely branching neurons throughout the medulla, pons, and midbrain and send diffusely branching axons throughout the brain. The midbrain is composed of the tectum (or roof), on which are the two superior colliculi and the two inferior colliculi, involved in sensory processing; and the tegmentum, containing extensions of neural systems of the hindbrain and also the substantia nigra, degeneration of which causes Parkinson's disease. The forebrain includes the limbic system, a number of interlinked structures important for motivational and emotional behaviors; the thalamus, which is the main source of sensory input to the cerebral cortex; the hypothalamus, important for motivational and hormonal regulation; the pituitary or "master gland"; the basal ganglia, which influence motor movements, emotional expression, memory, and reasoning; the hippocampus, important in memory functions; and the cerebral cortex, which surrounds the rest of the brain and is responsible for complex sensory analysis and integration, language processing, motor control, and social awareness. The ventricles are fluid-filled cavities within the brain.

The cerebral cortex consists of up to six laminae, or layers, of cell bodies parallel to the surface of the brain. The cells are organized into columns, perpendicular to the laminae; each column contains cells with similar response properties. The occipital lobe of the cerebral cortex is the site of primary visual processing. The parietal lobe processes somatosensory information and contributes to several complex processes, including attentiveness to stimuli. The temporal lobe processes auditory information and is important for perception of complex visual patterns and comprehension of language. The frontal lobe contains the motor cortex, which controls fine movements, and prefrontal cortex, which contributes to social awareness, the expression of emotion, memory for recent details (working memory), and calculation of actions and their outcomes.

Each part of the brain accomplishes a set of more or less specific functions; yet, a sense of unified experience emerges from these separate operations. The question of how the brain integrates various kinds of sensory information into the perception of a unified object is known as the binding problem. How are the various aspects bound together? One possibility is that binding depends on precisely simultaneous activity (gamma waves) in the different brain areas. The inferior temporal cortex may coordinate this activity. However, we still do not understand how synchronized gamma waves bind the different aspects into a unified perception.

KEY TERMS AND CONCEPTS

Module 4.1 The Divisions of the Vertebrate Nervous System

1. Some terminology
    Central nervous system (CNS): brain and spinal cord
    Peripheral nervous system (PNS): somatic and autonomic nervous systems
    Dorsal (toward the back)
    Ventral (toward the stomach)
    Dorsal-ventral axis of human brain at right angles to dorsal-ventral axis of spinal cord

2. The spinal cord
    Sensory nerves
    Motor nerves
    Bell-Magendie Law
    Dorsal root ganglion
    Gray matter
    White matter

3. The autonomic nervous system
    Sympathetic nervous system ("fight or flight")
        Sympathetic chains of ganglia
        Thoracic and lumbar regions
        Norepinephrine
        Gooseflesh: erection of hairs by sympathetic nervous system
    Parasympathetic nervous system (energy conserving)
        Cranial and sacral regions (craniosacral system)
        Ganglia near organs
        Acetylcholine

4. The hindbrain (rhombencephalon): medulla, pons, cerebellum
    Brain stem (medulla, pons, midbrain, some forebrain structures)
    Medulla
        Vital reflexes
        Cranial nerves
        Reticular formation
        Raphe system
    Pons ("bridge")
        Fibers crossing

Cranial nerves
Reticular formation
Raphe system
Cerebellum
Control of movement
Balance and coordination
Shifting attention
Timing

5. The midbrain (mesencephalon)
Tectum
Superior and inferior colliculi
Tegmentum
Cranial nerves
Reticular formation
Substantia nigra

6. The forebrain (prosencephalon)
Limbic system: border around brain stem
Olfactory bulb
Hypothalamus
Hippocampus
Amygdala
Cingulate gyrus of cerebral cortex
Thalamus
Transmit sensory information (except olfaction) to cortex
Hypothalamus
Motivated behaviors
Control of pituitary gland
Pituitary gland
Controls other glands
Basal ganglia
Caudate nucleus
Putamen
Globus pallidus
Connections with frontal cortex
Control of movement
Aspects of memory and emotional expression
Parkinson's disease
Huntington's disease
Basal forebrain
Nucleus basalis: acetylcholine to cortex
Arousal, wakefulness, attention
Parkinson's disease
Alzheimer's disease
Hippocampus
Storing new memories
Fornix: hippocampus to hypothalamus

7. The ventricles

Central canal
Cerebrospinal fluid (CSF)
Choroid plexus
Meninges
Subarachnoid space
Hydrocephalus

Module 4.2 The Cerebral Cortex

1. Hemispheric interconnections
    Corpus callosum
    Anterior commissure

2. Organization of the cerebral cortex
    Laminae and columns

3. The occipital lobe (posterior, or caudal, end of cortex)
    Primary visual cortex
        Striate cortex
    Cortical blindness

4. The parietal lobe (between occipital lobe and central sulcus)
    Central sulcus
    Postcentral gyrus
    Primary somatosensory cortex
        Two light-touch bands
        One deep-pressure band
        One light-touch and deep-pressure band
    Effects of right-hemisphere damage
        Neglect of opposite side of body

5. The temporal lobe (lateral, near temples)
    Primary auditory cortex
    Language comprehension
    Complex visual patterns
    Kluver-Bucy syndrome

6. The frontal lobe (from central sulcus to anterior end of brain)
    Primary motor cortex
        Precentral gyrus
    Prefrontal cortex
        The rise and fall of prefrontal lobotomies: Walter Freeman
            Lack of initiative
            Failure to inhibit unacceptable impulses
            Impaired facial expression of emotion
            Impairment of some aspects of memory
                More important for working memory than reference memory
                Delayed response task
        Shifting of attention
        Calculating actions and outcomes

7. How do the pieces work together?
   Operation as a whole vs. collection of parts
       Role of central amygdala in fear
           Specificity of function
       Karl Lashley
           Amount of damage more important than location
           May be true only for complex tasks
   The binding problem
       How brain areas influence one another to produce perception of single object
       Synchronized gamma waves
       Inferior parietal cortex

8. In closing: Functions of the cerebral cortex
   Elaborating sensory material

SHORT-ANSWER QUESTIONS

Module 4.1 The Divisions of the Vertebrate Nervous System
1. *The spinal cord*
   a. Draw a cross section of the spinal cord, including sensory and motor nerves, dorsal root ganglia, and dorsal and ventral directions.

   b. What is the Bell-Magendie Law?

   c. What makes up gray matter? White matter?

2. *The autonomic nervous system*
   a. Of what two parts does the autonomic nervous system consist? Give the location and basic function of each.

   b. Which transmitter is used by the postganglionic parasympathetic nerves? Which is used by most sympathetic postganglionic nerves?

3. *The hindbrain*
   a. What are the three components of the hindbrain? Give one "specialty" of each.

   b. What are cranial nerves? Where are their nuclei?

   c. What are the anatomical location and functions of the reticular formation and the raphe system?

4. *The midbrain*
   a. What are the two major divisions of the midbrain? Name two structures in each division.

5. *The forebrain*
   a. What are the major structures comprising the limbic system? What are the general functions of this interconnected system?

   b. Describe the relationship of the thalamus to the cerebral cortex.

   c. Where is the hypothalamus, and what kinds of behavior does it help regulate?

   d. Where is the pituitary? What is its function? What structure largely controls it?

   e. Where are the basal ganglia? Which structures make up the basal ganglia? Briefly describe their function.

f.   Where is the hippocampus? To what psychological process has it been linked?

6.   *The ventricles*
    a.   What are the ventricles? Where is cerebrospinal fluid (CSF) formed? In which direction does it flow? Where is it reabsorbed into blood vessels?

    b.   What are the functions of CSF?

Module 4.2 The Cerebral Cortex
1.   *Organization of cerebral cortex*
    a.   What is the relationship of gray matter to white in the cortex? Compare this relationship to that in the spinal cord.

    b.   How many layers (laminae) does human neocortex have? Describe the input to lamina IV and the output from lamina V.

c. What is the relationship of columns to laminae? What can be said about all the cells within one column?

2. *The occipital lobe*
   a. What are the location and functions of the occipital lobe?

3. *The parietal lobe*
   a. What are the location and functions of the parietal lobe?

4. *The temporal lobe*
   a. Where is the temporal lobe? What are some temporal lobe functions?

5. *The frontal lobe*
   a. What are the location and functions of the frontal lobe? Distinguish between the precentral gyrus and the prefrontal cortex.

b.   What were the results of prefrontal lobotomies?

c.-   What is the difference between working memory and reference memory? Which shows
greater impairment after prefrontal lesions?

d.   What is the delayed response task, and how is it affected by prefrontal lesions? Is this
primarily a test of working or reference memory?

6.   *How do the pieces work together?*
a.   How would you answer the question of whether the brain operates as an undifferentiated
whole or a collection of independent parts?

b.   What is the binding problem?

c. What are gamma waves? What may be the role of the inferior temporal cortex in binding the different aspects of sensory objects?

POSTTEST

Multiple-Choice Questions

1. Which is true concerning the spinal cord?
   a. Sensory neurons enter on the ventral side; motor neurons exit on the dorsal side.
   b. Cell bodies of sensory neurons lie outside the CNS in the dorsal root ganglia.
   c. Cell bodies of motor neurons lie outside the CNS in the ventral root ganglia.
   d. All of the above are true.

2. The parasympathetic system
   a. is sometimes called the "fight or flight" system.
   b. has a chain of interconnected ganglia along the thoracic and lumbar parts of the spinal cord.
   c. uses norepinephrine as its transmitter; the sympathetic system uses acetylcholine.
   d. is an energy-conserving system.

3. Concerning the cranial nerves,
   a. nuclei for the first four enter the forebrain and midbrain; nuclei for the rest are in the medulla and pons.
   b. nuclei for all twelve are in the medulla and pons.
   c. all have both sensory and motor components.
   d. all have only sensory or only motor components.

4. The hindbrain
   a. consists of four parts: the superior and inferior colliculi, the tectum, and the tegmentum.
   b. contains the reticular formation and raphe system.
   c. controls the pituitary gland.
   d. consists of the pons, which is adjacent to the spinal cord; the medulla, which is rostral to the pons; and the cerebellum, which is anterior to the pons.

5. The medulla
   a. contains prominent axons crossing from one side of the brain to the other.
   b. is part of the limbic system.
   c. contains nuclei that control vital functions.
   d. is especially important for working memory.

6. The cerebellum
   a. contributes to the control of movement, shifting of attention, and timing.
   b. is concerned mostly with visual location in space.
   c. is located immediately ventral to the pons.
   d. all of the above.

72

7. The components of the midbrain include
    a. the superior and inferior colliculi in the tectum, involved in sensory processing.
    b. the tegmentum, containing nuclei of the third and fourth cranial nerves, part of the reticular formation, and pathways connecting higher and lower structures.
    c. the substantia nigra, origin of a dopamine-containing pathway that deteriorates in Parkinson's disease.
    d. all of the above.

8. The limbic system
    a. is a set of isolated areas that are important for different aspects of memory.
    b. is a set of interlinked structures that are important for motivated and emotional behaviors.
    c. is another term for the basal ganglia.
    d. gets its name from the Latin word for bridge.

9. The hypothalamus
    a. contains parts of the reticular formation and raphe system.
    b. is part of the basal ganglia.
    c. is important for motivated behaviors and hormonal control.
    d. is connected only with the brain stem.

10. The basal ganglia
    a. are composed primarily of the caudate nucleus, putamen, and globus pallidus.
    b. control movement directly via axons to the spinal cord.
    c. are primarily concerned with sensory processing.
    d. all of the above.

11. The hippocampus   memories
    a. controls breathing, heart rate, and other vital reflexes.
    b. provides the major control for the pituitary gland.
    c. is part of the basal ganglia.
    d. none of the above.

12. The thalamus contains
    a. the superior and inferior colliculi.
    b. nuclei that project to particular areas of cerebral cortex.
    c. nuclei that regulate the pituitary.
    d. nuclei having to do with motivated behaviors, such as eating, drinking, sex, fighting, arousal level, and temperature regulation.

13. Cerebrospinal fluid
    a. is formed by cells lining the four ventricles.
    b. flows from the lateral ventricles to the third and fourth ventricles, and from there either to the central canal of the spinal cord or to the subarachnoid space, where it is reabsorbed into the blood vessels.
    c. cushions the brain and provides buoyancy.
    d. all of the above.

14. The laminae of the cortex
    a. usually consist of only two layers, one of axons and one of cell bodies.
    b. are the same thickness throughout the brain of a given species, but differ across species.
    c. consist of up to six layers, which vary in thickness across the various brain areas.
    d. are present only in humans; other mammals have cortical cells and axons mixed together.

15. Which of the following is true of cortical columns?
    a. Columns run parallel to the laminae, across the surface of the cortex.
    b. There are six columns in the human brain, and only one or two in other mammals.
    c. Cells within a column have similar response properties.
    d. The properties of cells within a column change systematically from top to bottom; cells at the top may respond to one stimulus, while those at the bottom respond to a different one.

16. Which is true of the occipital lobe?
    a. It is located at the posterior end of the cortex and contains primary visual cortex.
    b. It is located at the sides of the brain and is concerned mostly with perception of complex visual patterns.
    c. It is located immediately behind the central sulcus and contains the postcentral gyrus.
    d. It is located at the top of the brain and contributes to somatosensory processing.

17. Which is true of the parietal lobe?
    a. It contains the primary receiving area for axons carrying touch sensations and other skin and muscle information.
    b. It has a somewhat complicated spatial representation of the body on the postcentral gyrus.
    c. Damage to it on the right side can produce neglect of the opposite side of the body.
    d. All of the above are true.

18. The temporal lobe
    a. is located immediately in front of the central sulcus.
    b. is involved in some complex aspects of visual processing as well as auditory processing.
    c. has as its only function the processing of simple auditory information.
    d. none of the above.

19. Damage to the frontal lobe
    a. may cause losses of initiative and of social inhibitions and produce difficulties with delayed response tasks.
    b. is still a widely used surgical technique for mental patients because of its remarkable calming and normalizing tendencies without noticeable side effects.
    c. produces drastic impairments in intelligence.
    d. all of the above.

20. Gamma waves
    a. are synchronized waves of activity (30 to 80 per second) in various brain areas, which may reflect binding of sensory aspects into a unified perception.
    b. are synchronized by the prefrontal cortex, indicating that prefrontal cortex is the site of unified experience.
    c. are seen in the central amygdala during fearful experiences, and therefore are the basis for our sense of fear.
    d. are synchronized waves of activity localized within a specific brain area, and are important for shifting attention to the sensory aspect that is processed by that area.

Answers to Multiple-Choice Questions

1. b	6. a	11. d	16. a
2. d	7. d	12. b	17. d
3. a	8. b	13. d	18. b
4. b	9. c	14. c	19. a
5. c	10. a	15. c	20. a

Helpful Hints

1. To remember the 12 cranial nerves, use this mnemonic device:

1. On	(Olfactory)	7. Firm,	(Facial)
2. Old	(Optic)	8. Staid	(Statoacoustic)
3. Olympia's	(Oculomotor)	9. German	(Glossopharyngial)
4. Towering	(Trochlear)	10. Viewed	(Vagus)
5. Tops,	(Trigeminal)	11. A lot of	(Accessory)
6. A	(Abducens)	12. Hops	(Hypoglossal)

2. To remember the functions of the hypothalamus, think of the "4 Fs": Fighting, Fleeing, Feeding, and Reproductive Behavior.

Diagrams

1. In the following diagram of a sagittal section through the human brain, label the following structures: cerebral cortex, parietal lobe, occipital lobe, frontal lobe, cingulate gyrus, corpus callosum, thalamus, hypothalamus, superior and inferior colliculi, midbrain, cerebellum, pons, pituitary gland, tissue dividing the lateral ventricles, medulla, spinal cord, central canal of the spinal cord.

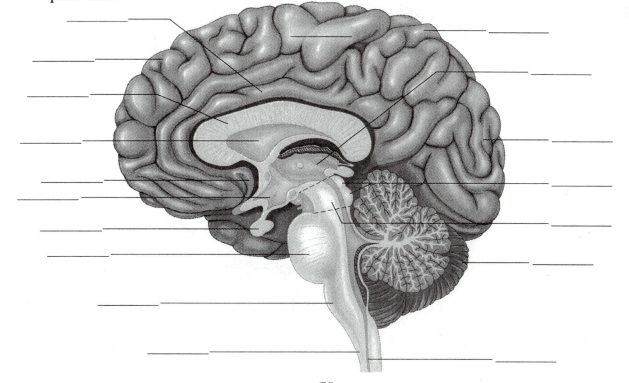

75

2. In the following diagram of a cross section through the spinal cord, label the following directions or structures: dorsal, ventral, sensory nerve, dorsal root ganglion, motor nerve, white matter, gray matter, central canal.

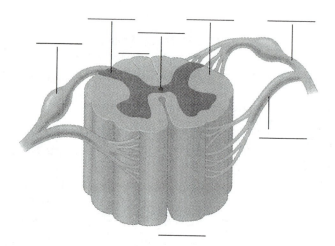

3. In the following diagram of the human cerebral cortex, label the following structures: central sulcus, precentral gyrus, postcentral gyrus, occipital lobe, frontal lobe, parietal lobe, and temporal lobe. Give the functions of each brain area.

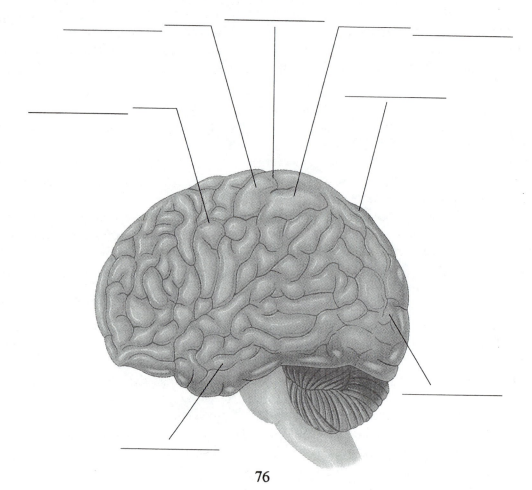

5

DEVELOPMENT AND PLASTICITY OF THE BRAIN

INTRODUCTION

The central nervous system develops from two long thin lips on the surface of the embryo that merge to form a fluid-filled tube. The forward end of the tube enlarges to become the forebrain, midbrain, and hindbrain; the rest becomes the spinal cord. Cerebrospinal fluid continues to fill the central canal of the spinal cord and four hollow ventricles of the brain.

There are four major stages in the development of neurons: proliferation, migration, differentiation, and myelination. During proliferation, cells lining the ventricles divide. Some of the new cells remain in place and continue dividing, whereas others migrate to their new destinations. Differentiation includes formation of the axon and dendrites and determination of shape and chemical components. Myelination is the formation, by glial cells, of insulating sheaths around axons, which increase the speed of transmission. Brain growth consists of both the expansion of old units and the addition of new ones, such as the glomeruli of the olfactory bulb and columns of cerebral cortex.

There is an initial overproduction of neurons; those that fail to form synapses with appropriate target cells die. The process of programmed cell death, or apoptosis, can be prevented if the neuron receives a neurotrophin from the target cell. Rita Levi-Montalcini discovered the first neurotrophin, nerve growth factor (NGF), which promotes survival of neurons of the sympathetic nervous system. Several additional neurotrophins have been discovered, including brain-derived neurotrophic factor (BDNF) and neurotrophins 3, 4/5, and 6. In addition to preventing apoptosis, neurotrophins may also enhance axonal branching and promote regrowth of axons after injury.

As the brain grows, axons must travel long distances to reach their appropriate targets. They are guided by concentration gradients of chemicals, such as the protein TOP_{DV}, which guides retinal neurons to the appropriate part of the tectum. After axons reach the general area of their target, they begin to form synapses with postsynaptic cells. These target cells receive an overabundance of synapses; they gradually strengthen some synapses and reject others. Initially, there are many tentative connections between axons and target cells; later, fewer but stronger attachments develop. The overproduction of neurons and subsequent pruning of unsuccessful connections provide a process of selection of the fittest or most informative connections.

Environmental enrichment results in a thicker cortex, more dendritic branching, and enhanced performance on learning tasks. Effects of enrichment, or of sensory deprivation, have been observed in species as diverse as honeybees, fish, and humans, although it is sometimes difficult to determine cause and effect relationships. Some experiences, such as environmental enrichment, have greater effects if they occur early in life. Song learning in birds is accompanied by a decrease in the number of dendritic spines, but an increase in the size of surviving spines. The large number of spines initially may allow for learning of an unpredictable variety of songs; but after the first year the circuitry for certain songs is strengthened, at the expense of that for new songs. In humans, early music training may increase the size of certain cortical areas. However, developing brains are not only more responsive to environmental stimuli, they are also more vulnerable to malnutrition, toxic chemicals, and disease. Although most neurons are formed early in life, adult brains have some ability to generate new neurons. Undifferentiated stem cells lining the ventricles can generate daughter cells that migrate to the olfactory bulbs. There is also evidence for new olfactory receptors and new neurons in the hippocampus and parts of the cerebral cortex of adults.

Brain damage can be caused by a variety of factors, including closed head injury and stroke. Stroke can result either from ischemia due to a blood clot that obstructs an artery, or from hemorrhage, caused by rupture of an artery. Strokes kill neurons either by depriving them of oxygen and glucose or by overexcitation, which allows excess sodium, calcium, and zinc ions to enter the neuron, resulting in swelling or bursting of the membrane and interfering with normal processes. Cell death can be minimized by the use of drugs that break up clots and perhaps those that block glutamate receptors, if given early after the stroke. Potential new treatments include cooling the brain, food restriction, and the administration of neurotrophins, cannabinoids, or drugs that trap free radicals.

Recovery may depend on a number of possible physiological mechanisms. Learned adjustments in behavior allow an individual to make better use of abilities unaffected by the damage and to improve abilities that were impaired by the damage, but not lost. Diaschisis, or decreased activity of neurons after loss of input, contributes to impairment following brain damage. It can be reduced by administration of stimulant drugs. Regrowth of axons can be guided by myelin sheaths in the periphery. However, axons in the central nervous system do not regenerate, in part because of formation of scar tissue and in part because of growth-inhibiting proteins. Sprouting of axons occurs in response to normal cell death, as well as after brain damage; axons from undamaged neurons develop new terminals that occupy the vacant synapses. Denervation supersensitivity refers to the increased sensitivity to a neurotransmitter by a postsynaptic cell that is deprived of synaptic input. Reorganization of sensory representations can occur by postsynaptic adjustments of synaptic strength or by collateral sprouting, sometimes over surprisingly long distances. However, these reorganizations may not be beneficial, as in the case of phantom-limb sensations.

Very old people have less potential for recovery after brain damage than do young adults. Furthermore, after recovery from brain damage in a young adult, the recovered behavior may be disrupted during old age. This suggests that damage to infant brains should be less debilitating than similar damage to adult brains. Under some circumstances this is true, and the infant's brain development can be modified to compensate for damage. On the other hand, damage to an infant brain may be more disruptive than that to an adult brain, depending on the age, brain area affected, and type of damage. Prenatal and infant brains are most vulnerable.

Therapies for brain damage include behavioral interventions that help people to reaccess memories or skills or to make better use of their unimpaired abilities. More recently, researchers have experimented with brain grafting and with drug treatments, such as calcium channel blockers, gangliosides, and progesterone. While these treatments are still in experimental stages, there is optimism for future improvements.

KEY TERMS AND CONCEPTS

Module 5.1 Development of the Brain
1. Growth and differentiation of the vertebrate brain
   Early development of the nervous system
       Neural tube
       Hindbrain
       Midbrain
       Forebrain
       Spinal cord
       Central canal of spinal cord
       Ventricles of brain
       Cerebrospinal fluid (CSF)

Growth and development of neurons
    Proliferation of new cells
    Migration toward eventual destinations
    Differentiation, forming axon first and then dendrites
    Myelination of some axons, continuing for years
    Organization of brain areas
        Olfactory bulb glomeruli
        Cortical columns
        Addition of new units
        Expansion of old units
Determinants of neuron survival
    Nerve growth factor (NGF)
        Sympathetic nervous system
        Rita Levi-Montalcini
        Promotes survival and growth, not neuronal birth
        Apoptosis vs. necrosis
    Other neurotrophins
        Brain-derived neurotrophic factor (BDNF)
        Neurotrophins 3, 4/5, 6
    Functions of neurotrophins
        Prevent apoptosis
        Increase branching of incoming axons
        Decrease pain and increase axon regrowth after injury
    Overproduction of neurons and massive cell death
        Error correction
        Match incoming axons to number of recipient cells

2.   Pathfinding by axons
   Chemical pathfinding by axons
       Specificity of axon connections
       Axons to extra leg of salamander
       Optic tract axons to tectum of newts
   Chemical gradients
       TOP_{DV}
   Competition among axons as a general principle
       Neural Darwinism

3.   Fine-tuning by experience
   Effects of experience on dendritic branching
       Enriched environment
           Thicker cortex
           More dendritic branches
           Improved learning
           Extensive education in humans
       Bird song learning
           Decreases number, but increases size, of dendritic spines
   Generation of new neurons
       Olfactory receptors
       Stem cells
           Lining of ventricles

Daughter cells→olfactory bulb
Hippocampus
Parts of cerebral cortex
Enhanced by diverse experience
Effects of experience on human brain structure
Early music training
Retain absolute pitch
Larger area in left temporal cortex
Playing stringed instruments (fingering with left hand)
Larger area in right postcentral gyrus
Methods 5.1: Magnetoencephalography
Magnetic fields generated by brain activity
Good temporal resolution, poor spatial resolution
Combinations of chemical and experiential effects
Two-stage process
Chemical gradients guide axons to approximate target
Strengthen some connections, discard others in response to experience
Spontaneous action potentials
Simultaneous activity of axons from nearby retinal areas
Lateral geniculate

4. Proportional growth of brain areas
Size of brain areas
Rate and duration of neuron proliferation
Parallel growth across brain areas (logarithmic)
Brain size and IQ
Significant correlation in one study
Men: larger brains than women, but similar IQ
Brain-to-body ratio: partial answer
Methods 5.2: MRI scans: magnetic resonance imaging
Atoms with odd-numbered atomic weights: inherent rotation
Magnetic field → alignment of axes of rotation
Brief radio frequency field → tilt axes
Turn off radio frequency field → atomic nuclei relax and release electromagnetic energy
Advantage: good spatial resolution without radioactivity
Disadvantage: lie motionless in confining, noisy apparatus

5. The vulnerable developing brain
Greater vulnerablilty to malnutrition, toxic chemicals, infections
Impaired thyroid function in infancy: permanent mental retardation and slow body growth
Anesthetics: apoptosis
Fetal alcohol syndrome
Short, less branched dendrites
Maternal cocaine or cigarette smoking
ADHD (attention-deficit/hyperactivity disorder) and ADD (attention-deficit disorder)
Difficult diagnosis
Decreased frontal cortex activity
Methylphenidate (Ritalin) or amphetamine
Increase availability of dopamine
Increase attention span of ADD and normal children

Module 5.2 Recovery of Function after Brain Damage
1. Causes of human brain damage
    Closed head injury
    Stroke (cerebrovascular accident)
        Ischemia (blood clot closes artery)
            Area of direct damage: loss of oxygen and glucose
            Penumbra: loss of much, but not all, oxygen and glucose
        Hemorrhage (rupture of artery)
            Area of direct damage: loss of oxygen and glucose
            Penumbra: excess oxygen, calcium, blood products
        Penumbra, following both ischemia and hemorrhage
            Waste from dead cells in area of direct damage
            Extracellular potassium
            Edema
            Glial cells release stored glutamate →
            Overstimulation →
            Accumulation of sodium, calcium, and zinc →
            Interference with chemical processes and swelling or bursting of membrane
        Means of lessening damage
            Tissue plasminogen activator (tPA): breaks up blood clots
            Glutamate antagonists and calcium channel blockers: mixed results
                Deficient glutamate and calcium → apoptosis
                Time course of MK-801 (glutamate receptor antagonist)
            Animal studies
                Neurotrophins
                Drugs that trap free radicals
                Food restriction
                Cannabinoids
                Cooling brain—most effective

2. Adjustments and potential recovery after brain damage
        Learned adjustments in behavior
            Deafferented limbs
                One deafferented limb: lack of spontaneous use
                Two deafferented limbs: monkey learns to use both
            Diaschisis
                Amphetamine (releases dopamine and norepinephrine): enhanced recovery
                Haloperidol (blocks dopamine receptors): impaired recovery
                Tranquilizers (decrease dopamine and norepinephrine release): impair recovery
        Methods 5.3: Lesions
            Ablation
            Stereotaxic instrument
            Sham lesion
        The regrowth of axons
            Myelin sheaths as guides
            Inhibiting growth of scar tissue: little effect
            Myelin
                Inhibits axon regrowth in CNS
                Stimulates axon regrowth in periphery
            CNS astrocytes → growth-inhibiting proteins

Antibodies to those proteins → regeneration of axons
Graft peripheral glia into CNS
Hemiplegia
Sprouting
Collateral sprouts
Locus coeruleus
Normal condition, not just response to damage
Cut connections from left entorhinal cortex to left hippocampus →
Right entorhinal cortex sprouts →
Recovery
Then cut path from right entorhinal cortex →
Impairs recovery
Denervation supersensitivy
Disuse supersensitivity
6-OHDA (6-hydroxydopmine)
Amphetamine: increased release of dopamine mostly on intact side of brain
Apomorphine: stimulated supersensitive dopamine receptors on brain-injured side
Methods 5.3: Autoradiography
Application of radioactive chemicals to thin brain sections
Sections placed against film → records amount of radioactivity in various brain areas
Reorganized sensory representations and the phantom limb
Based on collateral sprouting or increased receptor sensitivity
Amputation of finger: cortical responsiveness to adjacent fingers
Deafferentation of forelimb: cortical responsiveness to face
Phantom limb sensations in humans
Touch face → feel phantom hand
Sexual activity → feel phantom foot
Use mirror to reduce phantom pain
Methods 5.4: Histochemistry
Horseradish peroxidase (HRP)

3. Effects of age
Loss of "recovered" behaviors in old age
Kennard principle: more extensive recovery after early damage
Applies only to certain kinds of damage
Young brain more plastic, also more vulnerable
Effects on still-developing neurons
Remove one hemisphere: increased thickness of other hemisphere
Remove anterior cortex: less development of posterior cortex
Early orbital frontal cortex damage: later developing areas compensate
Early dorsolateral prefrontal cortex damage: effects more apparent later

4. Therapies
Behavioral interventions
Reaccess lost skills or memories
Practice impaired skills
Remove distracting stimuli

Drugs
    Nimodipine
        Calcium channel blocker
        Prevent damage due to excess NMDA stimulation
    Gangliosides (glycolipids)
    Progesterone
Brain grafts

SHORT-ANSWER QUESTIONS

Module 5.1 The Development of the Brain
1. *Growth and differentiation of the vertebrate brain*
    a.   Describe the formation of the central nervous system in the embryo. What happens to the fluid-filled cavity?

    b.   What are the three main divisions of the brain?

    c.   What are the four major stages in the development of neurons? Describe the processes in each.

    d.   What technical development by LaMantia and Purves increased our understanding of brain development? What was their major finding?

e.   What is apoptosis? What type of chemical can prevent apoptosis?

f.-   Who discovered nerve growth factor? What happens if a neuron in the sympathetic nervous system does not receive enough nerve growth factor?

g.   List five neurotrophins. What three functions do they serve?

2.   *Pathfinding by axons*
    a.   What did Weiss observe in his experiments on salamanders' extra limbs? What principle did he conclude directed the innervation of the extra limb? Is this principle still believed to be correct?

    b.   What did Sperry observe when he damaged the optic nerve of newts? What happened when he rotated the eye by 180 degrees? How did the newt with the rotated eye see the world?

c.   What conclusion did these results suggest?

d.   What is TOP_{DV}? What is its role in directing retinal axons to the tectum?

e.   What happens to axons that form active synapses? What happens to axons that do not form active synapses?

f.   Describe the principle of neural Darwinism. How does this relate to the initial overproduction and subsequent death of large numbers of neurons?

3. *Fine-tuning by experience*
    a.   Describe the effects of environmental "enrichment".

    b.   What physiological process appears to be correlated with song learning in mynah birds?

c. In what brain areas have new neurons been found in adulthood? What are stem cells and where are they found?

d. What is a brain correlate of absolute pitch? What evidence suggests that this may result from extensive early musical training?

e. What brain area is frequently larger in people who had extensive experience playing stringed instruments?

f. How does a lateral geniculate neuron "know" which axons originated near one another in the retina?

4. *Proportional growth of brain areas*
    a. What two factors determine the development of each brain area?

b.   Describe the neural development across various brain areas. Is this relationship linear or logarithmic?

c.   Describe the evidence for a correlation between brain size and intelligence in humans. How does this apply to men vs. women? To short people vs. tall people?

5.   *The vulnerable developing brain*
     a.   What are the effects of thyroid deficiency in adulthood? Compare these with the effects of thyroid deficiency in infancy.

     b.   Describe fetal alcohol syndrome. How are dendrites affected? How much alcohol is necessary to produce the syndrome?

     c.   What are the effects of prenatal cocaine exposure? Cigarette smoking during pregnancy?

d.   What types of behavioral and physiological abnormalities are associated with ADHD and ADD? What are the effects of Ritalin and amphetamine on behavior and neurochemistry?

Module 5.2 Recovery of Function after Brain Damage

1.   *Causes of human brain damage*
a.   What are the two types of stroke and the cause of each?

b.   In what two ways does a stroke kill neurons?   Describe the sequence of destructive processes in the penumbra.

c.   What are six treatments that may minimize damage from stroke?

2.   *Adjustments and potential recovery after brain damage*
a.   List six potential mechanisms for recovery from brain damage.

b. How may learned adjustments in behavior be promoted?

c. What is diaschisis? How is recovery from diaschisis affected by amphetamine or haloperidol?

d. How may crushed, but not cut, axons in the peripheral nervous system form appropriate connections when they regenerate? Why don't axons in the central nervous system regenerate? How might this lack of regeneration be overcome?

e. Under what conditions is sprouting most likely to be useful? What evidence suggests that sprouting produces beneficial results?

f. What is denervation supersensitivity?

g. What are the effects of 6-OHDA? Explain the differential effects of amphetamine and apomorphine after 6-OHDA lesions.

h. What evidence is there that sensory representations may be reorganized during recovery? What surprised investigators about the brain of a monkey whose limb had been deafferented 12 years earlier?

i. What are some sources of sensory input that can give rise to phantom limbs? What is the relationship between reorganization of somatosensory cortex and the likelihood of phantom sensations?

3. *Effects of age*
    a. Why is recovery from brain damage more difficult in old age? What sometimes happens in old age to functions that had been recovered in young adulthood?

    b. What is the Kennard principle? What evidence supports or refutes it?

c. What are some factors that may determine whether an infant brain is better or less able to recover from brain damage, compared to an adult brain?

d. What are the differences in the time courses of recovery from early damage to the orbital frontal cortex and the dorsolateral prefrontal cortex?

4. *Therapies*
   a. How may behavioral interventions facilitate recovery from brain damage?

   b. What are three potential drug therapies for brain damage? How may they work?

   c. How successful have brain transplants for Parkinson's disease been?

5. *Methods boxes*
    a. What does the magnetoencephalograph (MEG) measure? What is an advantage and a disadvantage of the MEG?

    b. What is the principle behind magnetic resonance imaging (MRI)? What is an advantage and a disadvantage of this technique?

    c. What is a stereotaxic instrument? Why is important to compare sham lesions with actual lesions?

    d. How is autoradiography used? What kind of data does it provide?

    e. How can histochemistry be used?

POSTTEST

Multiple-Choice Questions

1. The neural tube
   a. arises from a pair of long thin lips that merge around a fluid-filled cavity.
   b. develops into the spinal cord; the brain arises from a separate structure.
   c. eventually merges to form a solid structure, squeezing out the primitive cerebrospinal fluid.
   d. none of the above.

2. The four major stages in the development of neurons, in order, are
   a. proliferation, differentiation, migration, myelination.
   b. proliferation, growth, myelination, migration.
   c. proliferation, migration, myelination, growth.
   d. proliferation, migration, differentiation, myelination.

3. Which of the following is true?
   a. Myelination is complete by the end of the first year in humans.
   b. Neurons experimentally transplanted from one site to another at an intermediate stage of development may keep some properties of cells in the old location and develop some that are characteristic of their new location.
   c. Dendrites usually form before axons, and are usually fully formed before migration begins.
   d. Neurons are incapable of conducting action potentials until they are fully myelinated.

4. As the olfactory bulbs grow
   a. the number of glomeruli stays the same, but the size of each glomerulus increases.
   b. the glomeruli that were characteristic of the infant brain merge to form one continuous functional unit in the adult.
   c. the size of each glomerulus increases considerably, but the number of glomeruli actually decreases.
   d. the size of each glomerulus expands and new glomeruli are added.

5. Apoptosis
   a. is caused by an excess of neurotrophin.
   b. occurs in only a few areas of the brain.
   c. is the "suicide program" of the cell.
   d. was the first neurotrophin to be discovered.

6. Nerve growth factor
   a. is important for the health of all neurons throughout life.
   b. is important for the survival and growth of sympathetic neurons.
   c. is important for the survival of all sensory neurons, but not motor neurons.
   d. is important for the initial survival of all neurons but becomes less important after synapses are formed.

7. When Paul Weiss grafted an extra leg onto a salamander
   a. the extra leg received no neurons and therefore could not move.
   b. the extra leg moved in the opposite direction from the normal adjacent leg.
   c. the extra leg moved in synchrony with the normal adjacent leg.
   d. the leg degenerated because the immune system rejected it.

8. Sperry's work with the eyes of newts led him to conclude that
    a. neurons attach to postsynaptic cells randomly, and the postsynaptic cell confers specificity.
    b. axons follow a chemical trail that places them in the general vicinity of their target.
    c. innervation in the sensory system is guided by specific genetic information, whereas that in the motor system is random.
    d. neurons follow specific genetic information that directs each of them to precisely the right postsynaptic cell.

9. TOP_{DV}
    a. is a trophic factor necessary for the survival of neurons of the sympathetic nervous system.
    b. is a protein that guides axons to the developing legs of newts.
    c is a protein that causes a group of neurons that possess it to fire together, thereby increasing their chance of survival.
    d. is a protein that is more concentrated in neurons of the dorsal retina and the ventral tectum than in the ventral retina and dorsal tectum.

10. Massive cell death early in development
    a. would be so maladaptive that it hardly ever occurs.
    b. occurs only when the sensory environment has been highly restricted or when the fetus has been exposed to toxins.
    c. occurs as a result of genetic mistakes, which fail to direct the cells to their genetically programmed target. As a result the neurons wander aimlessly until they die.
    d. is a normal result of unsuccessful competition for synapses and growth factors.

11. Neural Darwinism
    a. was formulated by Roger Sperry.
    b. has recently been shown to be false.
    c. proposes that synapses form somewhat randomly at first; those that work best are kept, while the others degenerate.
    d. all of the above.

12. Environmental enrichment
    a. produces greater dendritic branching.
    b. produces changes in the structure of neurons, but no changes in their function.
    c. produces changes in the function of neurons, but no changes in their structure.
    d. has beneficial effects only in primates.

13. During their first year, mynah birds
    a. have decreasing numbers of dendritic spines in the song control areas of the brain.
    b. have an increase in size of the surviving dendritic spines.
    c. learn many songs, but, by year's end, have decreased ability to learn additional songs.
    d. all of the above.

14. Stem cells
    a. are hippocampal neurons that are especially resistant to damage.
    b. are undifferentiated cells lining the ventricles that sometimes generate daughter cells that migrate to the olfactory bulb and become glial cells or neurons.
    c. are glial cells that guide neurons during migration.
    d. are neurons that develop especially long axons that resemble the stems of plants.

15. Which of the following is true?
    a. Adults who have absolute pitch have larger than usual development in one area of the left temporal cortex.
    b. People with extensive experience playing stringed instruments also have larger than usual development in one area of the left temporal cortex.
    c. During early development the lateral geniculate neurons become responsive to inputs that are active out of phase with each other, in order to maximize the diversity of inputs.
    d. All of the above are true.

16. Which of the following is true concerning brain size?
    a. All brain components increase in direct (linear) proportion with one another.
    b. There is one experiment showing that people with larger brains have higher IQ scores.
    c. Men have larger brains, and therefore have higher IQ scores than do women.
    d. Short people have higher brain/body ratios, and are therefore smarter than tall people.

17. Mental retardation
    a. can be caused by thyroid deficiency during adulthood.
    b. results directly from excessively high levels of thyroid hormones during infancy.
    c. can be caused by thyroid deficiency in infancy.
    d. almost never results from genetic mutations.

18. Fetal alcohol syndrome
    a. results in decreased alertness, hyperactivity, varying degrees of mental retardation, motor problems, heart defects, and facial abnormalities.
    b. is observed even in children whose mothers took a single alcoholic drink during pregnancy.
    c. results from excessively long, heavily branched dendrites.
    d. all of the above.

19. Children of mothers who smoked during pregnancy have greater risk for
    a. low birth weight and many illnesses during life.
    b. Sudden Infant Death Syndrome (SIDS).
    c. intellectual deficits, ADHD, and impairments of the immune system.
    d. all of the above.

20. The most common cause of brain damage in young adults is
    a. stroke.
    b. disease.
    c. a sharp blow to the head.
    d. a brain tumor.

21. Which of the following occurs in the penumbra surrounding the area of direct damage from stroke?
    a. It is invaded by waste products from the dead or dying cells in the area of direct damage.
    b. Potassium ions and fluid accumulate outside the neurons.
    c. Glutamate released from glial cells overstimulates neurons, resulting in sodium, calcium, and zinc ions accumulating in the cells, which in turn impairs normal processes and causes the membranes to swell or burst.
    d. All of the above are true.

22. Damage from strokes can be minimized by
    a. activating glutamate synapses immediately after the stroke.
    b. giving tissue plasminogen activator, if the stroke is due to ischemia.
    c. creating a fever, which will increase the temperature of the brain and therefore enhance repair processes.
    d. all of the above.

23. Research on recovery from brain damage has shown that
    a. recovery can sometimes occur when an individual is forced to make full use of remaining capabilities.
    b. a person has to completely relearn the skills and memories that were lost when brain cells were killed.
    c. the primary means of recovery is having some other area of the brain take over the function of the damaged area.
    d. injections of transmitters is the best way to restore lost memories.

24. Amphetamine improves recovery by
    a. reducing diaschisis.
    b. producing denervation supersensitivity.
    c. relieving stress.
    d. stimulating regrowth of axons.

25. Adequate regrowth of an axon does **not** occur if
    a. the damaged axon is in the spinal cord of fish.
    b. an axon in the peripheral nervous system of mammals is crushed.
    c. the damaged axon is in the central nervous system of mammals.
    d. all of the above.

26. Research on regrowth of axons in mammals has shown that
    a. inhibiting the formation of scar tissue is a highly successful new technique.
    b. myelin in the peripheral, but not central, nervous system helps axons regenerate.
    c. the mammalian central nervous system has evolved advanced chemical stimuli to promote better axon regrowth than that seen in fish.
    d. the reason that neurons in the central nervous system fail to regenerate is that there are no myelin sheaths there.

27. Sprouting
    a. occurs only in response to traumatic brain damage.
    b. is always maladaptive, since the wrong axons make connections.
    c. may be adaptive if sprouts come from closely related axons.
    d. is enhanced by haloperidol.

28. Denervation supersensitivity is the result of
    a. increased output from other presynaptic cells adjacent to the one that has been damaged.
    b. postsynaptic neurons producing receptors for a different transmitter.
    c. changes in the chemical composition of the transmitter, making it more potent.
    d. an increased number of receptors on the postsynaptic cell and other changes within the cell.

29. After 6-OHDA lesions were made on the left side of a rat's brain
    a. amphetamine increased the release of dopamine mostly on the intact right side and thereby caused the rat to turn left.
    b. amphetamine directly stimulated supersensitive postsynaptic receptors on the intact right side, causing the rat to turn to the right.
    c. both amphetamine and apomorphine stimulated postsynaptic receptors on both sides of the brain, causing the animal to walk in a straight line.
    d. the primary means of recovery was collateral sprouting of neurons containing acetylcholine.

30. After amputation of one finger of an owl monkey
    a. neurons that had previously responded to it died because of lack of input.
    b. neurons that had previously responded to it became more responsive to other parts of the hand.
    c. reorganization caused the adjacent fingers to feel like the lost one.
    d. no reorganization could occur because connections become permanently fixed during the early critical period.

31. Aging is associated with
    a. shrinking of dendrites in certain brain areas in senile people, but not in alert older people.
    b. impaired recovery from brain damage, in part because remaining neurons modify their branching less readily than in younger people.
    c. loss of previously recovered functions due to damage that occurred long ago.
    d. all of the above.

32. The Kennard principle
    a. states that infants have less ability than adults to recover from brain damage, since their brains are more fragile.
    b. is true only for the peripheral nervous system.
    c. is only partly correct, since fetal and infant brains are actually more vulnerable than adults' brains to the effects of malnutrition, toxic chemicals, and infections; also recovery depends on the brain area damaged and the tested behavior.
    d. is entirely correct, since infants always have greater ability to recover from any sort of brain damage.

33. Which of the following statements about recovery from damage in infant brains is **not** true?
    a. The main reason that infant brains appear to recover from damage more fully than adults is that they cannot be tested as thoroughly.
    b. Performance deficits may not be noticed for more than a year after damage to dorsolateral prefrontal cortex of monkeys.
    c. During early development, damage to one set of neurons may alter the survival and connections of other neurons.
    d. Damage to infant brains can result in altered connections by the spared neurons.

34. Nimodipine
    a. is a type of ganglioside that can decrease the amount of damage caused by a stroke.
    b. is a calcium channel blocker that can decrease the amount of damage caused by a stroke, if administered after the stroke.
    c. is a neurotoxin that destroys catecholamine neurons.
    d. is an immune suppressant that stops rejection of brain grafts.

97

35. Brain grafting
    a. is by now a well established way of treating numerous disorders.
    b. has had its greatest successes in treating Alzheimer's disease.
    c. is never used any more, because the brain has such an effective immune system that the transplants never live.
    d. provides measurable, but somewhat disappointing, benefits to patients with Parkinson's disease.

Answers to Multiple-Choice Questions

1. a	6. b	11. c	16. b	21. d	26. b	31. d
2. a	7. c	12. a	17. c	22. b	27. c	32. c
3. b	8. b	13. d	18. a	23. a	28. d	33. a
4. d	9. d	14. b	19. d	24. a	29. a	34. b
5. c	10. d	15. a	20. c	25. c	30. b	35. d

Brain Parts and Development

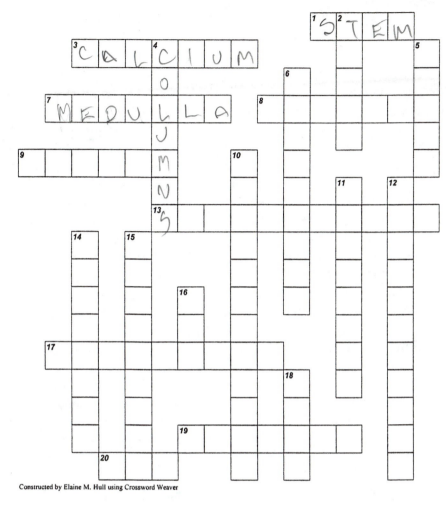

Constructed by Elaine M. Hull using Crossword Weaver

ACROSS

1 _____ cells: type of cells that line the ventricles and produce new neurons and glia
3 _____ channel blockers: drugs used after a stroke to prevent damage due to excess NMDA stimulation
7 Portion of brainstem that controls vital reflexes
8 _____ problem: How we construct a single object out of many aspects
9 Roof of midbrain
13 "Fight or flight" system
17 "Hole in the brain" filled with cerebrospinal fluid
19 Nucleus that is part of basal ganglia
20 Fluid that fills the ventricles and cushions the brain

DOWN

2 Chemical gradient that guides retinal axons to proper area of tectum
4 Units of cortex
5 Substantia _____: midbrain structure, degeneration of which causes Parkinson's disease
6 Stage of development in which neurons move to their final destination
10 Forebrain structure important for motivation and hormone control
11 Area surrounding site of direct stroke damage
12 Forebrain structure important for memory
14 Cortex lobe that processes somatosensory input
15 Neural "suicide program"
16 Imaging system based on use of a magnetic field to tilt rotation axes of atoms with odd-numbered atomic weights
18 Type of matter composed mostly of cell bodies and dendrites

6

VISION

INTRODUCTION

Sensory systems, including vision, are concerned with reception (absorption) of physical energy and transduction of that energy into neural activity that encodes some aspect of the stimulus. The structure of each kind of sensory receptor allows it to be stimulated maximally by one kind of energy, and little or not at all by other forms of energy. The brain interprets any information sent by nerves that synapse with those receptors as being about that form of energy. This principle was described by Müller as the law of specific nerve energies. This principle has been updated with three additional stipulations: (1) increases and decreases from a spontaneous rate of firing may signal different stimuli; (2) the timing of action potentials may code certain kinds of sensory information; and (3) perception is determined by activity of the whole system.

Light is focused by the cornea and lens onto the retina, which contains two kinds of receptors. Cones are most densely packed in the fovea, an area in the center of the retina with the most acute (detailed) vision. This acuity is largely the result of the small number of cones that synapse with each bipolar cell. Rods are located more peripherally in the retina than are cones and are more sensitive to low levels of light. Furthermore, each bipolar receives input from a large number of rods. This improves sensitivity to dim light but sacrifices acuity.

All mammalian photopigments contain 11-cis-retinal bound to one of several opsins. Light converts 11-cis-retinal to all-trans-retinal, which in turn activates second-messenger molecules. This results in the closing of sodium channels, which hyperpolarizes the receptor. In the dark the receptor steadily discharges an inhibitory transmitter; light decreases the output of that transmitter.

Cones mediate color vision because three different photopigments are found in three types of cones. Each photopigment is maximally sensitive to one wavelength of light but responds less readily to other wavelengths. Thus, each wavelength produces a certain ratio of responses from the three receptor types; the ratio remains essentially constant regardless of brightness. Rods, in contrast to cones, contain only one photopigment and therefore do not contribute directly to our perception of colors. Processing of color vision beyond the receptor level depends on an opponent-process mechanism, in which a given cell responds to one color with increased firing and to another color with a decrease below its spontaneous rate of firing.

A receptive field of a neuron in the visual system is that area of the retina (or in the visual field) in which the presence or absence of light affects that neuron's activity. A receptive field beyond the receptor level represents a composite of the receptive fields of neurons that provide its input. Many contain both excitatory and inhibitory regions. The receptive fields of bipolar, ganglion, and geniculate cells are concentric circles. For some cells light in the center is excitatory, and for other cells it is inhibitory; light in the surround has the opposite effect. Cells in the visual cortex (occipital lobe) have bar shaped receptive fields as a result of summing the receptive fields of their lateral geniculate cell inputs.

Visual input is processed neurally in order to provide an organized, useful representation of the environment. To understand the more complex processing later in the system, we begin with the retina. A visual receptor is able not only to stimulate its own bipolar(s) but also to inhibit activity in neighboring bipolars. It accomplishes this feat through the cooperation of horizontal cells, which receive input from a number of receptors and synapse with a number of bipolars. Electrical activity can flow in all directions in horizontal cells. The advantage of this arrangement is that borders are enhanced at the expense of redundant input. The process is called lateral inhibition.

100

Ganglion cells have been divided into two major types. Parvocellular neurons are relatively small cells, located in or near the fovea, that respond differentially to colors. Because they have small receptive fields, they are highly sensitive to details. Magnocellular neurons are larger, are spread evenly across the retina, and respond best to moving stimuli. Because their receptive fields are large, they are not sensitive to small details; they also do not respond differentially to colors. A smaller group of cells, koniocellular neurons, respond weakly to light and are poorly understood. At the lateral geniculate nucleus of the thalamus, most parvocellular ganglion cell axons synapse with parvocellular geniculate neurons, and most magnocellular ganglion cell axons synapse with magnocellular geniculate neurons.

Most of the input from the lateral geniculate goes to the primary visual cortex (area V1), which in turn projects to secondary visual cortex (area V2). From area V2, information branches out to numerous additional areas. At the cortex, the parvocellular and magnocellular systems split into three pathways. One pathway processes shape information from the parvocellular system. Another processes movement information from the magnocellular system. The third pathway processes brightness input from the magnocellular system and color information from the parvocellular system. Beyond the occipital cortex, shape information is sent to the inferior temporal cortex, which responds preferentially to highly complex shapes such as hands or faces. This path is referred to as the ventral stream, or the "what" pathway. Cells in this area are specialized to recognize objects. Other neurons project to a part of the parietal cortex, referred to as the dorsal stream, or the "where" or "how" pathway. It primarily helps the motor system to find objects and manipulate them.

David Hubel and Torsten Wiesel received the Nobel Prize for their pioneering work on feature detectors in the visual cortex. They distinguished three categories of neurons: simple, complex, and end-stopped, or hypercomplex. Simple cells respond maximally to a bar oriented in a particular direction and in a particular location on the retina. Their receptive fields can be mapped into fixed excitatory and inhibitory areas. Complex cells, on the other hand, have larger receptive fields, respond to correctly oriented bars located anywhere within the field (i.e., they do not have fixed excitatory and inhibitory areas), and respond best to stimuli moving perpendicular to the receptive field axis. End-stopped, or hypercomplex, cells are like complex cells, except for an area of strong inhibition at one end of the field. Cortical cells with similar properties are grouped in columns perpendicular to the surface.

It has been suggested that neurons in areas V1 and V2 are feature detectors. However, although each neuron has a preferred stimulus, it will respond to other similar stimuli. Therefore, the response of any cell must be compared with responses of many other cells. Furthermore, many cells in V1 and V2 respond best to sine wave gratings; however, it is obvious that we do not perceive the world as an assembly of sine waves. Therefore, the roles of V1 and V2 in visual perception probably provide preliminary analyses for other areas that actually identify objects.

Additional processing of shape information is accomplished by the inferior temporal cortex (in the ventral stream, or "what" pathway), which responds preferentially to highly complex shapes such as hands or faces. Cells in this area ignore changes in location, size, and perspective; they may contribute to our capacity for shape constancy. Damage to the pattern pathway results in visual agnosia, the inability to recognize visual objects. Some people have difficulty identifying almost all objects; others experience agnosia for only one or a few classes of stimuli. An area in the inferior temporal lobe (the fusiform gyrus) and part of the prefrontal cortex are activated during recognition of complex figures, but not when the same figures are seen but not recognized.

Area V4, or a nearby area, is especially important for color constancy. Animals with damage to this area retain some color vision, but lose the ability to recognize the color of an object across lighting conditions. Area V4 receives input from the "blobs" of area V1, which in turn receive input from parvocellular color processing cells and magnocellular brightness cells. Area V4 also contributes to visual attention.

Some cells in the magnocellular system are specialized for depth perception. They are sensitive to the amount of discrepancy between the images from the two eyes. Another branch of the magnocellular system detects motion. It projects to area V5 (middle temporal cortex, or MT) and an adjacent area (medial superior temporal cortex, MST). Neurons in these areas respond preferentially to different speeds and directions of movement, without analyzing the object that is moving. Many cells in MT respond best to moving borders of single objects, while cells in the dorsal part of MST prefer expanding, contracting, or rotating large scenes. These two types of cells send their output to the ventral part of MST, which allows us to perceive the motion of an object against a stationary field. ·

The shifting of visual attention from one object to another is correlated with increased activity in part of the parietal lobe. As a result, neural activity in visual cortex is altered, so that areas most relevant to the focused stimulus show increased activity, which then decreases when attention is shifted to a different stimulus. Much of the processing of visual information is unconscious. Furthermore, there appears to be no single area of the brain that puts together all the information about a given object. Perhaps simultaneous synchronized activity in the various areas is sufficient to bind the multiple aspects of an object into a unified perception.

Cells in the mammalian visual cortex are endowed at the individual's birth with certain adultlike characteristics. However, normal sensory experience is necessary to develop these characteristics fully and to prevent them from degenerating. If only one eye is deprived of vision during an early sensitive period, the brain becomes unresponsive to that eye. Input from the active eye displaces the early connections made by the inactive eye. It is likely that axons from the active eye compete successfully for neurotrophins provided by the postsynaptic cells. If both eyes are kept shut, cortical cells remain at least somewhat responsive to both eyes, though their responses are sluggish. Visual experience after the sensitive, or critical, period does not restore responsiveness to the previously inactive eye, unless the previously active eye is covered for a prolonged time. Other aspects of vision that require early experience for proper development are stereoscopic depth perception, ability to see lines of a given direction, and motion perception. If there is a total lack of visual stimulation throughout the sensitive period, the cortical areas that would have analyzed visual stimuli may become responsive to auditory or touch stimuli.

KEY TERMS AND CONCEPTS

Module 6.1 Visual Coding and the Retinal Receptors
1. Reception, transduction, and coding
    Reception: absorption of physical energy by receptors
    Transduction: conversion of physical energy to electrochemical pattern in neurons
    Coding: one-to-one correspondence between an aspect of stimulus and nervous system activity
    From neuronal activity to perception
        Receptor potential
        Shape of object not duplicated in brain
    General principles of sensory coding
        Law of specific nerve energies
        Spontaneous rate of firing
        Timing of action potentials
        Which other neurons are active

2. The eye and its connections to the brain
    Parts of the eye
        Cornea

        Pupil
        Lens
        Retina
        Macula
    The fovea (pit)
        Birds: two foveas per eye
        Few receptors send input to each bipolar cell
            Good acuity but relatively poor sensitivity to dim light
        Periphery of retina
            Many receptors converge on each bipolar cell
                Poor acuity but good sensitivity to dim light
    The route within the retina
        Receptors → bipolar cells → ganglion cells
        Optic nerve
            Blind spot

3. Visual receptors: Rods and cones
    Rods
        Most abundant in periphery
        Responsive to faint light, less useful in bright light
    Photopigments
        11-cis-retinal
        All-trans-retinal
        Opsins
        Conversion of 11-cis-retinal to all-trans-retinal →
            Second messenger molecules →
            Close sodium channels →
            Hyperpolarization

4. Color vision
    Dependent on patterns of responses by different neurons
    The trichromatic (Young-Helmholtz) theory
        Psychophysical color matching
        Three different opsins bound to 11-cis-retinal in three types of cones
        More long- and medium-wavelength than short-wavelength cones
    The opponent-process (Hering) theory
        Negative color afterimage
        Color opponent
    The retinex theory
        Color constancy
        Edwin Land
    Color vision deficiency
        Most common form: difficulty distinguishing red from green
            Sex linked (gene on X chromosome)

Module 6.2 The Neural Basis of Visual Perception
1. An overview of the mammalian visual system
    Retina
        Receptors (rods and cones)
        Horizontal cells

Bipolar cells
Amacrine cells
Ganglion cells
Axons form optic nerve
Optic chiasm
Lateral geniculate nucleus
Cerebral cortex: many visual areas with distinct functions

2. Mechanisms of processing in the visual system
Receptive fields
Receptive field of ganglion cell: composite of receptive fields of its inputs
Lateral inhibition
Horizontal cells
Bipolar cells

3. Concurrent pathways in the visual system
In the retina and lateral geniculate
Parvocellular
Small cell bodies
Small receptive fields
Located in or near fovea
Good acuity and color discrimination
Magnocellular
Larger cell bodies
Larger receptive fields
Even distribution
Best response to moving stimuli
No color discrimination
Koniocellular: least responsive, least understood
Lateral geniculate
Parvocellular geniculate cells: input from parvocellular ganglion cells
Magnocellular geniculate cells: input from magnocellular ganglion cells
In the cerebral cortex
Primary visual cortex, striate cortex (V1)
Secondary visual cortex (V2)
30-40 brain areas receiving visual input
Three pathways
Details of shape (mostly parvocellular)
Movement (mostly magnocellular)
Brightness (magnocellular) and color (parvocellular)
Beyond occipital cortex
Ventral stream ("what" pathway): temporal cortex
Input from shape, movement, and brightness/color pathways
Dorsal stream ("where" or "how" pathway): parietal cortex
Coordinates with motor system

4. The cerebral cortex: The shape pathway
Methods 6.1: Microelectrode recordings
Electrode types
Thin metal wire, insulated except for tip

Narrow glass tube, filled with salt solution and a metal wire
Hubel and Wiesel's cell types in the primary visual cortex
Binocular receptive fields, bar- or edge-shaped receptive fields
Simple cells (V1)
Fixed excitatory and inhibitory zones in receptive fields
Complex cells (V1 and V2)
Larger receptive fields
Cannot be mapped into excitatory and inhibitory zones
Response to moving bar of light
End-stopped or hypercomplex cells
Strong inhibitory area at one end of bar-shaped receptive field
The columnar organization of the visual cortex
Columns perpendicular to surface
Similar response properties within a column
Are visual cortex cells feature detectors?
Prolonged exposure: decreased sensitivity to feature
Ambiguity of response of a single cell
Spatial frequencies, sine-wave gratings
Shape analysis beyond areas V1 and V2
Inferior temporal cortex
Huge receptive fields, always include fovea
Shape constancy
Disorders of object recognition
Visual agnosia
Prosopagnosia
Fusiform gyrus in inferior temporal cortex
Part of prefrontal cortex
Methods 6.2: fMRI scans (functional magnetic resonance imaging)
Hemoglobin: different response in magnetic field after releasing oxygen
Good spatial and temporal resolution
No radiation hazard

5. The cerebral cortex: The color pathway
Area V1 "blobs"
Input from parvocellular (color) and magnocellular (brightness) pathways
Output to V2, V4, and posterior inferior temporal cortex
Area V4
Color constancy
Visual attention

6. The cerebral cortex: The motion and depth pathways
Stereoscopic depth perception
Magnocellular pathway
Structures important for motion perception
Area V5 (middle temporal cortex, MT)
Cells respond best to moving borders
Medial superior temporal cortex (MST)
Cells respond best to expansion, contraction, or rotation of large scene
Motion blindness

7. Visual attention
   Shifting attention
       Associated with activity in part of parietal lobe
       Results in increased or decreased activity in parts of visual cortex
   Suppressed vision during eye movements
       Temporal cortex: moving objects vs. visual changes due to head movements
       Visual cortex activity shuts down during eye movements

8. The binding problem revisited: Visual consciousness
   Blindsight
       Superior colliculus
       Islands of healthy tissue in otherwise damaged cortex
       Input from thalamus to other cortical areas
   Binding: synchronized simultaneous activity?

9. In closing: Coordinating separate visual pathways
   Simultaneous processing of different aspects by different brain areas

Module 6.3 Development of the Visual System

1. Infant vision
   More time looking at patterns
   Difficulty shifting attention

2. Effects of experience on visual development
   Effects of early lack of stimulation of one eye
       Binocular input to cortex, normally
       Blindness in deprived eye
   Effects of early lack of stimulation of both eyes
       Cortical cells
           Sluggish response to both eyes
           No sharp receptive fields
       Difficulty identifying objects visually
       Sensitive, or critical, period
   Restoration of response after early deprivation of vision
       Lazy eye, or amblyopia ex anopsia
   Uncorrelated stimulation in both eyes
       Stereoscopic depth perception
       Retinal disparity
       Strabismus
       Synchronous messages
       Nerve growth factor (NGF) and other neurotrophins, including NT-4
   Effects of early exposure to a limited array of patterns
       Astigmatism
   Effects of not seeing objects in motion
       Stroboscopic illumination
       Motion blindness
   Effects of blindness on the cortex
       Kittens: visual part of parietal lobe became responsive to sound or touch
       Humans: parts of visual cortex became responsive to sound or touch

106

SHORT-ANSWER QUESTIONS

Module 6.1 Visual Coding and the Retinal Receptors
1. *Reception, transduction and coding*
    a.   Distinguish between reception, transduction, and coding.

    b.   What is a receptor potential?

    c.   State the law of specific nerve energies. Who formulated it?

    d.   How does this law apply to neurons with spontaneous firing rates?

    e.   What two additional modifications of this principle seem necessary in light of current knowledge?

2. *The eye and its connections to the brain*
   a. What is the fovea? How did it get its name?

   b. How have many bird species solved the problem of getting detailed information from two different directions?

   c. Trace the path of visual information from a receptor to the optic nerve. What is the blind spot?

3. *Visual receptors: Rods and cones*
   a. Compare foveal and peripheral vision with regard to acuity, sensitivity to dim light, and color vision.

   b. What is the specific role of light in the initiation of a response in a receptor? What is a photopigment?

c. What is the relationship of 11-cis-retinal to all-trans-retinal? What is an opsin?

d. What kind of electrical response is produced in the receptor, and how does this affect the bipolars with which it synapses?

4. *Color vision*
   a. Why does the presence of cones in the retina of a given species not guarantee color vision? Why does color vision necessarily depend on the pattern of responses of a number of different neurons?

   b. How did Young and Helmholtz propose to account for color vision? On what kind of data was their theory based?

   c. What kind of theory did Hering propose? What observations supported his theory?

d. What is the current relationship between the three-receptor and the opponent-process theories?

e. What visual ability does the retinex theory explain?

f. What is the genetic basis for the most common form of color vision deficiency? Why do more males than females have this form of color deficiency?

Module 6.2 The Neural Basis of Visual Perception
1. *An overview of the mammalian visual system*
    a. Draw a diagram showing the relationships among the rods and cones, the bipolar and horizontal cells, and the ganglion and amacrine cells.

    b. Axons of which kind of cell form the optic nerve? What is the name of the site where the right and left optic nerves meet? What percentage of axons cross to the opposite side of the brain in humans? In species with eyes far to the sides of their heads?

c. Where do most axons in the optic nerve synapse? Where do some other optic nerve axons synapse?

d. What is the destination of axons from the lateral geniculate nucleus?

2. *Mechanisms of processing in the visual system*
   a. What is the definition of the receptive field of a neuron in the visual system?

   b. What is lateral inhibition? How does it enhance contrast?

   c. How is lateral inhibition accomplished in the vertebrate retina?

   d. If several bipolar cells provide input to a certain ganglion cell, what can be said about the location of their receptive fields relative to that of the ganglion cell?

e. How do receptive fields of ganglion cells and lateral geniculate cells differ from those of visual cortical cells?

f. In what cortical area does the ventral stream of visual input end? What is its specialty?

g. In what cortical area does the dorsal stream of visual input end? What is its specialty?

3. *Concurrent pathways in the visual system*
    a. Describe the characteristics of parvocellular ganglion cells.

    b. How do they differ from magnocellular ganglion cells?

    c. Which ganglion cells provide input to parvocellular geniculate neurons? to magnocellular geniculate neurons?

d. What happens to the parvocellular and magnocellular pathways in the cortex? What type of information does each of the three main concurrent visual pathways process?

4. *The cerebral cortex: The shape pathway*
    a. For what accomplishment did David Hubel and Torsten Wiesel share the Nobel Prize?

    b. Describe the receptive fields of simple cells.

    c. What is the major difference between responses of simple and complex visual cortical cells?

    d. Describe the receptive field of an end-stopped, or hypercomplex, cell?

    e. What can be said about the receptive fields of neurons in a column in the visual cortex?

f.   What is a feature detector?

g.   What evidence suggests that neurons in areas V1 and V2 are feature detectors?

h.   What are the problems with that interpretation?

i.   What is the evidence for spatial frequency detectors? What is the problem with the view that neurons in V1 and V2 are primarily spatial frequency detectors?

j.   Which area, beyond V1 and V2, is important for shape analysis? What is its major contribution?

k.   Describe the symptoms of visual agnosia. What is prosopagnosia?

l.   Which area in the inferior temporal lobe increases its activity when people with intact brains recognize faces?

5.   *The cerebral cortex: The color pathway*
   a.   What are the sources of input to the "blobs" of area V1? Where do the "blobs" send their output?

   b.   What appears to be the special function of area V4?

   c.   What might the magnocellular pathway, which does not analyze color information directly, contribute to color constancy?

   d.   To what other function does area V4 contribute?

6. *The cerebral cortex: The motion and depth pathways*
    a. Cells of which pathway are specialized for stereoscopic depth perception? To what aspect of the visual stimulus are they highly sensitive?

    b. Which two areas of the cortex are specialized for motion perception? How "picky" are cells in these areas to the specific characteristics of the stimulus that is moving?

    c. Describe the response characteristics of some cells in area V5.

    d. Describe the preferred stimuli for many cells in the dorsal part of area MST.

    e. What is the role of cells in the ventral part of MST?

    f. Describe the symptoms of motion blindness.

g. What cortical area may be important for shifting visual attention? How does activity in the visual cortex change when attention is shifted?

h. What is blindsight? What are three potential explanations for it?

Module 6.3 The Development of the Visual System
1. *Infant vision*
    a. What is the evidence that newborn infants can perceive complex stimuli? Do they see better in the periphery or in the center of their visual field?

    b. How easy is it for infants to shift their attention to other visual stimuli?

2. *Effects of experience on visual development*
    a. What is the effect of depriving only one eye of pattern vision during the critical period?

b. For what human condition does this principle have relevance? What is the usual treatment for this condition? Why is it important to begin treatment as early as possible?

c. What happens if both eyes are kept shut early in life?

d. What is a sensitive or critical period?

e. Define retinal disparity. How does the brain use this information to produce stereoscopic depth perception?

f. What is strabismus? Does surgical correction in adulthood improve depth perception in people with this disorder?

g. What chemicals may normally promote survival of synapses from the most active eye?

h.   What is the effect of supplying excess neurotrophins during the time when one eye is closed?

i.   What happens to the response characteristics of visual cortical cells in a kitten exposed to only horizontal lines early in life?

j.   What is astigmatism? What happens if a child has severe, uncorrected astigmatism during the first few years of life?

k.   What was the effect of rearing kittens in an environment illuminated only by a strobe light?

l.   What changes occur in the cortex of kittens or people who have been blind since birth?

POSTTEST

Multiple-Choice Questions

1. The one-to-one correspondence between some aspect of the physical stimulus and some aspect of the nervous system activity is known as
   a. reception.
   b. transduction.
   c. coding.
   d. a receptor potential.

2. The law of specific nerve energies
   a. implies that if the visual receptors were connected to the auditory nerve, and the auditory receptors were connected to the optic nerve, we would "see" sounds and "hear" lights.
   b. states that the kind of message a nerve carries depends only on the kind of stimulus that initiated it; that is, light can give rise only to visual messages, and so on.
   c. is true as it was originally stated; therefore, both increases and decreases in firing rates of cells with spontaneous firing rates must signal the same thing.
   d. is no longer thought to be true, and is now only of historical interest.

3. The fovea
   a. is completely blind because axons from ganglion cells exit from the retina there.
   b. covers approximately half the retina.
   c. contains no rods and is bypassed by most blood vessels and axons of more distant ganglion cells.
   d. is color blind because it contains no cones but has good sensitivity to dim light.

4. Which of the following is true?
   a. The fovea is more sensitive to dim light than is the periphery.
   b. The fovea has more detailed vision because few receptors synapse with each bipolar.
   c. Cones mediate more detailed vision because of their shape.
   d. Cones are situated peripherally in the retina, rods more centrally, though there is overlap.

5. A photopigment molecule absorbs a photon of light whose energy converts
   a. all-trans-retinal to 11-cis-retinal. Somehow this leads to hyperpolarization of the receptor.
   b. opsin to all-trans-retinal. Somehow this leads to depolarization of the receptor.
   c. 11-cis-retinal to all-trans-retinal. Somehow this leads to depolarization of the receptor.
   d. 11-cis-retinal to all-trans-retinal. Somehow this leads to hyperpolarization of the receptor.

6. The opponent-process theory
   a. is now thought to describe color processing by neurons after the receptor level, whereas the Young-Helmholtz theory describes activity at the receptor level.
   b. is now thought to describe color processing at the receptor level, whereas the Young-Helmholtz theory describes processing at higher levels.
   c. states that each receptor is sensitive only to a narrow band of wavelengths of light and that wavelength bands of different receptor groups do not overlap.
   d. is true only for rods, not cones.

120

7. The most common form of color vision deficiency
    a. is more common in women than in men.
    b. has been well known since the earliest civilizations.
    c. is characterized by difficulty distinguishing blue from yellow.
    d. is characterized by difficulty distinguishing red from green.

8. Which of the following best describes the main route of visual information in the retina?
    a. receptor→ganglion cell→bipolar cell
    b. receptor→bipolar cell→ganglion cell
    c. receptor→ganglion cell→amacrine cell
    d. receptor→horizontal cell→amacrine cell

9. Which of the following is true concerning receptive fields?
    a. They are always defined as an area surrounding "their" neuron; the receptive field for a simple cortical cell is itself in the cortex.
    b. The presence of both excitatory and inhibitory areas in the same receptive field is maladaptive and is a holdover from an earlier, inefficient way of processing information.
    c. Receptive fields of simple cortical cells are circular.
    d. For mammalian ganglion cells, they are generally doughnut-shaped, with the center being either excitatory or inhibitory and the surround being the opposite.

10. Lateral inhibition
    a. increases sensitivity to dim light.
    b. ordinarily decreases contrast at borders.
    c. ordinarily heightens contrast at borders.
    d. interferes with processing of color information.

11. Horizontal cells
    a. send axons out of the retina through the blind spot.
    b. send graded inhibitory responses to neighboring bipolar cells.
    c. are located behind the receptors so that they are out of the way of incoming light bound for receptors.
    d. all of the above.

12. Parvocellular ganglion cells
    a. are highly sensitive to both detail and color.
    b. are located primarily in the periphery of the retina.
    c. are among the largest ganglion cells in the retina.
    d. respond only weakly to visual stimuli.

13. Parvocellular lateral geniculate neurons
    a. receive input primarily from parvocellular ganglion cells.
    b. receive input primarily from koniocellular ganglion cells.
    c. receive input primarily from magnocellular ganglion cells.
    d. receive more or less equal input from all types of ganglion cells.

14. The parvocellular and magnocellular systems
    a. merge in area V1 and remain one system for subsequent analysis.
    b. remain as two systems throughout visual processing.
    c. divide into three systems, with much of the parvocellular system continuing to analyze details of shape, most of the magnocellular system analyzing movement, and the third system containing parvocellular cells that analyze color and magnocellular cells that analyze brightness.
    d. divide into many concurrent pathways, each analyzing a different color, direction of movement, or shape, but then converge in one master area, where all of these aspects are put together into a unified perception.

15. Simple cells in the visual cortex
    a. respond maximally to bars of light oriented in one direction but not to bars of light oriented in another direction.
    b. respond to "correctly" oriented bars of light only when they are in the "correct" part of the retina.
    c. were first described by Hubel and Wiesel.
    d. all of the above.

16. Simple and complex cells differ in that
    a. the receptive field of a simple cell is larger than that of a complex cell.
    b. the receptive field of a complex cell cannot be mapped into fixed excitatory and inhibitory zones, but that of a simple cell can.
    c. a simple cell does not respond at all to small spots of light, whereas complex cells respond best to small spots of light.
    d. all of the above.

17. Simple and complex cells are similar in that
    a. most of them receive at least some input from both eyes.
    b. most respond maximally to bars of light oriented in a particular direction.
    c. both may be found in the striate cortex.
    d. all of the above.

18. End-stopped, or hypercomplex, cells
    a. have extremely small receptive fields.
    b. are similar to complex cells, except that there is a strong inhibitory area at one end of the receptive field.
    c. respond only to very complex stimuli, such as faces.
    d. respond best to small spots of light.

19. Neurons along the track of an electrode inserted perpendicular to the surface of visual cortex
    a. have response characteristics that vary widely, but systematically, from the top to the bottom.
    b. have a random distribution of response characteristics.
    c. have certain response characteristics in common.
    d. cannot have their responses recorded, since the electrode damages them severely.

20. The hypothesis that neurons in the visual cortex are feature detectors
    a. is supported by the observation that prolonged exposure to a given feature seems to fatigue the relevant detectors.
    b. is supported by the finding that each cell in the primary visual cortex responds only to one very precise stimulus, so its response is not at all ambiguous.
    c. is disproved by the observation that visual cortical cells respond only to sine-wave gratings, and not at all to bars and edges.
    d. is now known to be true for cells in area V1, but not for any other visual processing area.

21. The inferior temporal cortex
    a. has receptive fields that always include the fovea.
    b. is concerned with advanced pattern analysis and complex shapes.
    c. may provide our sense of shape constancy.
    d. all of the above.

22. A person with visual agnosia
    a. may have lost recognition only for a few kinds of stimuli, such as faces, as in prosopagnosia.
    b. has lost the ability to read.
    c. is blind.
    d. has had damage limited to the primary visual cortex (area V1).

23. Area V4
    a. seems to be especially important for face recognition.
    b. seems to be especially important for color constancy.
    c. seems to be especially important for shape constancy.
    d. receives input only from the parvocellular system.

24. Occipital area V5 (MT, middle-temporal cortex) and area MST (medial superior temporal cortex)
    a. analyze complex shapes.
    b. analyze colors.
    c. analyze speed and direction of movement.
    d. analyze stereoscopic depth cues.

25. Cells in the dorsal part of MST that respond to expansion, contraction, or rotation of a large visual scene
    a. probably help to record the movement of the head with respect to the world.
    b. probably help to keep track of a single object.
    c. are very particular about the specific objects in their receptive field.
    d. receive input primarily from the parvocellular system.

26. Cells in the ventral part of MST
    a. receive input from cells in MT that respond best to moving borders.
    b. receive input from cells in dorsal MST that respond best to expansion, contraction, or rotation of a large visual scene.
    c. respond whenever an object moves relative to its background.
    d. all of the above.

27. Which of the following is true?
    a. Shifting visual attention is associated with activity in part of the parietal cortex.
    b. Recognition of objects is associated with activity in the fusiform gyrus of the inferior temporal cortex.
    c. The dorsal stream, ending in the parietal cortex, helps the motor system find objects, move toward them and grasp them.
    d. All of the above are true.

28. Human infants
    a. are unable to see patterns for at least several weeks.
    b. see better in their central field of vision because their fovea develops before the periphery of the retina.
    c. have trouble shifting their attention before about 6 months of age.
    d. all of the above.

29. If a kitten's eyelid is sutured shut for the first 6 weeks of life, and the sutures are then removed, the kitten
    a. is totally blind in the inactive eye only if the other eye had normal visual input.
    b. is totally blind in the inactive eye regardless of the other eye's visual experience.
    c. is able to see horizontal and vertical lines, but not diagonal lines or curves.
    d. sees normally out of the eye, since all of its connections were formed before birth.

30. Children with lazy eye (amblyopia ex anopsia)
    a. should have the active eye covered continuously until adulthood.
    b. should have the active eye covered as early as possible, but only until the lazy eye becomes functional.
    c. should have the active eye covered only after they have reached normal adult size, in order to avoid reorganization of connections.
    d. should not be treated at all, since they will eventually outgrow the condition.

31. Retinal disparity
    a. is an abnormal condition that should be treated as early as possible.
    b. is a cue for depth perception only in people with strabismus.
    c. can be used as a cue for depth perception no matter what the organism's early experience was.
    d. can normally be used for stereoscopic depth perception because cortical cells respond differentially to the degree of retinal disparity.

32. Neurotrophin NT-4, if injected in large amounts into the brains of infant rats while one eye was surgically closed,
    a. decreased responsiveness to the closed eye, so that even extensive visual experience while the previously active eye was covered could not restore vision to the previously closed eye.
    b. cortical cells that received the NT-4 remained responsive to both eyes.
    c. cortical cells that received the NT-4 became unresponsive to either eye.
    d. resulted in astigmatism in the previously closed eye.

33. Experiments on abnormal sensory environments have shown that
   a. if kittens are reared in an environment in which they see only horizontal lines, at maturity all cells are completely normal, because receptive field characteristics are fully determined at birth.
   b. if kittens are reared with only horizontal lines, they will become so habituated to that stimulus that they soon lose their ability to see horizontal lines.
   c. if kittens are reared with only horizontal lines, they will lose the ability to see vertical lines.
   d. if the environment is illuminated only with a strobe light during development, kittens lose their ability to see either horizontal or vertical lines.

34. Astigmatism
   a. is caused by asymmetric curvature of the eyes and results in blurring of vision for lines in one direction.
   b. is caused by strabismus and results in color blindness.
   c. is caused by amblyopia and results in loss of binocular cells in the cortex.
   d. is caused by too much retinal disparity and results in loss of depth perception.

35. Blindness from birth
   a. in kittens, resulted in supersensitivity to visual stimuli when vision was restored in adulthood.
   b. in people, resulted in increased responsiveness of visual cortex to auditory and touch stimuli.
   c. in all mammalian species, results in inability to see colors when vision is restored in adulthood, but otherwise vision is normal.
   d. can be restored in adulthood by infusions of neurotrophins.

Answers to Multiple-Choice Questions

1. c	10. c	19. c	28. c
2. a	11. b	20. a	29. a
3. c	12. a	21. d	30. b
4. b	13. a	22. a	31. d
5. d	14. c	23. b	32. b
6. a	15. d	24. c	33. c
7. d	16. b	25. a	34. a
8. b	17. d	26. d	35. b
9. d	18. b	27. d	

Helpful Hint

Here is an analogy of the selective absorption of different wavelengths by the three types of cones. Think of three tennis nets with different sized holes. The one with the largest holes will easily "catch" a red foam-rubber ball about the same size as its holes. Larger or smaller balls will tend to either bounce back off the net or to go through it, though if they are hit just right, they may be caught in the net. A net with medium-sized holes will easily catch a yellow tennis ball, and a net with even smaller holes will catch a blue golf ball.

Diagrams

1. Label the following components of the vision pathways on this horizontal section of the brain: optic nerve, optic chiasm, lateral geniculate nucleus, primary visual cortex, superior colliculus.

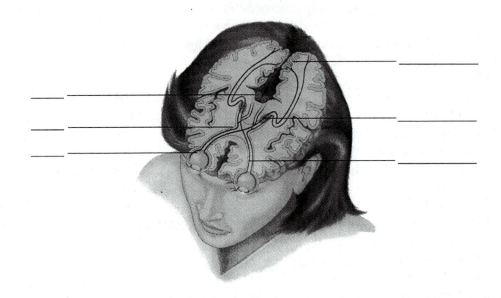

2. Does the following diagram represent the response characteristics of a retinal ganglion cell, a lateral geniculate cell, a "simple" cortical cell, or a "complex" cortical cell?

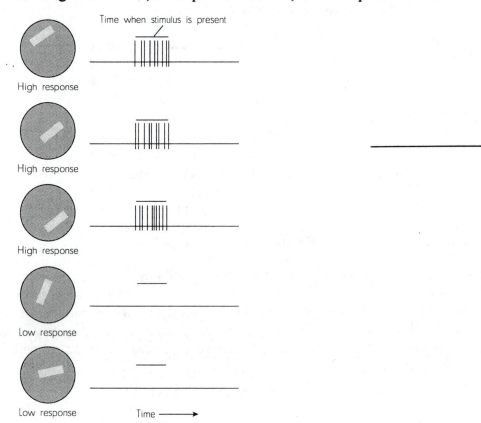

High response

High response

High response

Low response

Low response

Time when stimulus is present

Time ⟶

_____

7

THE NONVISUAL SENSORY SYSTEMS

INTRODUCTION

Sensory systems have evolved to provide information most useful for each species. Although humans can perceive a relatively wide range of stimuli, our sensory systems also show certain specializations.

The sense of hearing uses air vibrations to move the tympanic membrane and three middle ear bones (the hammer, anvil, and stirrup), which focus the force of the vibrations so that they can move the heavier fluid inside the cochlea. The basilar membrane forms the floor of a tunnel, the scala media. Receptor cells are embedded in the basilar membrane; hairs in the top of the receptors are in contact with the overlying tectorial membrane. Inward pressure of the stirrup on the oval window increases pressure in scala vestibuli, which presses down on scala media, which in turn bulges downward into scala tympani and pushes the round window outward. The opposite happens when the stirrup moves outward. The movement of the basilar membrane (the floor of scala media) relative to the tectorial membrane produces a shearing action that bends the hair cells, thereby generating a potential.

Pitch perception depends on a combination of three mechanisms. At low frequencies, neurons can fire with each vibration. At medium frequencies, neurons split into volleys, one volley firing with one vibration, another with the next, and so on. At higher frequencies the area of the basilar membrane with greatest displacement is used as a place code. The characteristics of the basilar membrane vary along the length of the cochlea. At the basal end a bony shelf occupies most of the floor of scala media, and the basilar membrane, which attaches to the shelf, is thin and stiff. At the apex, there is almost no bony shelf, and the basilar membrane is larger and floppier, even though the cochlea as a whole is smaller. The size and stiffness of the basilar membrane determine which part of the basilar membrane will respond to various frequencies of sound with the greatest-amplitude traveling wave. High-pitched tones cause maximal displacement near the base, and low-pitched tones cause maximal displacement closer to the apex. There is considerable overlap of pitches coded by frequency of firing and by place.

After passing through several subcortical structures, auditory information reaches the primary auditory cortex in the temporal lobes. Neurons with similar preferred tones cluster together there. Damage to the primary auditory cortex does not impair responses to simple sounds but does impair responses to combinations or sequences of sounds. Neurons in the secondary auditory cortex respond best to complex combinations of sounds, such as speech.

There are two categories of hearing impairment. Nerve, or inner ear, deafness is caused by damage to the cochlea, the hair cells, or the auditory nerve. Prenatal infections or toxins, inadequate oxygen during birth, diseases, reactions to drugs, and exposure to loud noises are frequent causes of nerve deafness. Conductive, or middle ear, deafness results from failure of the middle ear bones to transmit sound waves to the cochlea. It can be caused by diseases, infections, or tumorous growths in the middle ear.

Sound localization is accomplished by two methods. The difference in loudness between the two ears is used for high-frequency sounds, while the phase difference for sound waves arriving at the two ears is used for low-frequency sounds. However, for animals with small heads, there is little phase difference in the sound waves reaching the two ears. Therefore, it is difficult for them to localize low-frequency tones. Furthermore, they can use loudness differences only for higher frequencies than humans can. These animals have evolved the ability to perceive sounds that they can localize easily.

Vestibular sensation, based on the otolith organs and the semicircular canals in the inner ear, contributes to our sense of balance and guidance of our eye movements. Our auditory system may have evolved from the touch receptors of primitive animals.

The sense of touch is composed of several modalities, some of which are fairly well correlated with activity in specific receptor types. For example, free nerve endings are involved in sensations of pain, warmth, and cold. Hair-follicle receptors respond to movement of hairs; Meissner's corpuscles and Pacinian corpuscles signal sudden displacement of skin. Merkel's disks produce a prolonged response to steady indentation of the skin, while Ruffini endings respond to skin stretching.

Sensory nerves enter and motor nerves exit the spinal cord through each of 31 openings in the vertebral canal. These nerves innervate overlapping segments of the body (dermatomes). Several well defined pathways ascend from the spinal cord to separate areas of the thalamus, and thence to appropriate areas of somatosensory cortex in the parietal lobe. Thus, the various aspects of somatosensation are at least partially separate, from the receptor level to the cerebral cortex. Since bodily sensations depend on activity in the cerebral cortex, some people may experience a "phantom limb" after a part of the body has been amputated. In other patients damage to the somatosensory cortex may result in impairment of body perception.

Pain information is transmitted to the spinal cord by axons with little or no myelin, using substance P as their transmitter. From the spinal cord, pain information is sent to certain thalamic nuclei, and then to three cortical areas: the insula, cingulate cortex (which is linked to emotional responses), and somatosensory cortex. Capsaicin, derived from hot peppers, elicits the release of substance P and thereby produces a sensation of pain or heat. However, following application of capsaicin, there is a prolonged decrease in pain sensations. According to the gate theory, various kinds of nonpain stimuli can modify pain sensations. Pain sensations can be inhibited by release of the brain's endogenous opiates (endorphins), including leu- and met-enkephalin, dynorphin, beta-endorphin, and alpha-neoendorphin. In contrast, nociceptin actually increases pain. Endorphins are concentrated in the periaqueductal gray area of the midbrain. These neurons and others in the medulla block the release of substance P in the spinal cord and brainstem. Several stimuli can elicit the release of endorphins; these include pain, stress, acupuncture, and transcutaneous electrical nerve stimulation. However, some types of analgesia are dependent, not on endorphins, but on activity at certain glutamate synapses.

Morphine administered for serious pain is almost never addictive. Furthermore, although opiates inhibit the immune system temporarily, prolonged pain or stress weakens the immune system for a much longer time. The body sometimes increases the sensitivity to pain. Tissue damage results in the release of histamine, nerve growth factor, and other chemicals that help repair the damage. However, they also increase the number of sodium gates in receptors and axons, and may thereby enhance pain sensitivity.

Our understanding of the senses of taste and olfaction is plagued with many unresolved issues. There is lack of agreement as to whether there are a fixed number of primary stimuli, which send information to the brain via "labeled lines," or whether the brain analyzes patterns of firing across whole populations of neurons, with sensations varying along continuous dimensions. Compromises between the two positions will probably be required for both senses, but the exact nature of the compromises has not been specified. Studies of cross-adaptation suggest that we have at least four types of taste receptor: sweet, sour, salty, and bitter. There may also be a receptor for monosodium glutamate and additional receptors for bitter and sweet. The mechanisms of activation of some taste receptors have been discovered. Sodium ions activate salty receptors; acids close potassium channels in sour receptors; and sweetness and bitterness receptors respond to molecules that activate G proteins, which then release a second messenger within the cell. The anterior two-thirds of the tongue sends information via the chorda tympani, a branch of the seventh cranial nerve (facial nerve) to the nucleus of the tractus solitarius in the medulla. The posterior third of the tongue and the throat send input via branches of the ninth and tenth cranial nerves to different parts of the nucleus solitarius. From there the information is sent to numerous areas, including the pons, lateral hypothalamus, amygdala, ventral-posterior thalamus, and two areas of the cerebral cortex. The nucleus of the tractus solitarius in rats and the cerebral cortex in monkeys can respond differentially according to the acceptability of a taste.

Olfactory cells have cilia that extend into the mucous lining of the nasal passages. Odorant molecules must diffuse through a mucous fluid in order to reach the receptor sites on the cilia. There may be 1000 or more olfactory receptor proteins, which operate on the same principles as some neurotransmitter receptors. When activated by an odorant molecule, the receptor triggers a change in a G protein, which in turn elicits chemical activities within the cell. People with specific anosmias lack one or more of these receptors. Because there are so many types of receptor, olfaction has more of a labeled-line system of coding than does, for example, color vision, which has only three types of cones. However, even in olfaction, each receptor responds to other odorants that are similar to its preferred stimulus. Therefore, a single receptor can provide an approximate classification of an odorant, but related receptors provide more exact information. A population of varied receptors can provide information about complex mixtures of odors.

KEY TERMS AND CONCEPTS

Module 7.1 Audition
1. Sound and the ear
    Physical and psychological dimensions of sound
        Amplitude (physical intensity)
            Loudness (perception of intensity)
        Frequency (compressions per second)
            Pitch (perception related to frequency)
    Structures of the ear
        Outer ear
            Pinna
        Middle ear
            Tympanic membrane (eardrum)
                Middle ear bones
                    Hammer (malleus)
                    Anvil (incus)
                    Stirrup (stapes)
        Inner ear
        Oval window
        Cochlea
            Scala vestibuli
            Scala tympani
            Scala media
                Basilar membrane
                Hair cells (auditory receptors)
                Tectorial membrane
        Auditory nerve (part of eighth cranial nerve)

2. Pitch perception
    Frequency theory and place theory

Action potentials in synchrony with sound
Volley principle
Base: thin, stiff basilar membrane
Apex: larger, floppier basilar membrane
Traveling wave
Pitch perception in the cerebral cortex
Primary auditory cortex (temporal lobes)
Tonotopic map
Important for combinations or sequences of sounds
Secondary auditory cortex
Complex combination of sounds, such as speech
Different aspects of stimulus analyzed in different places
Ventral pathway (prefrontal cortex): what the sound represents
Dorsal pathway: where the sound originated in space

3. Hearing loss
Conductive deafness (middle-ear deafness)
Certain diseases or infections
Tumorous bone growth in middle ear
Can hear sounds that bypass middle ear, including own voice
Nerve deafness (inner-ear deafness)
Prenatal exposure to rubella, syphilis, or other contagious diseases, or to toxins
Inadequate oxygen to brain during birth
Inadequate thyroid activity
Diseases, including multiple sclerosis and meningitis
Childhood reactions to drugs, including aspirin
Repeated exposure to loud noises
Tinnitis: frequent or constant ringing in ears
Similarity to phantom limb

4. Localization of sounds
Difference in intensity
Sound shadow
High frequencies
Difference in time of arrival
Sudden onset sounds
Useful for any frequency
Phase difference
Low frequencies

Module 7.2 The Mechanical Senses
1. Vestibular sensation
Vestibular organ (adjacent to cochlea)
Otolith organs
Saccule
Utricle
Otoliths: calcium carbonate particles next to hair cells
Semicircular canals (three planes): filled with jellylike substance, lined with hair cells
Eighth cranial nerve, vestibular component
Brain stem and cerebellum

2. Somatosensation
    Somatosensory receptors
        Bare (or free) nerve ending
            Pain, warmth, cold
        Hair-follicle receptors
            Movement of hairs
        Meissner's corpuscles
            Sudden displacement of skin, low frequency vibration
        Pacinian corpuscles
            Sudden displacement of skin, high frequency vibration
        Merkel's disks
            Indentation of skin
        Ruffini endings
            Stretch of skin
        Krause end bulbs
            Uncertain function
    Input to the spinal cord and the brain
        31 sets of spinal nerves
        Dermatome
    Somatosensory thalamus
    Somatosensory cortex
        Parietal lobe
        Four parallel strips
            Two for touch
            Two for deep pressure and joint and muscle movement
        Most input from contralateral side, but some from opposite hemisphere via corpus callosum
        Impaired perception of body (damage to cortex)
    Tickle
        Can't tickle oneself
        Motor areas signal somatosensory areas

3. Pain
    Pain neurons and their neurotransmitters
        Substance P (unmyelinated and thinly myelinated fibers)
        Glutamate (cotransmitter)
        Capsaicin (induces release of substance P, stimulates heat receptors)
    Headaches
        Not serious
            Muscle tension
            Sinus infection
            Anxiety or depression
            Sleeplessness
            Withdrawal from caffeine
        Serious
            Brain tumor
            Encephalitis
            Burst blood vessel
            Head injury
            Migraine

4. Pain and the brain
    Spinal cord → thalamic nuclei → cerebral cortex
        Cingulate cortex → emotional content
        Somatosensory cortex → painful sensation
    Events that limit pain
        Gate theory
        Opioid systems (inhibit effects of substance P)
        Endorphins
            Enkephalins (met-enkephalin and leu-enkephalin)
            Dynorphin
            Beta-endorphin
            Alpha-neoendorphin
            Nociceptin (increases pain, unlike other endorphins)
            Periaqueductal gray area
            Analgesia for dull, but not sharp, pain
    Stimuli that produce analgesia
        "Runner's high," sexual activity, music
        Pain or stress
            Naloxone (blocks opioid receptors)
        Non-endorphin analgesia
        Acupuncture
        Transcutaneous electrical nerve stimulation (TENS)
    The pros and cons of morphine analgesia
        Rarely addicitve
        Less inhibition of immune system than pain
    Sensitization of pain
        Tissue damage →
        Release of histamine, nerve growth factor →
        Repair tissue and increase sodium gates in receptors and axons →
        Enhance pain sensitivity
        Touch receptors: substance P
        Sensitized cells in dorsal spinal cord

Module 7.3 The Chemical Senses
1. General issues about chemical coding
    Labeled-line principle
    Across-fiber pattern principle

2. Taste
    Taste receptors (modified skin cells)
        Taste buds (about 50 receptors per taste bud)
        Papillae (0-10 taste buds per papilla)
    How many kinds of taste receptors?
        Adaptation and cross adaptation
        Four main types: sweet, sour, salty, bitter
        Other possibilities
            Monosodium glutamate
            Umami
            Multiple bitter and sweet receptors

Mechanisms of taste receptors
    Salty: sodium influx
    Amiloride: blocks sodium entry → decreases salty taste
    Sour: acid closes potassium channels → depolarize membrane
    Sweet: G protein and second messenger
    Bitter: G protein and second messenger
    Umami: G protein and second messenger
Individual differences in taste
    Phenylthiocarbamate (PTC)
        Bitter, very bitter, or little taste
        Supertasters: most fungiform papillae
The coding of taste information
    Labeled-line theory
    Across-fiber pattern theory
Taste coding in the brain
    Information from anterior two-thirds of tongue
        Chorda tympani: branch of seventh cranial nerve (facial nerve)
    Information from posterior third of tongue and throat
        Ninth and tenth cranial nerves
        Anesthetize chorda tympani
            Lose taste in anterior tongue
            Increase bitter and salt sensitivity in posterior tongue
            "Phantoms"
    Nucleus of the tractus solitarius (NTS, in medulla)
    Pons, lateral hypothalamus, amygdala, ventral-posterior thalamus, two areas of cerebral
        cortex (taste and touch)
    Acceptability of a taste: altered by changes in response in NTS or cortex
Miracle berries and modification of taste receptors
    Miraculin
        Acids → sweet
    Gymnena sylvestre
    Theophylline
    Sodium laurel sulfate

3.   Olfaction
Olfactory receptors
    Olfactory cells: replaceable
    Olfactory epithelium
    Cilia
    Rapid adaptation
    Mucous fluid
    Olfactory bulb
        Coding by area of olfactory bulb excited
    Prefrontal cortex and other areas
Behavioral methods of identifying olfactory receptors
    Specific anosmias
    Isobutyric acid
    Musky, fishy, urinous, spermous, malty
    Up to 26 others

Biochemical identification of receptor types
    Similar to neurotransmitter receptors
        Seven transmembrane sections
        G proteins
    18 receptor proteins identified
    About 1000 receptor proteins in rodents
    Hundreds in humans
Implications for coding
    Each receptor: identify approximate nature of molecule
    Receptor population: more precise; identify complex mixture
    Variety of airborne chemicals, not on single dimension
    Space for many receptors not a problem
    Mostly labeled-line
    Some across-fiber pattern
Vomeronasal sensation and pheromones
    Vomeronasal organ: receptors located near, but separate from, olfactory receptors
        7-transmembrane receptor proteins
        Few types
        Nonadapting
    Pheromones: chemicals released by animals, affect conspecifics
        Different pheromones: infants, adult males, females in estrus or not in estrus
        Influence sexual or maternal behavior, puberty, or estrous or menstrual cycle

SHORT-ANSWER QUESTIONS

Module 7.1 Audition
1. *Sound*
    a. What is the relationship between amplitude and loudness? Between frequency and pitch?

2. *Structures of the ear*
    a. What is the role of the tympanic membrane and the hammer, anvil, and stirrup?

b.   Where are the auditory receptors located? How are they stimulated?

3. *Pitch perception*
    a.   What led to the downfall of the frequency theory of pitch discrimination in its simple form?

    b.   What is the volley theory?

    c.   What observation led to the downfall of the place theory as originally stated?

    d.   What is the current compromise between the place and frequency theories of pitch discrimination?

    e.   At which end of the cochlea is the basilar membrane stiffest?

f. How does the traveling wave along the basilar membrane lead to place coding?

g. Describe the location and function of the primary auditory cortex.

h. What are the preferred stimuli for cells in the secondary auditory cortex?

i. How do the dorsal and ventral pathways of analysis in the auditory cortex compare with those in the visual system?

4. *Hearing loss*
   a. For which type of deafness can one hear one's own voice, though external sounds are heard poorly?

   b. For what type of deafness is hearing impaired for a limited range of frequencies?

c. What are some causes of nerve deafness? Of conductive deafness?

5. I *alization of sounds*
    a. For which frequencies is the "sound shadow" method of localization best? Why?

    b. What characteristic of sound is necessary to be able to localize sounds on the basis of difference in time of arrival? Are some frequencies easier to localize on this basis than others?

    c. Describe the basis of localization on the basis of phase difference. For which frequencies is it most effective?

    d. Which method of sound localization is best for a species with a small head? Why?

Module 7.2 The Mechanical Senses
1. *Vestibular sensation*
    a. What are the main parts of the vestibular organ? What are otoliths? What is their function?

    b. What are the semicircular canals? How do they differ from the otolith organs?

2. *Somatosensation*
    a. List the somatosensory receptors and their probable functions.

    b. How many sets of spinal nerves do we have?

    c. What is a dermatome?

    d. Describe briefly the cortical projections of the somatosensory system.

e. Describe the loss of body sense that may accompany Alzheimer's disease.

3. *Pain*
   a. What is substance P? What sensation would be produced by an injection of substance P into the spinal cord?

   b. What is capsaicin? How does it work? What food contains capsaicin?

   c. What theory did Melzack and Wall propose to account for variations in pain responsiveness? What is its main principle?

   d. What are endorphins? How was the term derived?

   e. List the endorphins. Which one increases pain, unlike the rest?

f.   Where are endorphin synapses concentrated? What is their function there?

g.   List six kinds of stimuli that can reduce pain.

h.   What is naloxone? How is it used experimentally?

i.   What are the pros and cons of morphine analgesia in cases of serious pain?

j.   Describe the process by which tissue damage results in pain sensitization.

Module 7.3 The Chemical Senses
1.   *General issues about chemical coding*
     a.   Describe the labeled-line type of coding. Give an example.

b. Describe the across-fiber pattern type of coding. Give an example.

2. *Taste*
    a. Where are the taste receptors located? What is the relationship between taste buds and papillae?

    b. How can cross-adaptation be used to help determine the number of taste receptors?

    c. What are the four major kinds of taste receptor? What additional kind may we have?

    d. What are the mechanisms of activation of salty, sour, sweet, bitter, and umami receptors? How does amiloride affect salty tastes?

    e. Describe the individual differences in taste of phenylthiocarbamate (PTC). What is the physiological basis of increased sensitivity in supertasters?

f. What evidence favors the labeled-line theory of taste? The across-fiber pattern theory?

g. Describe the changes in taste sensitivity that occur if the chorda tympani is anesthetized.

h. Which structures in the brain process taste information?

i. What property is classified by the nucleus of the tractus solitarius of rats? Which area performs this function in monkeys?

3. *Olfaction*
    a. Describe the olfactory receptors. Why is there a delay between inhaling a substance and smelling it?

    b. What is a specific anosmia? What can we conclude about the number of olfactory receptors, based on information about specific anosmias?

c. How are olfactory receptors similar to neurotransmitter receptors? How many olfactory receptor proteins are estimated to exist in rodents, based on isolation of these proteins? in humans?

d. What can we say about the labeled-line theory vs. the across-fiber pattern theory for smell?

e. What is the vomeronasal organ? What type of molecules does it detect?

f. What classes of individuals can be distinguished, based on their pheromones?

g. What are some functions of pheromones in mice?

h. What are two functions of pheromones that have been demonstrated in humans?

POSTTEST

Multiple-Choice Questions

1. Which of the following is true of auditory perception?
    a. Loudness is the same thing as amplitude.
    b. Pitch is the perception of intensity.
    c. Perception of low frequencies decreases with age.
    d. Perception of high frequencies decreases with age.

2. The function of the tympanic membrane and middle-ear bones is to
    a. directly stimulate the auditory receptors.
    b. move the tectorial membrane to which the stirrup is connected.
    c. focus the vibrations on a small area, so that there is sufficient force to produce pressure waves in the fluid-filled cochlea.
    d. none of the above

3. The auditory receptors
    a. are called hair cells.
    b. are embedded in the basilar membrane below and the tectorial membrane above.
    c. are stimulated when the basilar membrane moves relative to the tectorial membrane; displacement of the hair cells by about the diameter of one atom opens ion channels in the membrane of the neuron.
    d. all of the above

4. The frequency theory
    a. in its simplest form cannot describe coding of very high-frequency tones because the refractory periods of neurons limit their firing rates.
    b. can be modified by the volley principle to account for pitch discrimination of all frequencies, up to 20,000 Hz.
    c. is now thought to be valid for high-frequency tones, whereas the place theory describes pitch coding of lower tones.
    d. is a form of labeled-line theory.

5. The place theory
    a. received experimental support from demonstrations that the basilar membrane was composed of a series of separate strings.
    b. has been modified so that a traveling wave produces a greater displacement at one area of the basilar membrane than at others.
    c. cannot be true at all, because the basilar membrane is the same throughout its length and therefore cannot localize vibrations.
    d. cannot be true at all, because the basilar membrane is too loose and floppy to show any localization.

6. The basilar membrane
    a. is smallest and stiffest at the apex (farthest, small end) of the cochlea.
    b. is smallest and stiffest at the base (large end) of the cochlea.
    c. has the same dimensions and consistency throughout its length.
    d. shows maximum displacement for low tones near its base.

7. Pitch discrimination
   a. depends on a combination of mechanisms: frequency coding for low pitches, place coding for high pitches, and both mechanisms for intermediate pitches.
   b. depends on a combination of mechanisms: frequency coding for high pitches, place coding for low pitches, and both mechanisms for intermediate pitches.
   c. cannot be satisfactorily explained by any theory.
   d. is accomplished only by place coding.

8. Damage to primary auditory cortex results in
   a. inability to hear anything.
   b. inability to hear high tones, but not low tones.
   c. inability to hear low tones, but not high tones.
   d. inability to recognize combinations or sequences of sounds, as in music or speech.

9. Inner-ear deafness
   a. is frequently temporary; if it persists, it can usually be corrected by surgery.
   b. is characterized by total deafness to all sounds.
   c. may result from exposure of one's mother to rubella or other contagious diseases during pregnancy.
   d. is characterized by being able to hear one's own voice but not external sounds.

10. A "sound shadow"
   a. is useful for sound localization only for low-pitched sounds.
   b. is useful for sound localization only for wavelengths shorter than the width of the head (that is, higher pitches).
   c. is a means of sound localization that uses differences in time of arrival between the two ears.
   d. cannot be used at all by small-headed species such as rodents.

11. Vestibular sensation
   a. arises from free nerve endings in the inner ear.
   b. is produced by a traveling wave along a membrane in the otolith organs.
   c. arises from hair cells in the otolith organs and the semicircular canals.
   d. plays only a minor role in balance and coordination.

12. Which of the following pairs of receptors and sensations is most correct?
   a. free nerve endings: pain, warmth, cold
   b. Merkel's disks: sudden movement across skin
   c. Pacinian corpuscles: steady indentation of skin
   d. Ruffini endings: movement of hairs

13. Dermatomes
   a. are sharply defined, nonoverlapping areas innervated by single sensory spinal nerves.
   b. are overlapping areas innervated by single sensory spinal nerves.
   c. are symptoms of a skin disorder, much like acne.
   d. are found only on the trunk of the body, not the arms, legs, or head.

14. Somatosensory information
    a. travels up a single pathway to one thalamic nucleus, which projects to one strip in the parietal lobe.
    b. travels up different pathways to separate thalamic areas, which project to four parallel strips in the parietal lobe.
    c. travels directly from the spinal cord to the parietal lobe, without any synapses on the way.
    d. travels to separate thalamic areas, which project to four parallel strips in the temporal lobe.

15. Substance P
    a. is an endogenous opiate.
    b. activates receptors that are normally blocked by capsaicin.
    c. is released in the spinal cord by unmyelinated and thinly myelinated axons carrying pain information.
    d. none of the above

16. The gate theory of pain
    a. was proposed by Melzack and Wall.
    b. states that nonpain input can close the "gates" for pain messages.
    c. may explain why athletes and soldiers may report little pain from a serious injury.
    d. all of the above

17. Leu- and met-enkephalin
    a. have chemical structures virtually identical to morphine.
    b. are two nociceptins in the brain.
    c. are peptide neurotransmitters, consisting of five amino acids each, that have opiate-like effects.
    d. all of the above

18. Which of the following is true of the periaqueductal gray area?
    a. Stimulation of enkephalin receptors there leads to blockade of substance P release in pain pathways.
    b. It is an area in the spinal cord where substance P is released to cause pain.
    c. Stimulation of it reduces sharp pain, but not slow, dull pain.
    d. It is a major site for the induction of pain sensitization.

19. Naloxone
    a. blocks opiate receptors.
    b. is one of the enkephalins.
    c. is released by transcutaneous nerve stimulation (TENS).
    d. depletes substance P.

20. Which of the following is true of analgesia?
    a. All forms are blocked by naloxone.
    b. Morphine administered for serious pain is especially addictive, and should be avoided.
    c. It can be produced by long distance running, sexual activity, some music, some kinds of painful stimuli, acupuncture, and transcutaneous electrical nerve stimulation.
    d. Morphine seriously weakens the immune system for as long as it is administered.

21. Which of the following is true?
   a. Even low doses of morphine can suppress breathing, so it is better for a patient to suffer the pain of an injury rather than risk loss of the control of breathing.
   b. Transcutaneous electrical nerve stimulation (TENS) works by releasing capsaicin in the spinal cord.
   c. Because pain is an evolutionarily old sense, it is very simple in its mechanisms.
   d. Sensitization of pain results when damaged tissue becomes inflamed and triggers the release of histamine and other chemicals that help repair damage; those chemicals increase the number of sodium gates in nearby receptors and axons.

22. The labeled-line principle
   a. states that each receptor responds to a wide range of stimuli and contributes to the perception of each of them.
   b. states that each receptor responds to a narrow range of stimuli and sends a direct line to the brain.
   c. describes color coding better than does the across-fiber pattern principle.
   d. describes most sensory systems in vertebrates.

23. Which of the following is true concerning taste receptors?
   a. There are about 50 receptor cells in each taste bud, and 0 to 10 or more taste buds in each papilla.
   b. Each receptor has its own taste bud.
   c. Taste receptor cells are true neurons that send axons directly to the thalamus.
   d. In adult humans taste buds are located mainly in the center of the tongue.

24. Cross-adaptation studies have suggested that
   a. there are at least four kinds of taste receptors.
   b. there may be a separate receptor for monosodium glutamate.
   c. there may be more than one kind of receptor for both bitter and sweet tastes.
   d. all of the above

25. Which of the following is an appropriate pairing of receptor type with its method of activation?
   a. salty: sodium inflow
   b. sweet: closing potassium channels
   c. sour: activation of G protein
   d. bitter: sodium outflow

26. Amiloride
   a. facilitates sodium flow across the membrane and intensifies salty tastes.
   b. blocks sodium flow across the membrane and intensifies salty tastes.
   c. blocks sodium flow across the membrane and reduces the intensity of salty tastes.
   d. facilitates potassium flow across the membrane and intensifies sweet tastes.

27. The across-fiber pattern principle of taste
   a. assumes that there are seven basic taste qualities.
   b. holds that taste is coded in terms of a pattern of neural activity across many neurons.
   c. has been disproven by the finding that every receptor responds only to one taste.
   d. none of the above

28. The nucleus of the tractus solitarius (NTS)
    a. is located in the medulla and projects to the pons, lateral hypothalamus, amygdala, thalamus, and cerebral cortex.
    b. is responsible only for information about the physical identity of substances; acceptability of tastes is classified only at the level of the cerebral cortex, even in rats.
    c. is located in the medulla and sends its output primarily to cranial nerves.
    d. is located in the cerebral cortex and projects to the medulla.

29. Olfactory receptors
    a. are not replaceable, once they die.
    b. each responds to only one specific odor.
    c. respond equally well to a great many odors.
    d. have cilia that extend into the mucous surface of the nasal passage; odorant molecules must pass through a mucous fluid to reach the receptor site.

30. Specific anosmias
    a. are usually very debilitating.
    b. have shown that there are only 4 kinds of olfactory receptors.
    c. suggest that there are probably a fairly large number of kinds of olfactory receptors.
    d. suggest that identification of odors depends entirely on an across-fiber pattern code.

31. Which of the following is true of olfactory receptors?
    a. They are similar to neurotransmitter receptors in that they have seven transmembrane sections and trigger changes in a G protein, which then provokes chemical activities inside the cell.
    b. There are as many as 1000 olfactory receptor proteins in mice and hundreds in humans.
    c. They send their axons to specific areas of the olfactory bulb.
    d. All of the above are true.

32. Pheromones
    a. are detected by standard olfactory receptors, which have an especially rapid adaptation.
    b. can synchronize or regularize women's menstrual cycles.
    c. are used in lower mammals, but not in humans.
    d. are especially important for locating sources of food.

Answers to Multiple-Choice Questions

1. d	7. a	13. b	19. a	25. a	31. d
2. c	8. d	14. b	20. c	26. c	32. b
3. d	9. c	15. c	21. d	27. b	
4. a	10. b	16. d	22. b	28. a	
5. b	11. c	17. c	23. a	29. d	
6. b	12. a	18. a	24. d	30. c	

Diagram

1. Label the following structures of the inner ear: scala vestibuli, scala media, scala tympani, basilar membrane, tectorial membrane, hair cells, and cochlear neuron.

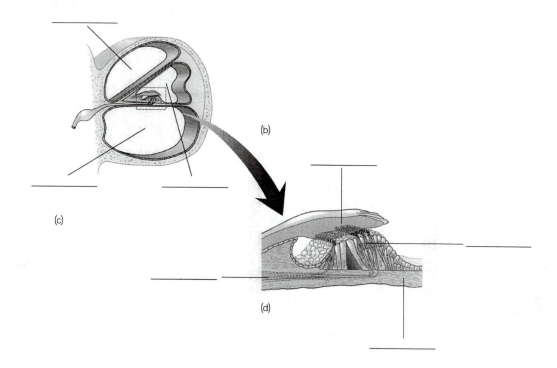

(b)

(c)

(d)

Sensational Senses

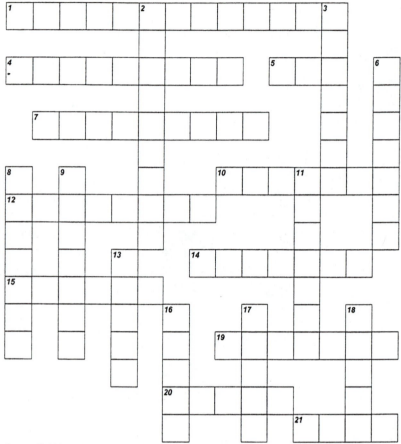

Constructed by Elaine M. Hull using Crossword Weaver

ACROSS

1 Small cell in visual system, sensitive to color and detail

4 Endogenous opiate

5 Cortex area responding to expansion, contraction, or rotation of large scene (abbr.)

7 Portion of body innervated by a nerve

10 Retinal neuron between receptor and ganglion cell

12 Type of retinal cell whose axons go to LGN or tectum

14 Type of visual cortex cell responding to specific line of light anywhere in its receptive field

15 Type of visual cortex cell whose receptive field can be mapped with spot of light

19 Organ consisting of 3 canals and containing auditory receptors

20 Visual receptors mediating color vision

21 Type of information processed by ventral stream (See 6 Down)

DOWN

2 Chemical in hot peppers that stimulates pain receptors

3 11-cis-_____: part of photopigments in dark-adapted state

6 Neural stream (path) of visual input to inferior temporal lobe

8 Inability to recognize certain objects

9 Inability to smell a substance

11 Calcium carbonate particle next to hair cell

13 _____ spot: site where ganglion cell axons leave retina

16 Quality of tone determined by frequency of vibration of sound waves

17 Area of retina with no rods and high acuity

18 One of 3 cochlear canals, the floor of which is the basilar membrane

8

MOVEMENT

INTRODUCTION

All movements of the body result from muscle contractions. Acetylcholine is the neurotransmitter released at the neuromuscular junction; it always results in contraction of the recipient muscle. Myasthenia gravis is a disease characterized by weakness and fatigue. It results from autoimmune destruction of acetylcholine receptors on muscle fibers. It may be treated either with immune-suppressant drugs or with drugs that inhibit the enzyme acetylcholinesterase, which breaks down acetylcholine. We manage to move our limbs in two opposite directions by alternately contracting antagonistic muscles, such as flexors and extensors. There are three categories of muscle: smooth, skeletal (or striated), and cardiac. Skeletal muscles may be either fast or slow. Fish have three types of muscle: red, slow, fatigue-resistant; pink, intermediate-speed, moderately fatigue-resistant; and white, fast, easily fatigued. Birds have dark and light muscles that correspond to the red and white muscles of fish. Mammals have muscles composed of mixed fast-twitch and slow-twitch fibers. Muscles consist of many fibers, each of which is innervated by one axon; however, each axon can innervate more than one fiber. Greater precision of movement can be achieved if each axon innervates few muscle fibers.

Two kinds of receptors signal change in the state of muscle contraction. The muscle spindle is a stretch receptor located in fibers parallel to the main muscle. Whenever the main muscle and spindle are stretched, the spindle sends impulses to the spinal cord that excite the motor neurons innervating the main muscle. This results in contraction of the main muscle, opposing the original stretch. The Golgi tendon organ is located at both ends of the main muscle and responds to increased tension in the muscle, as when the muscle is contracting or being actively stretched by an external stimulus. Its impulses to the spinal cord inhibit the motor neuron, leading to relaxation of the muscle. Combinations of activity in these two receptors allow one to maintain steady positions, to resist external forces, and to monitor voluntary movement.

Most behaviors are complex mixtures of voluntary and involuntary, or reflexive, components. Some movements are ballistic, which means that they proceed automatically once triggered. Other movements require constant sensory feedback. Central pattern generators control rhythmic movements, such as wing flapping and scratching. Motor programs are fixed sequences of movements; they may be learned or innate, rhythmic or not.

The cerebral cortex coordinates complex plans of movement. The primary motor cortex sends axons to the medulla and spinal cord, which in turn innervate the muscles. It has overlapping areas that control different parts of the body. The posterior parietal cortex responds to visual and somatosensory input and to future or current movements; it is important for converting perception into action. The primary somatosensory cortex provides the primary motor cortex with sensory information and also sends axons directly to the spinal cord. Several other cortical areas guide the preparation for movement. Prefrontal cortex responds mostly to sensory stimuli that lead to movement; premotor cortex is active before a movement; supplementary motor cortex is active before a rapid series of movements. Neurons in primary motor cortex respond differentially to movements in different directions; a movement vector is a representation of the relative activity of a group of neurons, each of which has a preferred direction of movement.

Output from the cortex to the spinal cord can be divided into two tracts. The dorsolateral tract controls movements in the periphery of the opposite side of the body. It includes axons from the primary motor cortex and adjacent areas and from the red nucleus, all of which cross from one side to the other in bulges in the medulla called the pyramids. These axons extend without synapsing to targets in the medulla and spinal cord. The ventromedial tract controls movements near the midline of the body that require bilateral control. It consists of some axons from primary and supplementary motor cortex, others from widespread areas of cortex, and those from the midbrain tectum, reticular formation, and vestibular nucleus. None of them cross within the brain, although some axons branch to both sides of the cord. They control muscles of the neck, shoulders, and trunk, whose movements are necessarily bilateral.

The cerebellum is important for learning, planning and coordinating complex movements, especially rapid ballistic sequences that require accurate timing and aiming. It also contributes to sensory and cognitive processes, especially those that guide movement and integrate several problem-solving steps into a smooth sequence. Damage to the cerebellum impairs rapid alternating movements, saccades, the ability to touch one's nose with one's finger, and the ability to shift attention. Parallel fibers in the cerebellar cortex activate Purkinje cells, which in turn inhibit the cerebellar and vestibular nuclei. Inhibiting these nuclei for shorter or longer times determines the duration and distance of a movement. Output from these nuclei is then sent to the midbrain and thalamus.

The basal ganglia are a group of subcortical structures that contribute to the selection and organization of movements, the control of muscle force, and habit learning. The caudate nucleus and putamen receive sensory input from the thalamus and cerebral cortex and send information to the globus pallidus, which in turn sends output to the thalamus, which finally sends the output to motor and prefrontal cortex. The basal ganglia may synchronize outputs from the cortex by activating certain movements and inhibiting others.

The symptoms of Parkinson's disease include muscle rigidity and tremor, slow movement, difficulty initiating physical or mental activity, depression, and cognitive deficits. Parkinson's disease results from degeneration of dopamine neurons ascending from the substantia nigra in the midbrain to the caudate nucleus and putamen, which are part of the basal ganglia. There is also degeneration in the amygdala. Loss of dopamine stimulation of D_1 and D_{12} receptors in the basal ganglia results in increased inhibition from globus pallidus to the thalamus, which then leads to less excitation from the thalamus to the cortex. Therefore, the cortex is less able to initiate movements. Genetic factors contribute to early-onset Parkinson's disease, but play less of a role in late-onset disease. One possible cause of this disease is MPTP in the environment, possibly in the form of herbicides and pesticides, including paraquat. MPTP is converted in the body to MPP+, which accumulates in dopamine neurons and destroys them. On the other hand, nicotine may decrease risk of the disease. The symptoms of Parkinson's disease can be lessened with L-dopa, the precursor of dopamine, although such treatment frequently results in undesirable side effects. Furthermore, L-dopa does not prevent the further loss of neurons. One possible reason for the variable results of L-dopa treatment is that some neurons may be transformed into "orphan" cells, which lack their normal connections. They may produce random leakage of dopamine at inappropriate times and places, while failing to deliver dopamine to correct sites. Other possible treatments include antioxidants, drugs that stimulate dopamine receptors or inhibit glutamate receptors, drugs that decrease apoptosis, nicotine, and inactivation of the globus pallidus. Brain grafts of fetal substantia nigra tissue have produced promising results in laboratory animals, but have produced only modest benefits in humans. Research is continuing on the possible use of genetically altered stem cells, substantia nigra tissue from other species, and neurotrophins.

Whereas Parkinson's disease results from degeneration of the dopaminergic input to the basal ganglia, Huntington's disease results from degeneration of the postsynaptic neurons there and in the cortex. Symptoms begin with a facial twitch and progressively lead to tremors in other parts of the body and to writhing movements and psychological disorders. An autosomal dominant gene on chromosome 4 has been identified as the ultimate cause of the disease. In people with Huntington's disease this gene contains extra repetitions of a sequence of bases in the genetic code for a protein called huntingtin. Huntingtin is found inside neurons, and the mutant form interferes with the expression of numerous genes.

KEY TERMS AND CONCEPTS

Module 8.1 The Control of Movement
1. Muscles and their movements
    Categories of muscle
        Smooth
        Skeletal or striated
        Cardiac
    Precise movements: few muscle fibers innervated by each axon
    Neuromuscular junction
        Acetylcholine
        Muscle contraction
    Antagonistic muscles
        Flexor
        Extensor
    Myasthenia gravis
        Autoimmune attack on acetylcholine receptors at neuromuscular junctions
        Progressive weakness and rapid fatigue
        Depletion of acetylcholine after several action potentials in rapid succession
        Treatment
            Drugs that suppress immune system
            Drugs that inhibit acetylcholinesterase (enzyme that breaks down acetylcholine)
                Prolongs action of acetylcholine
    Fast and slow muscles
        Fish
            Red, slow, resistant to fatigue
            Pink, intermediate speed, moderately resistant to fatigue
            White, fast, forceful, fatigue quickly
        Birds: white and dark muscles
        Humans and other mammals: mixed fibers in each muscle
            Fast-twitch fibers
            Slow-twitch fibers
    Muscle control by proprioceptors
        Stretch reflex
        Muscle spindle
            Stretch receptor parallel to muscle
            Causes muscle to contract: decreases stretch
        Golgi tendon organ
            In tendons at opposite ends of muscle
            Inhibits muscle: brake against too vigorous contraction
        Location of body parts

2. Units of movement

    Voluntary and involuntary movements
        Reflexes: consistent automatic responses to stimuli
            Involuntary

Many behaviors: mixture of voluntary and involuntary influences

Movements with different sensitivity to feedback

    Ballistic movement: executed as a whole; cannot be altered after initiated

    High sensitivity to feedback

        Threading needle

        Singing

            Delayed auditory feedback

Infant reflexes

    Grasp reflex

    Babinski reflex

    Rooting reflex

    Cerebral cortex damage in adults → infant reflexes released from inhibition

    Allied reflexes: several reflexes elicited together

Sequences of behaviors

    Central pattern generators

        Rhythmic movements

        Frequency of repetition: governed by spinal cord

    Motor program: fixed sequence of movements

        Learned or built in

        Birds: wing extension when dropped

        Humans: yawning

Categories of movement

    Spinal motor neuron: final common path

    Many brain areas control different patterns

Module 8.2 Brain Mechanisms of Movement

1.   The role of the cerebral cortex

Primary motor cortex: posterior frontal cortex, anterior to central sulcus

    General movement plans

    Overlapping areas of control

Areas near the primary motor cortex

    Posterior parietal cortex

        Position of body relative to the world

        Converting perception into action

    Primary somatosensory cortex

        Sensory information to motor cortex

        Direct output to spinal cord

    Prefrontal cortex

        Response to sensory signals that lead to a movement

    Premotor cortex

        Preparation for movement

    Supplementary motor cortex

        Preparation for rapid series of movements

Connections from the brain to the spinal cord

    Dorsolateral tract of spinal cord

        Axons from primary motor cortex and surrounding areas and from red nucleus of midbrain

        Direct connection to spinal cord

        Cross in pyramids of medulla

        Controls peripheral movements on opposite side of body

Ventromedial tract of spinal cord
Uncrossed axons from cortex, tectum, reticular formation and vestibular nucleus
Axons branch to both sides of spinal cord
Controls midline movements requiring bilateral influence

2. The role of the cerebellum ("little brain")
More neurons than rest of brain combined
Learned motor responses
Rapid ballistic movements
Effects of damage to the cerebellum
Inability to link motions rapidly and smoothly
Tests of cerebellar functioning
Saccades
Finger-to-nose test
Move function: cerebellar cortex
Hold function: cerebellar nuclei
Slow movement: not dependent on cerebellum
Evidence of a broad role
Response to sensory stimuli that direct movement
Cognitive programs for problem solving
Programming sequence of actions as a whole
Precise timing of brief intervals
Aspects of attention
Cellular organization
Input from spinal cord, sensory cranial nerve nuclei, and cerebral cortex
Cerebellar cortex: precise geometrical pattern with multiple repetitions of same units
Parallel fibers (axons parallel to each other) activate Purkinje cells (flat cells in sequential planes)
Purkinje cells inhibit cerebellar nuclei and vestibular nuclei of brain stem
These then send information to midbrain and thalamus
Controls duration of response

3. The role of the basal ganglia
Component structures
Caudate nucleus
Putamen
Globus pallidus
Input from sensory thalamus and cortex to caudate nucleus and putamen
Output from globus pallidus to thalamus, which projects to motor and prefrontal cortex
Functions
Organize action sequences into automatic units
Select correct movement and inhibit other movements
Control of muscle force

4. Possibilities for the future
Bypass spinal cord in people with spinal cord injury

155

Module 8.3 Disorders of Movement
1.   Parkinson's disease
     Symptoms
          Rigidity
          Muscle tremors
          Slow movements
          Difficulty initiating physical and mental activity
          Depression and cognitive deficits
     Degeneration of dopamine neurons projecting from substantia nigra to caudate nucleus and
          putamen; also degeneration in amygdala
          Decreased dopamine at inhibitory D_2 receptors in caudate and putamen →
          Increased excitation of globus pallidus →
          Increased inhibitory output from globus pallidus to thalamus →
          Decreased excitation from thalamus to cerebral cortex
     Possible causes
          Low heritability of late-onset Parkinson's disease
               Higher heritability of early-onset Parkinson's disease
          Exposure to toxins
               MPTP, MPP$^+$
               Postsynaptic neurons increase dopamine receptors
                    Compensation for loss of dopamine
                    Result in overresponsiveness
               Herbicides, pesticides (including paraquat)
          Cigarette smoking: decreases risk before age 75, increases it after that
               Smoking: greater risk for lung cancer and emphysema
     L-dopa treatment
          Precursor to dopamine
          Effectiveness varies
          Does not prevent loss of neurons
          Side effects: nausea, restlessness, sleep problems, low blood pressure, stereotyped
               movements, hallucinations, delusions
          "Orphan" cells: between death and regeneration; lack usual connections
     Therapies other than L-dopa
          Antioxidant drugs
          Drugs that stimulate dopamine receptors
          Drugs that block glutamate
          Neurotrophins
          Drugs that decrease apoptosis
          Inactivation of globus pallidus by electrical stimulation
          Surgical damage to globus pallidus or parts of thalamus
          Nicotine
          Brain grafts
               Patient's adrenal gland
               Brain tissue from aborted fetuses
               Genetically altered fetal cells: produce much L-dopa
               Stem cells
               Fetal tissue from other species
               Transplanted tissue that produces neurotrophins

2. Huntington's disease (Huntington's chorea)
    Symptoms
        Twitches and tremors
        Writhing movements
        Impaired ability to learn new movements
    Extensive brain damage, especially in caudate nucleus, putamen, globus pallidus, and cortex
    Psychological symptoms: depression, memory impairment, anxiety, hallucinations and
        delusions, poor judgment, alcoholism, drug abuse, sexual disorders
    Heredity and presymptomatic testing
        Autosomal dominant gene on chromosome #4
        Extra repetitions of sequence of bases: the more repetitions, the earlier the onset
        Protein encoded: huntingtin
            Mutant form: interferes with gene expression

SHORT-ANSWER QUESTIONS

Module 8.1 The Control of Movement
1. *Muscles and their movements*
    a. List the three categories of muscle.

    b. What is the transmitter at the neuromuscular junction? What is its effect? How do we
        move our limbs in two opposite directions?

    c. Describe the symptoms and cause of myasthenia gravis.

    d. What are two kinds of treatment for this disease?

157

e. List the types and functions of skeletal muscle in fish and birds.

f. How are mammalian muscles different from those of fish and birds? Contrast the muscles of sprinters and marathon runners.

g. What is a proprioceptor? A stretch reflex?

h. What is a muscle spindle? What is its effect on the spinal motor neuron that innervates its associated muscle?

i. Explain the knee-jerk reflex in terms of the above mechanism.

j. What is a Golgi tendon organ? What is its effect on the spinal motor neuron that innervates its associated muscle? What is its functional role?

2. *Units of movement*
   a.   What is a reflex?

   b.   Describe some of the involuntary components of "voluntary" behaviors, such as walking or talking.

   c.   What is a ballistic movement?

   d.   What is the effect of delayed auditory feedback on a singer's ability to hold a single note for a long time?

   e.   What is a motor program? Give examples of "built-in" and learned motor programs.

   f.   Do humans have any built-in motor patterns?

Module 8.2 Brain Mechanisms of Movement

1.   *The role of the cerebral cortex*

   a.   Describe the role of the primary motor cortex in the control of movement.

   b.   To what two processes do neurons in the posterior parietal cortex respond? What is the result of damage there?

   c.   Describe the roles of the prefrontal, premotor, and supplementary motor cortex.

   d.   Where does the dorsolateral tract begin? Where does it cross from one side to the other?

   e.   From what structures does the ventromedial tract originate? What is the relationship between this tract and the two sides of the spinal cord?

f.   Which movements are controlled by the dorsolateral tract, and which by the ventromedial tract?

2. *The role of the cerebellum*
    a.   What kinds of movements are especially affected by cerebellar damage?

    b.   What are saccades? Describe the effect of cerebellar damage on the control of saccades?

    c.   Describe the motor control required to touch one's finger to one's nose as quickly as possible.

    d.   Why may a police officer use the finger-to-nose test to check for alcohol intoxication?

    e.   Describe the evidence for a broad role for the cerebellum, beyond motor performance.

f. From what sources does the cerebellum receive input? To which structures do its output fibers project?

g. Describe the relationship between the Purkinje cells and the parallel fibers. How does this affect movement?

3. *The role of the basal ganglia*
   a. What structures comprise the basal ganglia?

   b. Which are the main receptive areas? The main output area? Where does the sensory input come from, and where does the output go?

   c. What is the role of the basal ganglia in the learning of motor patterns?

   d. How does cerebellar function compare with that of the basal ganglia?

Module 8.3 Disorders of Movement
1. *Parkinson's disease*
    a. Describe the symptoms of Parkinson's disease.

    b. What is its immediate cause? What is the result of loss of dopamine stimulation of D_2 receptors in the caudate nucleus and putamen?

    c. How strong is the evidence for a genetic predisposition for Parkinson's disease?

    d. How did the experience with a heroin substitute lead to suspicion of an environmental toxin as a cause of this disease?

    e. How may herbicides and pesticides be implicated?

    f. What is a problem with the toxin-exposure hypothesis?

g. What was the unexpected finding concerning cigarette smoking and Parkinson's disease? What may be the basis for this effect?

h. What is the rationale for treatment of Parkinson's disease with L-dopa? What are the side effects of this treatment?

i. What are "orphan" cells, and how may they contribute to Parkinsonian symptoms?

j. List some other possible treatments for Parkinson's disease?

k. How successful have brain grafts been in treating Parkinson's disease in humans? What are some of the problems with the use of fetal tissue? From where in the brain is fetal tissue taken?

1. What kinds of tissue have been used for brain grafts to treat Parkinson's disease? What are some potential additional sources for tissue for such grafts?

2. *Huntington's disease*
   a. What are the physical and psychological symptoms of Huntington's disease?

   b. Which neurons degenerate in Huntington's disease?

   c. Discuss the role of genetics in Huntington's disease. On which chromosome is the gene for Huntington's disease located?

   d. What is huntingtin? What do we know about the base sequence of the gene that codes for it? What may it do inside the cell?

POSTTEST

Multiple-Choice Questions

1. Which of the following is true of nerves and muscles?
   a. There is a one-to-one relationship between axons and muscle fibers.
   b. Each axon innervates several or many muscle fibers.
   c. Each muscle fiber receives several or many axons.
   d. Each axon innervates many muscle fibers, and each muscle fiber receives many axons.

2. Acetylcholine
   a. has only inhibitory effects on skeletal muscles.
   b. has excitatory effects on some skeletal muscles and inhibitory effects on others.
   c. has only excitatory effects on skeletal muscles.
   d. is released only onto smooth muscles, never onto skeletal muscles.

3. Myasthenia gravis
   a. results from destruction of acetylcholine receptors at neuromuscular junctions by an autoimmune process.
   b. is helped by drugs that increase the effect of acetylcholinesterase.
   c. is helped by drugs that enhance the function of the immune system.
   d. all of the above

4. Which of the following is a type of skeletal muscle in fish?
   a. slow, white, fatigue-resistant
   b. fast, white, fatigue-resistant
   c. slow, pink, fatigue-prone
   d. slow, red, fatigue-resistant

5. Mammalian muscles
   a. can be classified as red, pink, and white, as in fish.
   b. contain either fast-twitch or slow-twitch fibers, but not both.
   c. contain both fast-twitch and slow-twitch fibers in the same muscles.
   d. show only genetic, and not any environmental, determination of the ratio of fast-twitch to slow-twitch fibers.

6. The muscle spindle
   a. is a stretch receptor located in parallel to the muscle.
   b. inhibits the motor neuron innervating the muscle when it is stretched; this leads to relaxation of the muscle.
   c. responds only when the muscle contracts.
   d. synapses onto the muscle to excite it directly.

7. The Golgi tendon organ
   a. is also located in the muscle spindle.
   b. affects the motor neuron in the same way as the muscle spindle, thereby enhancing its effect.
   c. responds when the muscle contracts.
   d. excites the motor neuron that innervates the muscle.

8. Ballistic movements
   a. are required when a singer holds a note for a long time.
   b. require feedback as they are being executed.
   c. are controlled largely by the basal ganglia.
   d. proceed automatically once triggered.

9. The frequency of repetition of a cat's scratch reflex
   a. varies, and is controlled by pattern generators in the brain.
   b. is constant at three to four scratches per second, and is determined by cells in the lumbar spinal cord.
   c. is constant and is determined by pattern generators in the brain.
   d. is an example of feedback control.

10. Which of the following is true?
    a. Feedback control must be at the root of all movements; otherwise we would be unable to modify our behavior.
    b. Singing a single note does not require feedback, although singing several notes in a sequence does require feedback.
    c. Even ballistic movements are in reality feedback controlled.
    d. There are involuntary components of many voluntary behaviors.

11. Which of the following is true of motor programs?
    a. Grooming behavior of mice is an example of a built-in motor program.
    b. Grooming behavior of mice is an example of a learned motor program.
    c. Species of birds that have not used their wings for flight for millions of years still extend their wings when dropped.
    d. Humans have only learned, and not built-in, motor programs.

12. The primary motor cortex
    a. sends axons to the brainstem and spinal cord.
    b. includes the somatomotor, prefrontal, premotor, and supplementary motor cortex, as well as the basal ganglia.
    c. controls isolated movements of individual muscles.
    d. all of the above

13. The order of activity in preparing for and executing a movement is
    a. primary motor, premotor, prefrontal cortex.
    b. prefrontal, premotor, primary motor cortex.
    c. premotor, prefrontal, primary motor cortex.
    d. primary motor, prefrontal, premotor cortex.

14. The posterior parietal cortex
    a. is the main receiving area for somatosensory information.
    b. helps us to program a series of rapid movements.
    c. helps us to convert perception into action.
    d. is part of the primary motor cortex.

15. The dorsolateral tract of the spinal cord
    a. originates mostly in the primary motor cortex and adjacent areas and in the red nucleus of the midbrain.
    b. controls movements in the periphery of the body.
    c. controls movements on the side of the body opposite the brain area where the fibers originate.
    d. all of the above

16. The ventromedial tract of the spinal cord
    a. contains crossed fibers from the primary motor cortex and adjacent areas and from the red nucleus of the midbrain.
    b. controls movements near the midline of the body that are necessarily bilateral.
    c. controls movements on the side of the body opposite the brain area where the fibers originate.
    d. works independently from the dorsolateral tract.

17. The pyramids of the medulla
    a. contain the cell bodies of the dorsolateral tract.
    b. contain the cell bodies of the ventromedial tract.
    c. are the site where axons of the dorsolateral tract cross from one side to the other.
    d. are the site where axons of the ventromedial tract cross from one side to the other.

18 The cerebellum
    a. is especially important for performance of rapid ballistic movement sequences that require accurate aiming and timing.
    b. is large and critical for the behavior of sloths.
    c. is important only for innate, not learned, motor responses.
    d. all of the above

19. Damage to the cerebellum produces
    a. Parkinson's disease.
    b. Huntington's disease.
    c. deficits in saccadic movements of the eyes.
    d. deficits in slow feedback-controlled movements.

20. In executing the "finger-to-nose" movement quickly
    a. the cerebellar cortex is important in the initial rapid movement.
    b. the cerebellar nuclei are important in maintaining the brief hold pattern.
    c. other structures are important in the final slow movement.
    d. all of the above

21. Purkinje cells in the cerebellum
    a. receive input from parallel fibers.
    b. send output to parallel fibers.
    c. excite cells in the cerebellar nuclei.
    d. send output to the basal ganglia and cerebral cortex.

22. The cerebellum
    a. shows most activity during purely motor tasks.
    b. contributes to any behavior that requires careful timing of brief intervals.
    c. is now thought to contribute only to cognitive tasks, and not to motor tasks.
    d. is especially important for controlling muscle force.

23. The basal ganglia consist of
    a. the caudate nucleus, the cerebellum, and the thalamus.
    b. the cerebellum, the putamen, and the thalamus.
    c. the putamen, the globus pallidus, and the pyramids of the medulla.
    d. the caudate nucleus, the putamen, and the globus pallidus.

24. The basal ganglia are important for
    a. rapid ballistic movements.
    b. selecting and organizing responses.
    c. wing flapping in birds.
    d. fine control of movement.

25. Parkinson's disease
    a. results from too much dopamine in the basal ganglia.
    b. results from too little acetylcholine at the neuromuscular junction.
    c. results from too little dopamine in the basal ganglia.
    d. is almost completely determined genetically.

26. MPTP
    a. has been used with some success in treating Parkinson's disease.
    b. may be an environmental cause of Parkinson's disease.
    c. may be an environmental cause of myasthenia gravis.
    d. has been used with some success in treating myasthenia gravis.

27. Which of the following is **not** a current or potential treatment for Parkinson's disease?
    a. dopamine pills.
    b. L-dopa.
    c. nicotine.
    d. antioxidants.

28. Brain grafts
    a. are currently the best treatment for Parkinson's disease.
    b. are most effective if they use tissue from the patient's own adrenal gland in order to prevent rejection.
    c. are able to produce behavioral recovery only if the implanted tissue survives and makes functional synapses.
    d. currently use fetal substantia nigra tissue, but may someday use stem cells genetically altered to produce large quantities of L-dopa.

29. Huntington's disease
    a. results from destruction of dopaminergic input to the basal ganglia.
    b. is characterized by great weakness.
    c. is caused by a dominant gene on human chromosome number 4.
    d. is caused by a recessive gene on human chromosome number 10.

30. Which of the following are not symptoms of Huntington's disease?
    a. weakness and difficulty initiating movements
    b. depression, anxiety, memory impairment, hallucinations, and delusions
    c. poor judgment, alcoholism, and drug abuse
    d. facial twitch and tremors

31. The gene associated with Huntington's disease
    a. in its normal form, contains a sequence of bases repeated at least 40 times; many of those repeats are lost in patients with Huntington's disease.
    b. in its normal form, does not contain any repeated sequences of bases.
    c. is now known to code for acetylcholine receptors.
    d. is now known to code for huntingtin, a protein, the mutant form of which interferes with the expression of many genes.

Answers to Multiple-Choice Questions

1. b	9. b	17. c	25. c
2. c	10. d	18. a	26. b
3. a	11. a	19. c	27. a
4. d	12. a	20. d	28. d
5. c	13. b	21. a	29. c
6. a	14. c	22. b	30. a
7. c	15. d	23. d	31. d
8. d	16. b	24. b	

Diagrams

1. Label the following components of the basal ganglia: caudate nucleus, putamen, globus pallidus (lateral part), globus pallidus (medial part), thalamus, subthalamic nucleus, amygdala, substantia nigra.

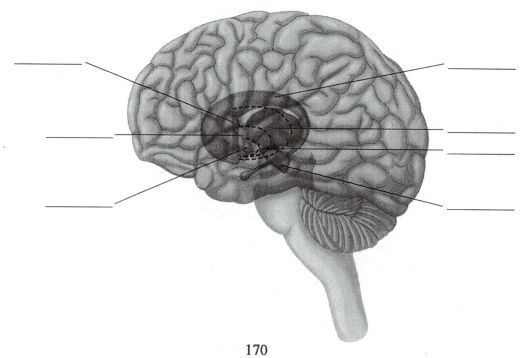

2. Label the principal areas of the motor cortex in the human brain: posterior parietal cortex, prefrontal cortex, premotor cortex, primary motor cortex, primary somatosensory cortex, supplementary motor cortex.

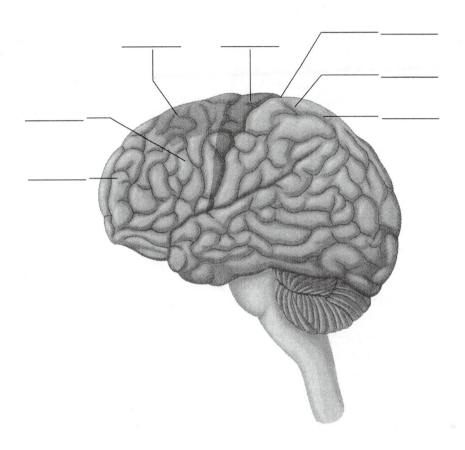

9

RHYTHMS OF WAKEFULNESS AND SLEEP

INTRODUCTION

Animals ranging from insects to humans exhibit endogenous rhythms of behavior. Circannual (approximately year-long) cycles govern hibernation, migration, and seasonal mating in some species. Circadian (approximately 24-hour) cycles regulate activity and sleep as well as other bodily functions. The "clock" governing these cycles generates the rhythm internally, although the external light cycles affect the specific settings. The mechanism of the clock is not understood; however the length of the rhythm may be altered by genetic mutation. The protein products of two genes in fruitflies build up during the day and produce sleepiness; high levels also decrease production of the proteins. Similar genes have been found in mice. Light appears to act on the suprachiasmatic nucleus (SCN) of the hypothalamus. If the axons from the retina to the SCN are damaged, light can no longer reset the biological clock. Melatonin, a hormone produced by the pineal gland, may be one means by which the SCN regulates sleeping and waking. Increased melatonin secretion begins 2 to 3 hours before the onset of sleepiness.

Relaxed wakefulness (with the eyes closed) is characterized by alpha waves at a frequency of 8-12 per second. Stage 1 of sleep is signaled by irregular, low-voltage waves, after which progression through stages 2, 3, and 4 is correlated with increasingly slow, large-amplitude waves. Throughout the night, there is a cyclic progression back and forth through the four stages. However, after the first period of stage 1, each return to stage 1 is correlated with rapid eye movements, relaxed muscles, and rapid and variable heart rate and breathing. Rapid eye movement (REM) sleep has also been called paradoxical sleep, because the EEG shows fast, low amplitude waves, as during wakefulness, and the heart rate and breathing are variable, but the postural muscles are completely relaxed.

Wakefulness and behavioral arousal depend, in part, on the reticular formation, a group of large, branching neurons running from the medulla into the forebrain. The pontomesencephalon is the part of the reticular formation that contributes to cortical arousal. It receives input diffusely from many sensory systems and generates spontaneous activity of its own. It sends output to the thalamus and basal forebrain. There are different types of arousal, requiring many brain areas. The locus coeruleus, in the pons, is active in response to meaningful events and may help to form memories. The basal forebrain is the site of nuclei that send acetylcholine-containing axons to widespread areas of the thalamus and cortex; these neurons also promote wakefulness. Finally, two paths from the hypothalamus increase arousal by releasing the neurotransmitter histamine.

Sleep results in part from reductions of sensory input and of activity in arousal systems. Adenosine accumulates during wakefulness and shuts off the basal forebrain neurons that produce arousal. Prostaglandins also increase during the day and inhibit hypothalamic cells that increase arousal. In addition, some brain areas actively promote sleep. Clusters of GABA-containing neurons in the basal forebrain send widespread axons that promote the onset of sleep. These neurons receive much of their input from the anterior and preoptic areas of the hypothalamus, which also regulate temperature.

During REM sleep, high-amplitude potentials can be recorded in the pons, geniculate, and occipital cortex (PGO waves). Animals maintain nearly constant amounts of PGO waves. If deprived of REM, PGO waves intrude into other sleep stages and even wakefulness. Animals compensate for lost PGO waves when allowed to sleep freely. Cells in the pons also inhibit the motor neurons that control postural muscles. Other sites that are active during REM are the limbic system and parts of

172

the parietal and temporal cortex; other cortical areas, including the primary visual, motor, and dorsolateral prefrontal cortex, become less active during REM. Two neurotransmitters regulate REM sleep. Acetylcholine induces its onset, and serotonin interrupts or shortens it.

There are three categories of insomnia: onset, maintenance, and termination. Causes of insomnia include abnormalities of biological rhythms, withdrawal from tranquilizers, and periodic limb movements. Sleep apnea, the inability to breathe during sleep, may be caused by obesity or impairment of brain mechanisms for respiration. Narcolepsy refers to periods of extreme sleepiness during the day. Additional symptoms of narcolepsy are cataplexy (extreme muscle weakness while awake), sleep paralysis (inability to move during transition into or out of sleep), and hypnagogic hallucinations (dreamlike experiences that are difficult to distinguish from reality). All of these symptoms can be interpreted as intrusions of REM sleep into wakefulness. In REM behavior disorder people appear to act out their dreams, possibly as a result of damage to the neurons in the pons that inhibit movement during REM. Nightmares are unpleasant dreams that occur during REM sleep; night terrors are experiences of extreme anxiety, occurring during non-REM sleep, from which a person wakens in terror. Sleep talking occurs with similar probability in REM and non-REM sleep, whereas sleepwalking occurs mostly during stages 3 and 4 slow-wave sleep.

Sleep serves two major functions. The repair and restoration theory stresses that restorative functions occur mostly during sleep, especially for the brain. The evolutionary theory proposes that sleep is basically an energy-conserving mechanism employed during times when activity would be either inefficient or dangerous. These two theories are complementary and compatible.

The function of REM sleep is not well understood. In general, the percentage of sleep spent in REM correlates positively with the total amount of sleep. REM deprivation has resulted in increased irritability, anxiety, and appetite, impaired concentration, and increased REM time on subsequent uninterrupted nights. REM may facilitate memory storage; however, non-REM (NREM) may also strengthen certain memories. The eye movements that characterize REM may also increase oxygen supply to the corneas. Dreams may result from the brain's attempt to make sense of its increased activity during REM episodes (activation-synthesis hypothesis). A clinico-anatomical hypothesis rests in part on the observations that during REM, neural activity in primary visual, motor, and prefrontal cortex is suppressed. Therefore, normal visual input cannot compete with self-generated stimulation, and motor activity is suppressed. Also, working memory and "use of knowledge," functions of prefrontal cortex, are inhibited. On the other hand, increased activity in inferior parietal cortex and higher visual areas may increase spatial perception and visual imagery.

KEY TERMS AND CONCEPTS

Module 9.1 Rhythms of Waking and Sleeping
1. Endogenous cycles
        Endogenous circannual and circadian rhythms
    Setting and resetting the cycle
        Biological clock
        Free-running rhythm
        Zeitgeber
    Duration of the human circadian rhythm
        Difficulties with experiments
        Ability to adapt to 23- or 25-hour days, but not 22- or 28-hour days
        Average: 24.2 hours

2. Resetting the biological clock
   Jet lag
       Worse going east
       Phase-delay: going west
       Phase-advance: going east
   Shift work
       Exposure to bright lights

3. The mechanisms of the biological clock
       Interfering with the biological clock
           Curt Richter
               Lack of effect of most procedures
   The suprachiasmatic nucleus (SCN)
       Main control of rhythms of sleep and temperature
       Endogenous rhythm
           Disconnected SCN still generates rhythms
           Single SCN cells generate rhythm
               Less steady than group of cells
           Genetic mutation that produces 20-hour rhythm
               Transplantation of mutant or normal SCN: animals followed rhythm of SCN
       Drosophila genes
           Build up during day and produce sleepiness
           Period (per)
           Timeless (tim)
               Inactivated by light
           Similar genes in mice
   How light resets the SCN
       Retinohypothalamic path
           Axons from optic nerve
       Animals with little or no vision: light still resets rhythms
           Mice with genetic defects
           Blind mole rats
       Light behind people's knees: reset rhythm
           Blood-borne factors
   Melatonin
       Pineal gland
       Peak 2 to 3 hours before sleepiness
       Melatonin pill in afternoon → phase advance
       Melatonin pill in morning → phase delay
       Risks unknown

Module 9.2 Stages of Sleep and Brain Mechanisms
1. The stages of sleep
   Alpha waves (8 - 12 per second): relaxed wakefulness
   Stage 1 sleep
       Irregular, low-voltage EEG waves
   Stage 2 sleep
       Sleep spindle
       K-complex
   Stages 3 and 4 slow-wave sleep

174

Synchronized EEG: slow, large amplitude waves

Cycling back through stages 3 and 2

Methods 9.1: Electroencephalography

    Electrodes attached to scalp

    Record average activity of population of cells under electrode

    Can determine: asleep, awake, dreaming, excited

    Abnormalities: epilepsy, tumor, other medical problems

2.   Paradoxical or REM sleep

    Characteristics

        Paradoxical sleep

            In some ways deepest and in some ways lightest sleep

        Rapid eye movements (REM)

        Irregular, low-voltage fast (desynchronized) EEG

        Postural relaxation

        Variable heart rate and breathing

        Penile erection or vaginal moistening

        Facial twitches

        Polysomnograph: EEG and eye movement records

        Sleep cycles

            90- to 100-minute cycles

            Stages 3 and 4 predominant early in night

            REM predominant late in night

            REM sleep and dreaming

                Dreams reported on 80-90% of awakenings from REM

                Some kind of thought process during non-REM sleep (NREM)

                REM: intensifies dreams but not synonymous with dreaming

                Ideas only loosely associated

3.   Brain mechanisms of wakefulness and arousal

    Brain structures of arousal

        Cut through midbrain: prolonged sleep

            Not due to loss of sensory input

        Reticular formation: interconnected network

        Pontomesencephalon

            Widespread sensory input

            Spontaneous activity

            Axons to thalamus and basal forebrain

                Acetylcholine: excitatory effects

                Arousal then relayed to cortex

        Arousal not a unitary process

            Locus coeruleus ("dark blue place")

                Bursts of impulses in response to meaningful events

                Norepinephrine

                May aid in memory formation

            Basal forebrain nuclei (anterior and dorsal to hypothalamus)

                Provides input to thalamus and cortex

                Transmitter: acetylcholine → mostly excitatory effects

                Damaged in Alzheimer's disease

           Paths from hypothalamus
                Histamine
       Getting to sleep
          Decrease temperature
             Shift blood to periphery
             Melatonin
          Decrease stimulation
             Gentle rocking: may help
          Inhibit arousal systems that are excited by acetylcholine
             Adenosine: inhibits basal forebrain arousal systems
                Metabolism: adenosine monophosphate (AMP) → adenosine
                Caffeine → inhibits adenosine → wakefulness
          Prostaglandins
             Build up during day, decline during sleep
             Increased by immune system during infection
             Inhibit hypothalamic neurons that increase arousal
          Basal forebrain nuclei that induce sleep
             Wide projections
             Transmitter: GABA → inhibitory effects
             Input from anterior and preoptic hypothalamus
                Temperature regulation
                Fever increases output to sleep-related cells

4. Brain function in REM sleep
Increased activity in pons and limbic system
Increased activity in parts of parietal and temporal cortex
Decreased activity in primary visual, motor, and dorsolateral prefrontal cortex
PGO (pons-geniculate-occipital) waves
       Compensation for lost PGO waves
Pons → spinal cord: inhibition of motor neurons
Neurotransmitters
       Acetylcholine → REM onset
          Carbachol
          Important for both waking and REM: activate brain
       Serotonin → interrupts or shortens REM

5. Abnormalities of sleep
Insomnia
       Onset insomnia
          Possible cause: phase-delayed temperature rhythm
       Maintenance insomnia
          Possible cause: circadian rhythm irregularity
       Termination insomnia
          Possible cause: phase-advanced temperature rhythm
          Early onset of REM sleep
          Depression
       Withdrawal from tranquilizers
Sleep apnea
       Sudden infant death syndrome
       Obesity

Narcolepsy
    Attacks of daytime sleepiness
    Cataplexy
    Sleep paralysis
    Hypnagogic hallucinations
    May be due to intrusion of REM into wakefulness
        Overactive acetylcholine synapses
    Treated with stimulants
        Pemoline (Cylert) or methylphenidate (Ritalin)
Periodic limb movement disorder (mostly during NREM sleep)
REM behavior disorder
    Acting out dreams
    Damage in pons and midbrain
    Motor neurons no longer inhibited
Night terrors, sleep talking, and sleepwalking
    Night terrors different from nightmares
        Occur in NREM sleep
    Sleep talking
        Occurs in REM or NREM sleep
    Sleepwalking
        Most common in children
        Mostly in Stages 3 and 4 (not during REM)

6. In closing: Stages of sleep
Usefulness of EEG recordings in identifying internal experiences

Module 9.3 Why Sleep? Why REM? Why Dreams?
1. The functions of sleep
The repair and restoration theory of sleep
    Effects of sleep deprivation
        Human (voluntary) experiments: dizziness, impaired concentration, irritability, hand
            tremors, hallucinations
        Animal (nonvoluntary) experiments
            Few days deprivation: increased temperature, metabolism, and appetite
            Longer deprivation: decreased immune function, decreased brain activity
    Little effect of physical exertion
    Variability of requirements
The evolutionary theory
    Hibernation: retards aging process and suppresses metabolism and temperature
    Energy conservation
    Time required for food search
    Safety from predators

2. The functions of REM sleep
Individual and species differences
    Percent of time in REM correlated with length of sleep
The effects of REM deprivation
    Humans
        Increased anxiety and irritability
        Decreased concentration

Increased appetite
REM rebound (increased REM in uninterrupted nights)
Paradoxical sleep deprivation in nonhumans (up to 70 days)
Severe impairments of behavior and health
Maybe due in part to falling into cold water
Hypotheses
Memory storage
Differential effects on types of learning
NREM also important for learning
Discard useless information
Increase oxygen to eyeballs

3. Biological perspectives on dreaming
The activation-synthesis hypothesis
Paralysis of postural muscles
Vague and hard to test
A clinico-anatomical hypothesis
Arousing stimuli processed in unusual ways
Suppression of activity in primary visual, motor, and prefrontal cortex
No normal visual stimuli or motor responses
Inhibited working memory and "use of knowledge"
Increased activity in inferior parietal cortex
Damage there → poor spatial perception and no dreams
Increased activity in "higher" visual areas
Damage there → dreams with no visual content
Also vague and hard to test; but is based on studies of patients

4. In closing: Our limited self-understanding
No need for conscious understanding of evolutionary reasons for behavion

SHORT-ANSWER QUESTIONS

Module 9.1 Rhythms of Waking and Sleeping
1. *Endogenous cycles*
   a. What do we know about the factors that initiate migration in birds?

   b. What are endogenous circannual rhythms? Endogenous circadian rhythms? How consistent are circadian rhythms within individuals in a given environment? Between individuals?

c.   How can circadian rhythms be demonstrated experimentally? What are some bodily and behavioral changes that occur in circadian rhythms?

d.   What is a Zeitgeber? What is the most effective Zeitgeber for land animals? For many marine animals?

e.   How easily can humans adapt to a new cycle length? What are the limits of adaptation?

2.   *Resetting the biological clock*
    a.   Is it easier to cross time zones going east or west? Why?

    b.   What is the best way to reset the biological clock when working a night shift?

3.   *The mechanisms of the biological clock*
    a.   What sorts of attempted interference with the biological clock were not effective?

b. What structure is the source of the circadian rhythms? What is its relationship to the visual system?

c. What is the evidence that the suprachiasmatic nucleus (SCN) generates rhythms itself?

d. What happened when SCN tissue from hamsters with a mutant gene for a 20-hour rhythm were transplanted into normal hamsters?

e. What two genes, discovered in Drosophila (fruitflies), govern circadian rhythms? How do they work? How common is this mechanism in other animals?

f. From what pathway does the SCN get its input from the visual system? Are blind mice and mole rats able to use light to reset their SCN? By what non-retinal path may light influence circadian rhythms in people?

g. What is melatonin? From which gland is it secreted? When does increased secretion of melatonin occur?

Module 9.2 Stages of Sleep and Brain Mechanisms
1. *The stages of sleep*
    a. Describe the usual behavioral correlate of alpha waves. What is their frequency?

    b. Describe the EEG in stage 1 sleep.

    c. What are the EEG characteristics of stage 2 sleep?

    d. Which stages of sleep are classed as slow-wave sleep (SWS)?

2. *Paradoxical or REM sleep*
    a. Why is REM sleep sometimes called paradoxical sleep? What are its characteristics?

181

b.   What is a polysomnograph?

c.   What is the typical duration of the sleep cycle? During which part of the night is REM predominant? During which part are stages 3 and 4 SWS predominant?

d.   How good is the correlation between REM and dreaming?

e.   What evidence suggests that REM states are characterized by "loose" associations?

3.   *Brain mechanisms of wakefulness and arousal*
   a.   What is the result of a cut through the midbrain on sleep and waking cycles? Was this result due simply to loss of sensory input or to damage to a particular brain structure?

   b.   Describe the input, output, and interconnections of the pontomesencephalon. What is its relation to the reticular formation?

c.   Give the location, neurotransmitter, and a major function of the locus coeruleus.

d.   What is the major neurotransmitter released by neurons in the basal forebrain that contribute to arousal?

e.   What is the neurotransmitter of two paths from the hypothalamus that stimulate arousal? What is the implication of this for allergy treatments?

f.   What is a good indicator of how fast a person will get to sleep? Explain this finding.

g.   How does adenosine contribute to sleepiness? How does caffeine increase arousal?

h.   What are prostaglandins? How do they provoke sleep?

i.   What neurotransmitter is released by neurons of the basal forebrain that promote sleep? What is a major source of input to those neurons? How is that source related to body temperature?

4.   *Brain function in REM sleep*
     a.   What are PGO waves? Where are they recorded? What happens to PGO waves after a period of REM deprivation?

     b.   Describe the mechanism for inhibiting motor activity during REM sleep.

     c.   Which neurotransmitter is important for REM onset? For interruption or shortening of REM? What is one effect of the drug carbachol?

5.   *Abnormalities of sleep*
     a.   List and describe the characteristics of the three categories of insomnia. What circadian rhythm disorders may cause each category?

184

b.   What are the pharmacological effects of most tranquilizers that are used as sleeping pills? How may sleeping pills contribute to insomnia?

c.   Describe the symptoms of sleep apnea. What is one cause of sleep apnea?

d.   What four symptoms are commonly associated with narcolepsy? What is a likely cause of narcolepsy?

e.   Define cataplexy. What tends to trigger it? Define hypnagogic hallucinations.

f.   Describe the symptoms of periodic limb movement disorder.

g.   What are the symptoms and possible cause of REM behavior disorder?

h. How do night terrors differ from nightmares? During which type of sleep are night terrors most common?

i. During which stages does sleep talking occur? Sleepwalking?

Module 9.3 Why Sleep? Why REM? Why Dreams?
1. *The functions of sleep*
    a. Describe the repair and restoration theory of sleep.

    b. What are some effects of sleep deprivation in humans? In rats?

    c. Describe the evolutionary theory of the need for sleep. What evidence supports it?

    d. How compatible are these two theories?

2. *The functions of REM sleep*
   a. What is the relationship between percentage of time in REM and total sleep time?

   b. What kinds of behavioral changes occur if people are selectively deprived of REM sleep? How does this compare with the effects on nonhuman animals?

   c. Describe the apparent relationship between learning and paradoxical sleep. For what kind of learning does paradoxical sleep seem to be most important? Does NREM also contribute to strengthening of memories?

   d. How may REM contribute to oxygen supply for the cornea?

3. *Biological perspectives on dreaming*
   a. What is the current view of Freud's assumptions concerning dreaming?

b. State the activation-synthesis hypothesis. What evidence supports this hypothesis? How widely accepted is it?

c. Summarize the basic ideas of the clinico-anatomical hypothesis.

d. What three cortical areas are suppressed during dreams? What would be the effects of these suppressions?

e. What two cortical areas are active during dreams? What would they contribute to dreams?

POSTTEST

Multiple-Choice Questions

1. Curt Richter suggested the revolutionary idea that
    a. nearly all behavior is a reaction to a stimulus.
    b. the body generates its own cycles of activity and inactivity.
    c. temperature fluctuations are the best Zeitgeber.
    d. animals wait till the first frost before preparing for winter so that they can enjoy summer longer.

2. Migratory birds
    a. respond only to temperature signals to begin migration.
    b. respond only to the ratio of light to dark, especially in spring.
    c. respond only to the availability of food.
    d. show migratory restlessness every spring and fall, even in captivity with constant light/dark cycles.

3. Circadian rhythms
    a. cannot be demonstrated if lights are always on or always off.
    b. always average within a minute or two of 24 hours in length, regardless of the light cycle.
    c. include cycles of waking and sleeping, eating and drinking, temperature, hormone secretion, and urine production.
    d. are very flexible and can be changed as soon as a different light cycle is established.

4. The human circadian rhythm
    a. can easily adjust to 22- or 28-hour days, but not to 20- or 30-hour days.
    b. has a mean of 24.2 hours, but can adjust to 23- or 25-hour days.
    c. can be most easily reset by using only dim lights in the evening.
    d. cannot be reset at all.

5. Which of the following is true?
    a. It is easier to adjust our biological rhythms to longer cycles and to travel across time zones going west.
    b. It is easier to adjust our biological rhythms to shorter cycles and to travel across time zones going east.
    c. People on irregular shifts tend to sleep the longest when they go to sleep in the morning or early afternoon.
    d. People on night shifts that were exposed to normal levels of room lighting found it easy to adjust their cycles.

6. Which of the following can totally disrupt the biological clock?
    a. food or water deprivation
    b. anesthesia
    c. lack of oxygen
    d. none of the above

7. The suprachiasmatic nucleus (SCN)
    a. is located in the brain stem.
    b. no longer generates a rhythm if it is disconnected from input from the optic nerve.
    c. if transplanted from fetal hamsters that have a mutant gene producing a 20-hour cycle, into normal hamsters, will produce 20-hour cycles in the recipients.
    d. is concerned only with the resetting of the clock, not with generating the rhythm.

8. Two genes in Drosophila known as *period* (*per*) and *timeless* (*tim*)
    a. produce proteins that are present in only small amounts early in the day, but increase throughout the day.
    b. produce proteins that make the fly sleepy, when present in high levels.
    c. are similar to genes found in mice.
    d. all of the above

9. Melatonin
    a. is secreted by the pituitary gland.
    b. is secreted primarily at the time of sleep onset.
    c. is secreted 2-3 hours before the time of sleep onset.
    d. has now been tested extensively and is known to have no side effects.

10. Alpha waves are characteristic of
    a. REM sleep.
    b. alert mental activity.
    c. relaxed wakefulness.
    d. slow-wave sleep.

11. Stages 3 and 4 sleep
    a. are characterized by sleep spindles and K-complexes.
    b. are known together as slow-wave sleep.
    c. are characterized by irregular, jagged, low-voltage waves.
    d. are the stages during which REM occurs.

12. Which of the following is **not** a sign of REM sleep?
    a. tenseness in postural muscles
    b. extreme relaxation of postural muscles
    c. variable heart and breathing rates
    d. irregular, low-voltage, fast EEG activity

13. Paradoxical sleep is paradoxical because brain waves suggest
    a. slow-wave sleep, when one is really dreaming.
    b. dreaming, when one is really in slow-wave sleep.
    c. sleep, when one is really awake.
    d. activation, when one's postural muscles are most relaxed.

14. REM sleep occurs
    a. only early in a night's sleep.
    b. cyclically, about every 90 minutes.
    c. randomly throughout the night.
    d. only after a period of physical exercise.

15. Dreams
    a. are highly correlated with sleep talking.
    b. are of greater duration and frequency during the early part of the night.
    c. may occur in NREM, but are more likely to include vivid visual imagery if they occur during REM.
    d. all of the above

16. A cut through the midbrain
    a. produced prolonged sleep because an area that promotes wakefulness was cut off from the rest of the brain.
    b. left the animal sleeping constantly because most sensory input was cut off from the brain.
    c. left the animal sleeping and waking normally, since structures that control these functions are anterior to the midbrain.
    d. left the animal more wakeful than usual because much of the reticular formation was still connected to the brain, but a sleep-promoting system had been damaged.

17. The pontomesencephalon, part of the reticular formation,
    a. is very discretely organized, with few interconnections.
    b. is important in generating slow-wave sleep.
    c. is primarily concerned with sensory analysis.
    d. none of the above.

18. The locus coeruleus
    a. is very active during REM sleep.
    b. is very active during slow wave sleep.
    c. is very active during meaningful events, and may be important for storing information.
    d. got its name from its dark red color.

19. Neurons in the basal forebrain that promote arousal
    a. use acetylcholine as their transmitter in most cases.
    b. use norepinephrine as their transmitter in most cases.
    c. use prostaglandin as their transmitter in most cases.
    d. are focused only on arousal and are not related to learning and attention or any other processes.

20. Adenosine
    a. is a major neurotransmitter producing arousal.
    b. builds up during wakefulness until it reaches a sufficient level to shut off.
       arousal neurons in the basal forebrain and thereby produce sleepiness.
    c. is the component of coffee that keeps us awake.
    d. is produced by neurons in the cortex during REM sleep.

21. Sleep-inducing nuclei in the basal forebrain
    a. use GABA as their neurotransmitter.
    b. use acetylcholine as their neurotransmitter.
    c. have very restricted projections to specific cortical areas.
    d. work by inhibiting nuclei in the anterior and preoptic hypothalamus.

22. PGO waves
    a. occur during REM sleep.
    b. are recorded in the pons, lateral geniculate, and occipital cortex.
    c. are compensated, if "lost" due to REM deprivation.
    d. all of the above

23. Neurons that are more active during REM are located in
    a. primary visual, motor, and dorsolateral prefrontal cortex.
    b. parts of the parietal and temporal cortex.
    c. neurons in the basal forebrain that release GABA as their neurotransmitter.
    d. the locus coeruleus.

24. Inhibition of motor neurons during REM is induced by neurons in
    a. the dorsolateral prefrontal cortex.
    b. the reticular formation.
    c. the pons.
    d. the amygdala.

25. Which of the following is true?
    a. Acetylcholine promotes the onset of REM sleep.
    b. Acetylcholine promotes slow-wave sleep.
    c. Carbachol inhibits REM sleep.
    d. Serotonin promotes the onset of REM sleep.

26. People with phase-delayed temperature rhythms who try to fall asleep at the normal time may experience
    a. excess sleep.
    b. maintenance insomnia.
    c. termination insomnia.
    d. onset insomnia.

27. Which of the following is a cause of insomnia?
    a. narcolepsy
    b. cataplexy
    c. repeated use of tranquilizers
    d. hypnagogic hallucinations

28. Which of the following is associated primarily with REM sleep?
    a. nightmares
    b. night terrors
    c. sleep talking
    d. all of the above

29. When people are deprived of sleep for a week or more,
    a. they usually suffer severe consequences, including death.
    b. some report dizziness, irritability, and difficulty concentrating, but no drastic consequences.
    c. their immune systems work overtime to compensate for the lack of sleep.
    d. they report no symptoms whatever.

30. The evolutionary theory of sleep
    a. states that species regulate their sleep time according to how much repair and restoration their bodies need.
    b. states that species evolved a mechanism to promote energy conservation at times when they are relatively inefficient.
    c. is incompatible with other theories concerning repair and restoration.
    d. is currently very well established.

31. Comparisons of sleep patterns across individuals and across species indicate that
    a. percentage of time spent in REM remains the same, no matter how long the individual sleeps.
    b. percentage of time in REM decreases as total amount of sleep increases.
    c. percentage of time in REM increases as total amount of sleep increases..
    d. percentage of time spent in REM is extremely variable, and shows no relationship to the total amount of sleep.

32. After about a week of REM deprivation, at least some subjects
    a. reported increased anxiety, irritability and impaired concentration.
    b. experienced increased appetite and weight gain.
    c. spent more sleep time on subsequent nights in REM sleep.
    d. all of the above.

33. The activation-synthesis hypothesis proposes that dreams result from
    a. unconscious wishes struggling for expression.
    b. the ego's attempt to gain control of the id.
    c. the brain's attempt to make sense of its activity.
    d. the brain's attempt to wake up.

34. The clinico-anatomical hypothesis is based on observations that during dreaming
    a. there is increased activity in the inferior parietal cortex, which contributes to spatial perception and integration of body sensations with vision.
    b. there is increased activity in prefrontal cortex, which contributes to the fantasy-like experience of dreams.
    c. there is increased activity in primary visual cortex, which contributes to visual dreams.
    d. there is decreased activity in the visual areas of the temporal lobe, which leaves the rest of the brain to create imagery of its own.

Answers to Multiple-Choice Questions

1. b	7. c	13. d	19. a	25. a	31. c
2. d	8. d	14. b	20. b	26. d	32. d
3. c	9. c	15. c	21. a	27. c	33. c
4. b	10. c	16. a	22. d	28. a	34. a
5. a	11. b	17. d	23. b	29. b	
6. d	12. a	18. c	24. c	30. b	

Doing and Dreaming

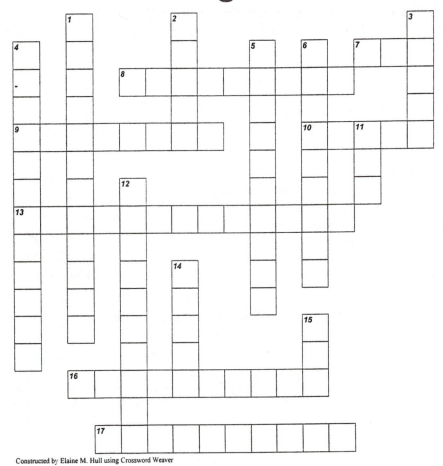

Constructed by Elaine M. Hull using Crossword Weaver

12 _____ gravis: disorder caused by autoimmune destruction of acetylcholine receptors

14 Tendon organ located at both ends of a muscle, responds to muscle contraction

15 The biological clock (abbr.)

ACROSS

7 Slow, fatigue-resistant muscle in fish

8 Stimulus that can reset the biological clock

9 Type of muscle, connected to bones

10 Type of EEG wave with 8-12 hertz rhythm

13 Transmitter at neuromuscular junction and used in tracts that arouse brain

16 Protein, mutation of which causes Huntington's disease

17 Disorder in which person falls asleep during emotional excitement

DOWN

1 Tract from numerous cortical areas to spinal cord with multiple synapses

2 Fast, easily-fatigued muscle in fish

3 Precursor of dopamine

4 Tract from motor cortex to spinal cord with no synapses

5 Part of hindbrain important for ballistic movements and timing

6 Hormone produced by pineal gland and promoting sleep

11 Type of brain wave produced during rapid eye movement sleep (abbr.)

194

10

THE REGULATION OF
INTERNAL BODY STATES

INTRODUCTION

Homeostatic drives are drives that tend to maintain certain biological conditions within a fixed range. Temperature regulation in mammals and birds is such a drive. Constant relatively high temperatures provide conditions in which chemical reactions can be regulated precisely and, by increasing the metabolic rate, increase capacity for prolonged activity. Several physiological mechanisms, including shivering, sweating, panting, and redirection of blood flow, raise and lower temperature appropriately. These are coordinated primarily by the preoptic area, which monitors both its own temperature and that of the skin and spinal cord. Behavioral regulation of temperature is used both by animals that are poikilothermic (body temperature matches that of environment) and by those that are homeothermic (body temperature is regulated within a few degrees of a constant setting). Fever is produced when leukocytes (white blood cells) release interleukin-1, which causes production of prostaglandins E_1 and E_2, which in turn cause the preoptic area to raise body temperature. Moderate fevers are helpful in combating bacterial infections. Body temperature of infant animals may be an important influence on their behaviors, such as the tonic immobility response.

Water balance is critical, both for regulating the concentration of chemicals in our bodily fluids (and therefore the rate of chemical reactions) and for maintaining normal blood pressure. If we have ample supplies of palatable fluids to drink, we may drink a great deal of them and let the kidneys discard the excess. If there is a shortage of fluids to drink, or a large loss of water, the posterior pituitary releases vasopressin (also known as antidiuretic hormone, or ADH), which increases both blood pressure and water retention by the kidneys. There are two major types of stimuli for thirst: decreased water content inside cells and decreased blood volume. When there are increased solutes in the blood, the blood and extracellular fluid become more concentrated. Water tends to flow out of cells into the area of higher osmotic pressure (extracellular fluid). The resulting loss of water from cells in the OVLT (organum vasculosum laminae terminalis) elicits neural responses that are relayed to several hypothalamic nuclei, including the supraoptic and paraventricular nuclei, which produce vasopressin (antidiuretic hormone, ADH), the hormone that is released from the posterior pituitary and that increases blood pressure and urine concentration. The OVLT also relays information to the lateral preoptic area, which gives rise to osmotic thirst. Thus, an increase in osmotic signals results in greater water retention, increased water intake, and higher blood pressure. If large amounts of whole blood are lost, the resulting hypovolemia (low volume of blood) is detected by baroreceptors in the large veins. The kidney also detects the hypovolemia and releases renin, which acts in the blood to produce angiotensin II. This hormone causes constriction of blood vessels to maintain blood pressure. It also stimulates neurons in the subfornical organ, which in turn relay the signal to neurons in the preoptic area, which produce hypovolemic thirst. The signals from the baroreceptors and angiotensin II are synergistic.

Loss of sodium and other solutes results in an immediate and automatic craving for sodium. This sodium hunger depends largely on two hormones, aldosterone and angiotensin II. Aldosterone, secreted by the adrenal glands, causes the kidneys, salivary glands, and sweat glands to conserve sodium; it also stimulates an increase in salt intake. Angiotensin II, as noted above, stimulates sodium hunger. The effects of aldosterone and angiotensin II are strongly synergistic.

195

The factors regulating hunger, satiety, and the selection of specific foods are very complex. Food selection is influenced by the digestive system (including intestinal enzymes), cultural factors, taste, familiarity, and memories of the consequences of consuming a particular food. Hunger and satiety depend on stimuli from the mouth, stomach, and duodenum, as well as blood levels of glucose and other nutrients. Blood glucose levels are maintained at an almost constant level by varying amounts of insulin, which enables glucose to enter cells, and glucagon, which converts stored glycogen into glucose. Damage to the lateral hypothalamus results in self-starvation, unless the animal is force-fed. The intact lateral hypothalamus contributes to feeding by modifying activity in the nucleus of the tractus solitarius (NTS), which may influence taste sensations and salivation, and also by facilitating ingestion and swallowing. It also sends axons to other brain structures that facilitate ingestion and swallowing, initiate and reinforce learned behaviors, and increase autonomic responses such as release of digestive juices. Damage to the ventromedial hypothalamus results in obesity. This results from faster emptying of the stomach and increased release of insulin, which promotes fat storage and inhibits its release for use as fuel. As a result, the animal consumes more frequent meals. Damage to the paraventricular nucleus (PVN) also results in overeating. However, rats with PVN damage eat larger meals, rather than more frequent meals.

Several chemicals have been found to influence eating and satiety. Leptin is a peptide produced by fat cells that increases energy expenditure and decreases feeding. However, leptin is not an effective treatment of obese people; apparently they produce leptin, but are insensitive to its effects. One means by which leptin decreases feeding is by inhibiting the release of neuropeptide Y (NPY), which normally increases feeding by inhibiting the PVN. Thus, the effect of NPY is similar to lesions of the PVN (failure to end meals appropriately), and leptin inhibits that effect. Several chemicals, including CCK and glucagon (similar to GLP-1 in the brain), have central and peripheral effects that are complementary. Another neurotransmitter that inhibits feeding is serotonin; drugs that stimulate serotonin $5-HT_{1B}$ or $5-HT_{2C}$ receptors may be useful for weight control. The effects of many of these chemicals are similar across species. Furthermore, the multiple messengers and pathways that control food intake and digestion provide an effective system of checks and balances.

Genes control body weight in many ways, including metabolic rate. Other genetic influences include the production of and sensitivity to peptides and other neuromodulators that regulate eating. However, social and other environmental influences, as well as exercise and eating habits, are important determinants of body weight.

Anorexia nervosa is a disorder in which people eat much less than they need, sometimes starving themselves to death. They are usually perfectionistic, most frequently women, and often are depressed; however, antidepressant drugs are seldom effective in treating anorexia. People with bulimia nervosa alternate between overeating and dieting, frequently eating a huge meal and then purging. People with bulimia have higher than normal levels of peptide YY (a neuromodulator similar to NPY), low levels of CCK, and/or decreased production of, or sensitivity to, serotonin. Drugs that increase serotonin may be effective in treating bulimia. However, it is not clear whether transmitter abnormalities precede or result from the bulimia.

KEY TERMS AND CONCEPTS

Module 10.1 Temperature Regulation
1. Homeostasis
    Set range
    Set point

2. Surviving in extreme cold
    Problem: formation of ice crystals → tear blood vessels and cell membranes

Some insects and fish: glycerol and other antifreeze chemicals in blood
Wood frogs: do freeze
    Withdraw most fluid from organs and blood vessels, store it in extracellular space
    Chemicals that regulate ice crystal formation
    Increased blood-clotting

3. Controlling body temperature
Poikilothermic: body temperature same as environment
Homeothermic: body temperature almost constant
The advantages of constant body temperature
    Easier to heat than to cool body
    $37°$ C close to warmest environmental temperature
    Warmer muscles work better
    Optimal temperatures for enzymes
    Reproductive cells: cooler environment
Brain mechanisms
    Hypothalamus
    Preoptic area
        Monitors own temperature
        Monitors temperature of skin and spinal cord
    Other parts of brain and spinal cord
Behavioral mechanisms
Fever
    Leukocytes
        Interleukin-1
    Prostaglandins E_1 and E_2
    Preoptic area
    Moderate fevers helpful
        Physiological and behavioral means
The development of animal behavior
    Improved behavioral capacities in warm environment
The tonic immobility response
    Terminated by increased temperature

4. In closing: Temperature and behavior
    Redundant mechanisms

Module 10.2 Thirst
1. Mechanisms of water regulation
Increasing intake
Decreasing output
Vasopressin or antidiuretic hormone (ADH)

2. Osmotic thirst
Osmotic pressure
    Semipermeable membrane
    Increase in solute concentration outside cell
        Water leaves cells
Brain areas
    OVLT (organum vasculosum laminae terminalis): detects osmotic pressure

Supraoptic nucleus: vasopressin release from posterior pituitary
Paraventricular nucleus: vasopressin release from posterior pituitary
Lateral preoptic area: drinking
Cell bodies and axons passing through

3. Hypovolemic thirst
Loss of blood volume
Satisfied best by salt water
Mechanisms
Baroreceptors
Hormones from kidneys
Renin
Angiotensinogen in blood
Angiotensin II
Subfornical organ → preoptic area → thirst
Synergistic effects of angiotensin and baroreceptors
Sodium-specific cravings
Automatic preference (not learned)
Aldosterone
Increased sodium retention by kidney, salivary glands, and sweat glands
Increased sodium hunger
Angiotensin II
Synergistic effects

4. In closing: The psychology and biology of thirst
Both skeletal (behavioral) and autonomic controls

Module 10.3 Hunger
1. How the digestive system influences food selection
Mouth
Saliva: carbohydrate digestion
Stomach
Hydrochloric acid
Enzymes for protein digestion
Small intestine
Protein, fat, and carbohydrate digestion
Absorption
Large intestine
Water and mineral absorption
Lubrication
Enzymes and consumption of dairy products
Lactose, milk sugar
Lactase enzyme
Other influences on food selection
Carnivore, herbivore, omnivore
Culture, taste, familiarity, learning
Conditioned taste aversions

2. How taste and digestion control hunger and satiety
Oral factors

198

    Desire to taste or chew
    Sham feeding
The stomach and intestines
    Vagus nerve (cranial nerve X)
        Information about stretching of stomach
    Splanchnic nerves
        Information about nutrient contents
    The duodenum
        Taste neurons in pons: food in duodenum decreases responsiveness to sweet taste
        Sugars → satiety faster than fats
        The hormone CCK (cholecystokinin)
            Inhibits stomach emptying
        CCK also released in brain
Glucose, insulin, and glucagon
    Insulin: facilitates glucose entry into cells
        In brain: satiety hormone
        Migratory and hibernating species: store fat and glycogen
        Diabetes: High blood glucose; little reaches cells, most is excreted
    Glucagon: liver converts stored glycogen to glucose

3. The hypothalamus and feeding regulation
    The lateral hypothalamus
        Lesions: starvation or weight loss
        Electrical stimulation: eating
        Neurons vs. dopamine axons passing through
            Damage to dopamine axons with 6-OHDA: loss of arousal
            Damage to cell bodies or lesions in very young rats: loss of feeding
        Mechanisms
            NTS (nucleus of the tractus solitarius in medulla): taste, salivation
            Forebrain structures: facilitate ingestion
            Dopamine-containing cells: initiation and reinforcement of learned behaviors
            Stimulation of autonomic responses, including digestive secretions
    Medial areas of the hypothalamus
        Ventromedial hypothalamus
            Lesions: weight gain to a new high set point
            Ventromedial hypothalamic syndrome
                Includes damage to nearby cells and axons
            Ventral noradrenergic bundle
            Effects of ventromedial hypothalamic lesions
                Finicky eaters
                More normal-sized meals per day
                Increased stomach motility and secretions
                Faster stomach emptying
                Increased insulin and fat storage
        Paraventricular nucleus
            Critical for ending meals
    Methods 10.1: Using multiple methods
        Lateral hypothalamus
            Lesions → decreased eating
            Stimulation → increased eating

199

Recording: increased activity during eating
Convergence of methods

4. Satiety chemicals and eating disorders
   Leptin
      Produced by fat cells
      Decreases hunger, increases energy expenditure and immune function
      Genetically obese mice: fail to produce leptin
         Administer leptin → more active, eat less, lose weight
      Obese people: more leptin than lean people; may be insensitive to it
   Neuropeptide Y (NPY)
      Inhibits paraventricular nucleus (PVN), which would otherwise end the meal
      Inhibited by leptin
   Other neuromodulators and hormones
      Methods 10.2: Microdialysis
         Double fluid-filled tube with thin membrane tip
         Fluid delivered through one tube, collected from other tube
            Chemicals diffuse across membrane into fluid
            Measure neurotransmitters released during behavior
      Similarity of function across species
         CCK → satiety in humans and snails
      Similarity of function in brain and periphery
         Glucagon and GLP-1 decrease feeding
         CCK in intestines and brain inhibits feeding
      Numerous chemicals affect feeding
         Serotonin 5-HT$_{2C}$ receptor mutants: normal weight until middle age, then obese
         Appetite suppressants: stimulate 5-HT$_{1B}$ or 5-HT$_{2C}$ receptors
         Complex interactions
   Genetics, metabolic rate, and body weight
      Human obesity: numerous genes
         Heat production vs. fat storage
         Genes and environment: Pima Indians
   Weight loss techniques
      Increase exercise
      Restrain eating
         Appetite suppressant drugs
            "Fen-phen"
               Fenfluramine: increase serotonin release and decrease reuptake
               Phentermine: blocks norepinephrine reuptake
               Medical complications
            Sibutramine (Meridia)
               Blocks reuptake of serotonin and norepinephrine
      Experimental drugs: block fat absorption
   Anorexia and bulimia
      Anorexia nervosa
         Hardworking perfectionists (obsessive-compulsive)
         Depression
         Elevated cortisol
         Antidepressant drugs: seldom effective
         Culture

200

Bulimia nervosa
    Eat enormous meal, then purge
    High levels of peptide YY (PYY)
    Low levels of CCK
    Decreased serotonin levels or receptor sensitivity
    Tryptophan deficient diet → mild depression and possible uncontrolled eating

5. In closing: The multiple controls of hunger
    Checks and balances

SHORT-ANSWER QUESTIONS

Module 10.1 Temperature Regulation

1. *Homeostasis*
   a. What is a homeostatic process?

   b. What are some physiological processes that are controlled near a set point? What are some homeostatic processes that anticipate future needs or that change under various conditions?

   c. Why does the scrotum of most male mammals hang outside the body? Why should pregnant women avoid hot baths?

2. *Controlling body temperature*
   a. Define the terms poikilothermic and homeothermic.

b. What is a major advantage of a constant body temperature? What is the cost to the animal for maintaining homeothermy?

c. What two kinds of stimuli does the preoptic area monitor for temperature control?

d. What prevents the temperature of fish, amphibians, and reptiles from fluctuating wildly?

e. What are prostaglandins E_1 and E_2, and what are their roles in producing a fever?

f. Of what benefit is a fever?

3. *Temperature regulation and behavior*
   a. What was the key to eliciting behaviors such as odor conditioning and certain controls of eating and drinking in baby rats?

b. Describe the tonic immobility response of baby birds. What is a major stimulus governing the duration of immobility?

Module 10.2 Thirst

1. *Mechanisms of water regulation*
    a. Describe the different mechanisms of maintaining water balance that have been developed by desert animals and by animals with an abundant water supply.

    b. What are the two functions of vasopressin when body fluids are low? What is its other name?

2. *Osmotic thirst*
    a. What is osmotic pressure?

    b. How does the body "know" when its osmotic pressure is low?

c. What are the roles of the OVLT, the supraoptic and paraventricular nuclei of the hypothalamus, and the lateral preoptic area?

3. *Hypovolemic thirst*
    a. Why is hypovolemia dangerous?

    b. Under what circumstances does hypovolemic thirst occur?

    c. Will an animal with hypovolemic thirst drink more pure water or more salt water with the same concentration as blood? Why?

    d. What is the role of baroreceptors in hypovolemic thirst?

    e. What steps lead to the production of antiotensin II? What are its two main effects?

f.   Which brain structures seem to mediate hypovolemic thirst?

g.   How may the effects of angiotensin II be enhanced?

h.   What two effects of aldosterone are beneficial in cases of sodium deficiency? What other hormone contributes to salt hunger?

Module 10.3 Hunger
1.   *How the digestive system influences food selection*
    a.   Enzymes for the digestion of what type of nutrient(s) are present in saliva? In the stomach? In the small intestine?

    b.   From which structure is digested food absorbed?

    c.   Why do newborn mammals stop nursing as they grow older?

d. Discuss the evidence that humans are a partial exception to the principle of lactose intolerance in adults.

e. List the factors that may influence food selection.

2. *How taste and digestion control hunger*
    a. Summarize the evidence for the importance of oral factors in hunger and satiety. What is the evidence that these factors are not sufficient to end a meal normally?

    b. How did Deutsch et al. show the importance of stomach distension in regulating meal size?

    c. Which two nerves convey the stomach's satiety signals?

    d. What is CCK? In what two places is it produced? What is one likely mechanism by which it induces satiety?

e.   What evidence suggests blood glucose is, or is not, important in the regulation of appetite?

f.   What is the effect of insulin on blood glucose? In what ways does insulin affect hunger? Compare the effects of glucagon with those of insulin.

g.   Why do people with untreated diabetes eat a lot but gain little weight? How is this similar to, and how is it different from, the effects of high levels of insulin?

3. *The hypothalamus and feeding regulation*
   a.   Describe the evidence that the lateral hypothalamus is important for hunger.

   b.   What is 6-hydroxydopamine? What kind of neuronal damage does it inflict when injected into the lateral hypothalamus? What are the behavioral results of such damage?

   c.   What is the result of damage to lateral hypothalamic cell bodies?

d.   By what four mechanisms may the lateral hypothalamus contribute to feeding?

e.   Describe the various behavioral changes produced by lesions of the ventromedial hypothalamus, ventral noradrenergic bundle, and surrounding areas. Can we say that animals with such lesions show an overall increase in hunger or a lack of satiety?

f.   To what factors can we attribute the obesity induced by ventromedial hypothalamus lesions?

g.   What are the effects of damage to the paraventricular nucleus (PVN)? How are these effects different from those of ventromedial hypothalamus damage?

4.   *Satiety chemicals and eating disorders*
    a.   What type of cells produce leptin? What message does leptin convey? Is there any evidence that overweight humans produce too little leptin?

b. What brain area is inhibited by neuropeptide Y (NPY)? What are the effects of NPY on feeding? What chemical inhibits the release of NPY?

c. What is microdialysis?

d. What are two means by which CCK inhibits feeding? What are the effects of glucagon and GLP-1?

e. What are two lines of evidence that serotonin influences feeding? What two types of serotonin receptors have been implicated?

f. Discuss the role of basal metabolic rate in weight regulation.

g.   Give one example a group of people who demonstrate the relationship of genetic and environmental factors in the control of weight. How important are exercise and restraint of eating?

h.   What are some appetite-suppressant drugs? What are their effects on neurotransmitters?

i.   Compare the symptoms of anorexia nervosa with those of bulimia nervosa.

j.   Describe the personality characteristics of many people with anorexia and their relatives.

k.   What chemical differences are seen in bulimics, compared to other people. Can we determine cause and effect relationships between these chemicals and the disorder?

l.   What was the result of the study that gave a tryptophan-deficient diet to recovering bulimics? What do these results suggest about a possible factor contributing to bulimia?

POSTTEST

Multiple-Choice Questions

1. Temperature regulation
   a. is an example of a homeostatic mechanism.
   b. is important in mammals and birds for increasing resting metabolic rate and, thereby, capacity for prolonged activity.
   c. maintains body temperature at levels that maximize the enzymatic properties of proteins.
   d. all of the above

2. The preoptic area monitors
   a. only its own temperature.
   b. only skin and spinal cord temperature.
   c. both its own and skin and spinal cord temperature.
   d. the temperature of internal organs via nerve input from those organs.

3. Behavioral means of temperature regulation
   a. are the only means of temperature regulation in poikilotherms.
   b. are the only means of temperature regulation in homeotherms.
   c. do not become functional until adulthood.
   d. are effective only for controlling temperature within the normal range, not to induce a fever.

4. Fever
   a. is harmful and should always be reduced with aspirin.
   b. is produced primarily by prostaglandins E_1 and E_2 acting on cells in the preoptic area.
   c. is produced directly by bacteria acting on the preoptic area.
   d. is especially high in baby rabbits, in response to infections.

5. Which of the following is true?
   a. Infant rats, in the first week of life, can exhibit odor conditioning and certain controls of eating and drinking, but only if tested at normal room temperature (20°-23°C).
   b. Infant rats, in the first week of life, can exhibit odor conditioning and certain controls of eating and drinking, but only if tested at room temperatures above 30°C.
   c. Chicks, when grabbed by a predator, will feign death for many hours, because the predator's warmth keeps the chick warm enough so that it does not have to move around.
   d. Chicks, when grabbed by a predator, will feign death because they know that this decreases the probability of being attacked.

6. Vasopressin
   a. raises blood pressure by constricting blood vessels.
   b. is also known as antidiuretic hormone, because it promotes water retention by the kidney.
   c. is secreted from the posterior pituitary, as a result of control by the supraoptic and paraventricular nuclei of the hypothalamus.
   d. all of the above.

211

7. The main reason that a salty meal makes us thirsty is that
   a. excess salt in extracellular fluid produces cellular dehydration; such dehydration of cells in the OVLT results in osmotic thirst.
   b. increased salt in extracellular fluid causes the fluid to enter OVLT cells, thus distending them and producing osmotic thirst.
   c. increased salt in blood causes liquid to enter cells, thus producing hypovolemia.
   d. the salt enters cells in the OVLT and stimulates them directly.

8. The lateral preoptic area
   a. controls hypovolemic, but not osmotic, thirst.
   b. is the site of receptors for osmotic thirst.
   c. receives input from the OVLT and controls drinking.
   d. primarily responds to signals concerning dryness of the throat.

9. After its blood volume has been reduced, an animal
   a. will drink more pure water than salt water of the same concentration as blood.
   b. will drink more salt water of the same concentration as blood than pure water.
   c. will not drink any more than usual, since both liquid and solute have been removed.
   d. will drink only highly concentrated salt water.

10. Angiotensin II
    a. is secreted by the kidney.
    b. causes water to leave cells in the preoptic area and thereby stimulates osmotic thirst.
    c. stimulates the subfornical organ, which relays the information to the preoptic area, which in turn can induce drinking.
    d. all of the above

11. Which of the following is not likely to induce drinking?
    a. application of angiotensin II to the OVLT
    b. application of angiotensin II to the subfornical organ
    c. low blood pressure signals from baroreceptors in the large veins
    d. a salty meal

12. Salt craving
    a. occurs automatically, without learning, when sodium is low.
    b. depends largely on aldosterone secreted by the adrenal glands.
    c. is enhanced by angiotensin II.
    d. all of the above

13. In the stomach
    a. food is mixed with hydrochloric acid and enzymes for the digestion of protein.
    b. food is mixed with hydrochloric acid and enzymes for the digestion of carbohydrates.
    c. food is mixed with enzymes that aid the digestion of fats.
    d. absorption of food through the walls of the stomach occurs.

14. Lactase
    a. is the sugar in milk.
    b. is an intestinal enzyme for the digestion of milk.
    c. is abundant in almost all adult humans, but is lacking in adults of other mammalian species.
    d. is abundant in birds and reptiles, but is lacking in mammals.

15. Oral factors
    a. contribute to satiety but are not sufficient to determine the amount of food consumed.
    b. are irrelevant to satiety.
    c. are the single most important factor in inducing satiety.
    d. include only the taste of food.

16. If a cuff closes the outlet from the stomach to the small intestine
    a. the animal will not eat because of the trauma of the cuff.
    b. the animal will continue eating indefinitely, since food must pass beyond the stomach to trigger satiety.
    c. the animal will eat a normal-sized meal and stop.
    d. the animal will eat a normal meal, wait for it to be absorbed through the walls of the stomach, and then eat again.

17. Splanchnic nerves
    a. carry information about the nutrient contents of the stomach.
    b. carry information about the stretching of the stomach walls.
    c. are stimulated directly by cholecystokinin (CCK).
    d. secrete CCK into the circulatory system.

18. CCK
    a. is produced by the duodenum in response to the presence of food there.
    b. works, in part, by closing the sphincter muscle between the stomach and duodenum, thus allowing the stomach to fill faster.
    c. is also produced in the brain, where it tends to decrease eating.
    d. all of the above

19. Which of the following is true?
    a. Glucose levels in the blood are the primary signal for hunger.
    b. Insulin reaches the brain and acts as a satiety hormone.
    c. Obese people produce less insulin than do people of normal weight.
    d. Glucose levels in the blood are elevated by insulin.

20. Insulin
    a. is secreted in response to low blood sugar.
    b. is released by the liver.
    c. is no longer secreted after VMH lesions.
    d. promotes entry of glucose into cells.

21. People with untreated diabetes eat more food because
    a. the vagus and splanchnic nerves are damaged.
    b. they store too much of their glucose, so it is unavailable for use.
    c. they excrete most of their glucose unused.
    d. their basal metabolic rate is too high.

22. Glucagon
    a. is high in the late autumn in migratory and hibernating species.
    b. is produced by the small intestine.
    c. stimulates the liver to convert stored glycogen to glucose for release into the blood.
    d. stimulates the liver to convert glucose to glycogen for storage.

213

23. Which of the following is true of lateral hypothalamic damage?
    a. It results in inactivity and decreased responsiveness to stimuli.
    b. At least some of the results are due to damage to axons passing through the area, rather than to cell bodies located there.
    c. At least some of the effects on eating are due to low levels of insulin and digestive juices.
    d. All of the above are true.

24. Obesity resulting from damage to the ventromedial hypothalamus and ventral noradrenergic bundle
    a. can be prevented by allowing the animals to eat only the same amount that they ate before the lesion.
    b. occurs because the stomach empties faster than normal and because insulin secretion is increased.
    c. results from a dramatic increase in the palatability of all foods, resulting in overeating even of bitter or untasty food.
    d. results from eating much larger meals than usual, because of lack of satiety.

25. Which of the following is true of the paraventricular nucleus (PVN)?
    a. It is important for ending a meal.
    b. It is important for beginning a meal.
    c. NPY excites neurons in the PVN.
    d. Leptin increases eating by increasing NPY release in the PVN.

26. Basal metabolic rate
    a. is increased when people diet, in order to generate more heat.
    b. is decreased when people diet, in order to conserve energy.
    c. is influenced almost exclusively by what we eat; genetic influence is minimal.
    d. is virtually identical in all people.

27. Leptin
    a. increases eating.
    b. is a neurotransmitter produced by the brain.
    c. is produced by fat cells.
    d. is reduced in quantity in overweight people.

28. Neuropeptide Y (NPY)
    a. is produced by fat cells and decreases feeding.
    b. directly increases metabolic rate.
    c. decreases fat storage by decreasing the production of leptin.
    d. inhibits activity in the PVN, similarly to a lesion, thereby increasing meal size.

29. Microdialysis
    a. is a means of detecting the release of neurotransmitters.
    b. is a technique used primarily for damaging cell bodies while leaving axons intact.
    c. is a technique used primarily for damaging axons while leaving cell bodies intact.
    d. has been used to demonstrate that serotonin is an important hunger signal.

30. Which of the following is true?
    a. A tryptophan-deficient diet given to recovering bulimics provoked mild depression and a sense that they could lose control over their eating.
    b. Bulimics have higher than normal levels of peptide YY (PYY).
    c. Bulimics have lower than normal levels of CCK and serotonin (or decreased sensitivity to serotonin).
    d. All of the above are true.

Answers to Multiple-Choice Questions

1. d	7. a	13. a	19. b	25. a
2. c	8. c	14. b	20. d	26. b
3. a	9. b	15. a	21. c	27. c
4. b	10. c	16. c	22. c	28. d
5. b	11. a	17. a	23. d	29. a
6. d	12. d	18. d	24. b	30. d

Diagram

1. Label the following structures: corpus callosum, cerebral cortex, lateral ventricles, third ventricle, basal ganglia, lateral hypothalamus, ventromedial hypothalamus, paraventricular hypothalamus.

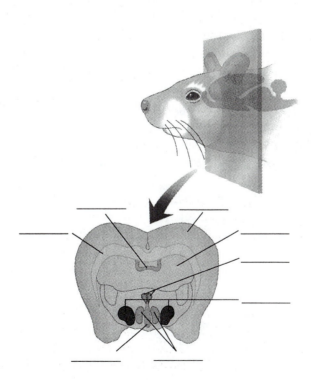

11

REPRODUCTIVE BEHAVIORS

INTRODUCTION

Sex hormones have two distinct kinds of effects, depending on the stage of development at which they are present. The absence of androgens during an early critical period results in female-typical appearance and behavior, and androgens administered to a genetic female masculinize her genitals and behavior. The SRY (sex region Y) gene on the Y chromosome causes the primitive gonads to develop as testes and to secrete testosterone, which increases growth of the testes and Wolffian ducts (seminal vesicles and vas deferens). The testes also secrete Mullerian inhibiting hormone, which causes the female reproductive tract to regress. In the absence of the SRY gene, mammals develop as females. Their gonads differentiate into ovaries, their Mullerian ducts differentiate into oviducts, uterus, and upper vagina, and their Wolffian ducts regress. In rodents androgen exerts its masculinizing effects on behavior mostly by being converted, intracellularly, to estrogen. A female is not masculinized by her own estrogen because it is bound to alpha-fetoprotein, which prevents it from entering cells. Hormones may also have organizing effects on the hypothalamus, on nerves and muscles that control the penis, and on nonsexual characteristics, such as body size, life expectancy, play patterns, and aggressiveness.

When sex hormones are administered during adulthood, they tend to activate whatever behavior patterns were organized during development. Estrogens enhance sensory responsiveness of the pubic area of female rats. The ventromedial nucleus and the medial preoptic area (MPOA) of the hypothalamus are important brain areas for the activational effects of hormones. Stimulation of the MPOA enhances female-typical behavior in female rats and male-typical behavior in males. Dopamine in the MPOA facilitates masculine sexual behavior. Dopamine is released in the MPOA of male rats before and during copulation; dopamine is not released in males that fail to copulate. Castrated males produce dopamine in the MPOA but fail to release it. Moderate levels of dopamine stimulate D_1 or D_5 receptors, which promote erection in males and receptivity in females; higher levels stimulate D_2 receptors and promote orgasm and ejaculation. Testosterone also increases men's sexual interest, and oxytocin may enhance sexual pleasure, especially at orgasm. Although decreases in testosterone generally decrease sexual activity, low testosterone is not always the source of impotence. Treatments that reduce testosterone production or block its receptors have been used to treat sex offenders.

In women and certain other female primates, menstrual cycles result from interaction between the hypothalamus, pituitary, and ovaries. Follicle-stimulating hormone (FSH) from the anterior pituitary stimulates the growth of ovarian follicles and the secretion of estrogen from the follicles. Increasing estrogen at first decreases the release of FSH, but near the middle of the cycle, it somehow causes a sudden surge of luteinizing hormone (LH) and FSH. These hormones cause an ovum to be released and cause the uterine lining to proliferate. They also cause the remnant of the follicle (the corpus luteum) to release progesterone, which further prepares the uterus for implantation of a fertilized ovum. Progesterone inhibits release of LH; therefore, near the end of the cycle, all hormones are low, resulting in menstruation if fertilization does not occur. If the ovum is fertilized, estradiol and progesterone increase throughout the pregnancy. Combination birth-control pills contain estrogen, which suppresses the release of FSH early in the cycle, and progesterone, which inhibits the secretion of LH. Women's sexual interest is somewhat higher during the periovulatory period, but hormones are less important for women's sexual response than for females

216

of other species. Sex hormones also affect women's preference for somewhat masculinized, as opposed to feminized, men's faces.

Hormones also have activational effects on nonsexual behaviors. Testosterone enhances aggression in many species. Estrogen increases the number of dendritic spines in the hippocampus, which may be related to memory. It also increases the numbers of certain dopamine and serotonin receptors in the nucleus accumbens and several cortical areas; these areas are thought to control reinforcement and emotion. Times of decreasing estrogen, such as before menstruation, after childbirth, and after menopause, may be associated with depression and irritability in some women. Premenstrual syndrome (PMS) may also be related to increased cortisol, decreased vasopressin, or decreased activity of several neurotransmitters. Finally, PMS may be related to decreased metabolism of progesterone to allopregnanolone, which has antianxiety effects. Estrogen also enhances verbal memory and manual dexterity, but decreases performance on spatial tasks. Testosterone given to older men improved their spatial skills. However, hormonal effects on cognitive abilities are small, and their functional significance is not understood.

Puberty is influenced by body weight. The hypothalamus begins to release bursts of luteinizing hormone releasing hormone (LHRH), which stimulates the pituitary to secrete LH and FSH, which in turn stimulate the gonads to release estradiol or testosterone.

Parental behavior in rodents can be rapidly induced by hormonal patterns characteristic of the time of delivery. This suggests that the immediate maternal behavior that occurs with delivery may be under hormonal control. Oxytocin and prolactin appear to be especially important. Hormones increase activity in the medial preoptic area, which is important for parental behavior, as well as for temperature regulation, thirst, and sexual behavior. Repeated exposure to pups can induce parental behavior after about six days, even in females without ovaries. However, brain areas that respond to pheromones from the young animals initially suppress parental behavior; their activity is inhibited in the later phase, thereby allowing parental behavior to occur. Males of some mammalian species also contribute to the care of the young and may undergo hormonal changes that promote parental behavior. However, hormonal changes are not necessary for parental behavior in humans, except to permit a woman to nurse a baby.

Early fetal gonadal structures differentiate in either a male or a female direction, depending on the presence or absence of the SRY gene. Some XY males have a mutation of the SRY gene, resulting in poorly developed genitals. Some XX females have an SRY gene translocated from their father's Y chromosome to an autosomal chromosome, which may result in some ovary and some testis tissue. If a female is exposed to excess androgen during the critical period for sex differentiation, she may develop structures intermediate between those of a normal female and a normal male. A similar condition may occur if a genetic male has low levels of testosterone or is unresponsive to it. Such individuals are called intersexes or pseudohermaphrodites. Most intersexes have been reared as females, since it is easier to feminize the genitals surgically than to masculinize them. However, the surgery frequently impairs genital sensation. A genetic male may develop a relatively normal female appearance and gender identity because of testicular feminization (androgen insensitivity), due to a lack of androgen receptors. In the Dominican Republic some genetic males lack an enzyme that converts testosterone to dihydrotestosterone. Because dihydrotestosterone is more effective than testosterone for masculinizing the genitals, these boys appeared to be girls early in life; however, they became masculinized by high levels of testosterone at puberty. They then developed male gender identity, which was consistent with their prenatal testosterone. It was not possible for a genetic male, whose penis was accidentally removed at birth, to develop a female identity, despite attempts by his parents to raise him as a girl. These cases suggest that prenatal hormones play an important role in determining gender identity, although environmental factors may have some influence.

Genetic factors may promote homosexual orientation in both men and women. Monozygotic (identical) twins of homosexuals are more likely to be homosexual than are dizygotic (fraternal) twins or other biological or adopted siblings. One study suggested that a gene that contributes to male homosexuality is on the X chromosome, and therefore is inherited from the mother; however, later studies did not replicate these results. A gene that increases homosexuality, and therefore decreases reproductive success, would be expected to be selected against in the course of evolution. However, it may be perpetuated through kin selection or by increasing the reproductive ability of the women who carry the gene. Homosexuality is not well correlated with hormone levels in adulthood. However, there is some evidence that low levels of prenatal testosterone, sometimes caused by stress, may predispose males to homosexuality in adulthood. In rats, similar stress effects appeared to be mediated by endorphins and were influenced by social experiences after birth. Some women whose mothers took diethylstilbestrol (DES) to prevent miscarriage may have increased bisexual or homosexual responsiveness. Some brain structures show sex differences in size. For some of these structures, including the anterior commissure, the suprachiasmatic nucleus, and the interstitial nucleus 3 of the hypothalamus, homosexual men have structures more similar in size to those of women than to those of heterosexual men. We do not know whether these differences are a cause or an effect of homosexuality, or indeed, if they are relevant at all.

KEY TERMS AND CONCEPTS

Module 11.1 The Effects of Sex Hormones
1. Organizing effects of sex hormones
    Organizing effects
        Permanent change
        Sensitive stage of development
    Activating effects
        Temporary activation of a response
        May last longer than hormone remains in organ, but not indefinitely
    Sex differences in the gonads and hypothalamus
        Chromosomes
            Female: XX
            Male: XY
        Gonads: identical in very early stage
        Male (XY)
            SRY gene (sex region Y) → testes → testosterone →
            Wolffian ducts → seminal vesicles and vas deferens
            MIH (Mullerian inhibiting hormone) → degeneration of Mullerian ducts
            Penis, scrotum
        Female (XX)
            Ovaries (egg-producing organs)
            Mullerian ducts mature → oviducts, uterus, upper vagina
            Wolffian ducts degenerate
    Hypothalamus
        Medial preoptic hypothalamus
            Sexually dimorphic nucleus: larger in males
        Cyclic pattern of hormone release in females
    Sensitive period for testosterone's effects
        Humans: third and fourth months of pregnancy
        Rats: last few days of pregnancy and first few postnatal days
        Masculinization of female rats by testosterone injections
        Little or no sex hormones: female development

218

Aromatization of testosterone to estradiol
  Alpha-fetoprotein: protects some female mammals from estradiol
  Primates: protected by metabolism of estradiol
  Estradiol injection → masculinizes female
    Exceeds normal binding by alpha-fetoprotein or metabolism
Survival of muscles and nerves of penis
Sexual differentiation in the spotten hyena
  Females larger and more aggressive than males
- Clitoris similar to penis
  Sexual intercourse and delivery of babies through canal in clitoris
    High mortality of babies
  Dominant females and young: first access to food
  High levels of androstenedione during pregnancy
    Most converted to testosterone, little converted to estrogen
Sex differences in nonreproductive characteristics
  Males > females
    Body size
    Aggressiveness
    Rough and tumble play
  Females > males
    Life expectancy
    Infant care
  Excessive adrenal androgens in girls: male-typical toys and activities
  Women > men
    Increased density of neurons in language area of temporal lobe
    Larger corpus callosum relative to total brain size

2. Activating effects of sex hormones
Sexual behavior in rodents
  Dependent on hormones
  Testosterone and its metabolites, dihydrotestosterone and estradiol → masculine behavior
  Estrogen followed by progesterone → feminine behavior
    Pudendal nerve: tactile stimulation from pubic area to brain
    Ventromedial nucleus
    Medial preoptic area
      Sexually dimorphic nucleus
      Stimulation → male-typical behavior in males, female-typical behavior in females
      Increase in activity during copulation
      Dopamine
        Released in male MPOA in presence of female
        Facilitates copulation
        Castration: impairs release of MPOA dopamine
      Female: activity primed by estradiol and oxytocin
      Moderate dopamine levels: D_1 and D_5 receptors
        Erection in male
        Receptivity in female
      Higher dopamine levels: D_2 receptors
        Ejaculation and orgasm

Behavior influences hormonal secretions
  Ring-necked doves
    Synchronized series of behaviors
    Each behavior → hormones that prepare for next stage of behavior
Sexual behavior in humans
  Effects on men
    Correlation of testosterone levels and sexual excitement
    Oxytocin release during orgasm
    Impotence not always due to low testosterone
    Sex offenders
      Cyproterone: blocks testosterone receptors
      Medroxyprogesterone: decreases production of gonadotropin and testosterone
      Triptorelin: blocks gonadotropin and decreases testosterone
  Effects on women
    Menstrual cycle
    FSH (follicle stimulating hormone)
      Promotes growth of follicle, which nurtures ovum
      Increases secretion of estradiol by follicle
    Estradiol
      Decreases FSH, then causes surges of LH (luteinizing hormone) and FSH
    LH and FSH
      Release ovum
      Increase secretion of progesterone by corpus luteum (remnant of follicle)
    Progesterone
      Prepares lining of uterus
      Inhibits LH release
    Menstruation: due to decreased hormone levels
    If pregnancy: estrogen and progesterone increase
    Birth-control pills
      Combination pill: suppresses FSH and LH release, prevents ovum from implanting
    Periovulatory period
      Maximum fertility and sexual interest
      Preferred less feminized faces than during luteal phase or menstruation
Nonsexual behavior
  Testosterone: increases aggression
  Estrogen
    Increases growth of dendritic spines in hippocampus
    Increases D_2 and $5HT_{2A}$ receptors in nucleus accumbens and cortex
      Increases sexual motivation, reinforcement, mood
  Premenstrual syndrome
    Decreased estrogen
    Increased cortisol
    Decreased neurotransmitter activity
    Decreased metabolism of progesterone to allopregnanolone, an antianxiety hormone
  Estrogen
    Improves verbal memory and manual dexterity
    Impairs spatial performance
    Menopause: estrogen replacement → better performance on memory tasks
    Transsexuals: estrogen treatment → better performance on verbal memory tasks

Testosterone: improved spatial performance in older men
Meadow voles: males roam more than females; better spatial performance
Pine voles: males and females similar in roaming and spatial performance

3. Puberty
Menarche
Influence of body weight
Luteinizing hormone releasing hormone → FSH and LH →
Estrogen in girls, testosterone in boys →
Growth spurt
Secondary sexual characteristics

4. Parental behavior
Species differences
Monkeys: increased interest in babies as pregnancy progresses
Rats: less responsive late in pregnancy; after birth: very responsive
Hormone-dependent early phase
Oxytocin
Prolactin
Medial preoptic area
Experience-dependent later phase
Decreased response to pheromones
Vomeronasal organ
Paternal behavior
Most species: no paternal behavior
Species with paternal behavior: father shows hormonal changes
Testosterone: increases near end of pregnancy, decreases after delivery
Prolactin levels high after birth

5. In closing: Sex-related behaviors and motivations
No need to understand purpose of behavior
Sexual activity feels good
Mother rat: licks pups to get salt

Module 11.2 Variations in Sexual Development and Orientation
1. Determinants of gender identity
Gender identity: sexual identification
Human characteristic
Gender role: characteristics encouraged by specific society for one sex or the other
Intersexes
Atypical chromosomes
XY, with mutation of SRY
XX, with translocated SRY from father's Y onto autosomal chromosome
Atypical hormone pattern
Excess androgens in females
Insufficient testosterone or responsiveness to it in males
True hermaphrodites: some testicular and some ovarian tissue
Intersexes or pseudohermaphrodites: intermediate appearance
Previously: usually reared as girls
"Corrective" surgery destructive of sexual sensation

Testicular feminization or androgen insensitivity
    XY genotype
    Lack of androgen receptors
    Female gender identity
Discrepancies of sexual appearance
    Penis development delayed until puberty
        Decreased 5 α-reductase 2 (enzyme that converts testosterone to
            dihydrotestosterone)
        Dihydrotestosterone more effective in masculinizing genitals
        Puberty: enough testosterone to masculinize penis
    Accidental removal of the penis

2. Possible biological bases of sexual orientation
Genetics
    Greater similarity of orientation in monozygotic (identical) twins
    Gene on X chromosome: increased male homosexuality
        Not replicated in later studies
    Possible indirect effects
    Evolutionary selection
        May increase reproductive success of women
        May be perpetuated by kin selection
Hormones
    No consistent differences in adult hormone levels
    Decreased testosterone during early development of males
    Prenatal stress or alcohol
        Endorphins: antitestosterone effects
        Social experiences in male rats
            Rearing in isolation or with only males → sexually responsive only to males
            Rearing with males and females → sexually responsive to both sexes
        Uncertain relationship in humans between stress and homosexual sons
    Diethylstilbestrol (DES) in females → masculinization
    Clicks in inner ear: heterosexual women > lesbian or bisexual women > heterosexual men
Brain anatomy
    Anterior commissure
        Larger in women and homosexual men
    Suprachiasmatic nucleus (SCN)
        Larger in homosexual than heterosexual men
    Interstitial nucleus 3 of anterior hypothalamus
        Larger in heterosexual men than in women and homosexual men
        Differences not due to AIDS
        Cause vs. effect
        Functions unclear

SHORT-ANSWER QUESTIONS

Module 11.1 The Effects of Sex Hormones

1. *Organizing effects of sex hormones*

   a. Distinguish between organizing effects and activating effects of hormones.

   b. What is the SRY gene? Describe the chain of events that result from its presence during development.

   c. What are Mullerian ducts? What are Wolffian ducts?

   d. What are two sex differences in the structure or function of the hypothalamus?

   e. Describe the effects of testosterone injections on female rats during the last few days before birth and the first few days after birth.

f.   What happens if a developing mammal is exposed to neither androgens nor estrogens during early development?

g.   When is the critical period for testosterone's effects on rats? On humans?

h.   By what mechanism does testosterone exert its effects on the hypothalamus in rodents?

i.   Describe the effects of injections of large amounts of estrogen on female rats during the critical period.

j.   What is the role of alpha-fetoprotein?

k.   Describe the organizing effects of testosterone on the nerves and muscles that control the penis.

1.   What are some nonreproductive characteristics that may be influenced by prenatal hormones?

2. *Activating effects of sex hormones*
    a.   Which hormones can restore male-typical sexual behavior following castration? What is the most effective hormone treatment for restoring female-typical behavior?

    b.   What is the pudendal nerve? What are estrogen's effects on its function?

    c.   What brain area may facilitate female-typical behavior in females and male-typical behavior in males?

    d.   What neurotransmitter in the MPOA stimulates male sexual activity? How does castration affect the release of that neurotransmitter in the MPOA?

e. What may be its role in the progression from the early stages of copulation, which require erection in males and the receptive posture in females, to the stage of orgasm?

f. Describe the relationship between testosterone levels and sexual activity in men. Which other hormone contributes to sexual pleasure?

g. Which two drugs have been used to treat sex offenders? What promising drug has more recently been used? What are the effects of these drugs?

h. List the chain of hormonal processes in the menstrual cycle.

i. What are the two effects of follicle-stimulating hormone (FSH)?

j. Rising levels of which hormone cause a sudden surge of LH and FSH near the middle of the cycle? What is the effect of the surge of LH and FSH on the ovum?

k.   What is the corpus luteum, and what hormone does it release?

l.-   What are the effects of progesterone? Describe the levels of the major hormones shortly before menstruation.

m.   How do combination birth-control pills work?

n.   Describe the effect of women's menstrual cycle on their preference for masculinized vs. feminized faces.

o.   The decline in which hormone may be associated with negative moods? What are some neural effects of this hormone?

p.   What cognitive effects have been demonstrated for estrogen and testosterone? How strong are these effects?

3. *Puberty*
   a. What is the role of weight in the age at which menarche occurs?

   b. What is the first sign of the onset of puberty? Describe the consequences of this process.

4. *Parental behavior*
   a. Describe the roles of hormones and experience in parental behavior of rodents.

   b. Which two hormones have been shown to promote maternal behavior in monkeys? In rats?

   c. What brain area is important for these hormonal effects?

   d. Describe the hormonal changes associated with parental behavior in male dwarf hamsters.

Module 11.2 Variations in Sexual Development and Sexual Orientation

1. *Determinants of gender identity*

    a. What is an intersex? What is the difference between a true hermaphrodite and an intersex or pseudohermaphrodite?

    b. What are some developmental influences that may produce an intersex individual?

    c. Why have most intersexes been reared as females?

    d. How successful is the surgical treatment of intersexes?

    e. Describe the chromosomal pattern and the genital appearance of individuals with androgen insensitivity, or testicular feminization. What causes the unresponsiveness to androgen? What two abnormalities appear at puberty?

f.   Describe two situations in which children were exposed to the prenatal hormonal pattern of one sex and then reared as the opposite sex. What can we infer from these situations about the relative importance of early rearing experiences and hormones as determinants of gender identity?

2.   *Possible biological bases of sexual orientation*
    a.   Describe the evidence for a genetic predisposition towards homosexuality.

    b.   What was the likely explanation for the increased incidence of homosexuality among maternal relatives of homosexual men? Has the early finding been replicated?

    c.   By what indirect routes might genes influence sexual orientation?

    d.   Discuss the problems concerning evolutionary selection of any genes predisposing toward homosexuality.

e. What are two possible explanations for the continued existence of those genes?

f. Describe the experiments on the effects of stress on sex differentiation of rats. What were their results?

g. How may endorphins be implicated in the effects of stress? What other factor may influence the effects of prenatal stress?

h. Summarize the evidence regarding possible prenatal stress effects on homosexual men.

i. How strongly does prenatal diethylstilbestrol (DES) influence homosexuality in women?

j. What are three brain structures that show a sex difference in size? In which direction is the size difference for each? How do homosexual men compare with heterosexual men and with women regarding the size of these structures?

k.   Describe LeVay's evidence implicating the interstitial nucleus 3 of the hypothalamus in homosexuality.

l.   If there is a consistent difference between homosexual and heterosexual men in the size of various brain nuclei, what can we conclude about the role of these nuclei in determining sexual orientation?

POSTTEST

Multiple-Choice Questions

1. The SRY gene
   a.   is present on the X chromosome and is responsible for the tendency of mammals to become female, unless the gene's effects are overridden by high levels of testosterone.
   b.   is present on the Y chromosome and causes the gonads to differentiate into testes, which then secrete testosterone, which then masculinizes the organism.
   c.   has been linked to homosexuality.
   d.   is the major gene that directly specifies the size of certain brain structures.

2. Wolffian ducts
   a.   are the precursors of the oviducts, uterus, and upper vagina.
   b.   are the precursors of the seminal vesicles and vas deferens.
   c.   are the precursors of the external genitals.
   d.   none of the above.

3. Sex differences in the hypothalamus include
   a.   the sexually dimorphic nucleus of the medial preoptic area, which is larger in males.
   b.   parts of the hypothalamus that generate a cyclic pattern of hormone release in females.
   c.   both a and b.
   d.   none of the above.

232

4. If a female rat receives testosterone injections during the last few days before birth or the first few postnatal days, then in adulthood
   a. her pituitary and ovary will produce steady levels of hormones rather than cycling in the normal manner.
   b. she will exhibit neither masculine nor feminine sexual behavior.
   c. she will exhibit normal feminine sexual behavior in spite of the full masculinization of her genitals.
   d. she will exhibit normal feminine sexual behavior, and her genitals will appear fully feminine.

5. A female pattern of development
   a. can be produced by giving a female mammal large amounts of estrogen during the sensitive period.
   b. can be produced in normal males by giving them estrogen in adolescence.
   c. can be produced in mammals of either sex by depriving the animal of testosterone during the sensitive period.
   d. all of the above.

6. Which of the following is true?
   a. Testosterone's organizing effects occur throughout the entire period of gestation.
   b. Alpha-fetoprotein is the enzyme that converts testosterone to estradiol.
   c. Estradiol masculinizes the hypothalamus by being aromatized to testosterone.
   d. Testosterone masculinizes the hypothalamus of rodents largely by being aromatized to estradiol.

7. High levels of testosterone during prenatal development
   a. cause female monkeys to display more rough and tumble play.
   b. may contribute to the shorter life spans of males.
   c. may contribute to the greater aggressiveness of males.
   d. all of the above.

8. Stimulation of the MPOA
   a. increases both male-typical behavior in males and female-typical behavior in females.
   b. decreases male-typical behavior in males and increases female-typical behavior in females.
   c. increases male-typical behavior in males and decreases female-typical behavior in females.
   d. produces homosexual behavior in both sexes.

9. Activation of female sex behavior by hormones
   a. is most easily elicited by injections first of progesterone and then dihydrotestosterone in females whose ovaries were removed.
   b. may be mediated in part by increasing the area of skin that activates the pudendal nerve.
   c. is mediated by a decrease in stimulation of D_1 and D_5 dopamine receptors in the MPOA.
   d. all of the above.

10. Dopamine in the MPOA of male rats
    a. is released when the male is exposed to a receptive female, but only for those males that do copulate when they are allowed to.
    b. is not released in normal amounts by castrated males.
    c. may act through different receptors to promote erection first and then ejaculation.
    d. all of the above.

11. Cyproterone, medroxyprogesterone, and a newer drug, triptorelin
    a. are common treatments for impotence.
    b. are common treatments for premenstrual syndrome.
    c. can be used to decrease sexual fantasies and offensive sexual behaviors of sex offenders.
    d. are sometimes used to elicit the maturation and release of an ovum in infertile women.

12. The corpus luteum
    a. is the remnant of the follicle, which releases progesterone.
    b. releases estrogen during the early part of the cycle, which causes the pituitary to release a surge of progesterone at midcycle.
    c. is the primary source of FSH.
    d. is the primary source of LH.

13. FSH
    a. is secreted from the uterus.
    b. is secreted from the follicle.
    c. stimulates the follicle to grow, nurture the ovum, and produce estrogen.
    d. stimulates the follicle to grow and produce LH.

14. Combination birth control pills
    a. contain both estrogen and progesterone.
    b. suppress the release of FSH.
    c. suppress the release of LH.
    d. all of the above.

15. Which of the following is true?
    a. The effects of "sex hormones" are limited to the control of reproductive behavior and the endocrine system.
    b. Increases in estrogen may result in increased production of D_2 and $5HT_{2A}$ receptors in the nucleus accumbens and cortex, which have been implicated in mood and reinforcement.
    c. Estrogen produces major enhancements in spatial performance.
    d. Testosterone treatments in older men impaired their spatial performance.

16. Puberty
    a. begins when the hypothalamus begins to secrete luteinizing hormone releasing hormone in hourly bursts.
    b. is influenced by weight.
    c. is accompanied by a growth spurt and induction of secondary sex characteristics caused by estradiol in girls and testosterone in boys.
    d. all of the above.

17. Which is true concerning rodent parental behavior?
    a. Hormones are important in eliciting parental behavior soon after giving birth for the first time.
    b. Hormones continue to be the most important factor in eliciting parental behavior throughout the entire period of care of the young.
    c. Male rats do not show any parental behavior unless they are given high doses of progesterone during prenatal development.
    d. Parental behavior is enhanced by lesions of the MPOA, since that area is concerned only with male sexual behavior, which would interfere with parental behavior.

234

18. Intersexes
    a. are extremely rare, no more than one in several million.
    b. usually have complete sets of both male and female structures.
    c. include genetic females who were exposed to elevated levels of androgens during fetal development.
    d. are usually genetic males who have been exposed to estrogens during fetal development.

19. Intersexes reared as females
    a. should always have surgical "correction" of their genitals immediately after birth.
    b. are sometimes resentful that surgical "correction" of their genitals destroyed sexual sensation and makes them feel violated.
    c. provide clear evidence that prenatal hormones are the only determinant of gender identity.
    d. provide clear evidence that prenatal hormones are unimportant in gender identity.

20. Androgen insensitivity (testicular feminization)
    a. is characterized by normal testosterone levels, but a lack of androgen receptors.
    b. results in an individual who appears to be completely female but fails to menstruate at puberty and has no pubic hair.
    c. cannot be alleviated by giving injections of testosterone.
    d. all of the above.

21. Certain genetic males in the Dominican Republic
    a. lack the enzyme that converts testosterone to dihydrotestosterone.
    b. lack the enzyme that converts testosterone to estradiol.
    c. are usually reared as boys, but adapt easily to a feminine sexual identity when they begin to produce high levels of estrogen at puberty.
    d. are usually reared as girls, but are completely unable to adapt to their new male gender identity when high levels of testosterone at puberty cause growth of a penis.

22. A genetic contribution to homosexuality
    a. may be carried by a gene on the X chromosome that promotes homosexuality in males, although the evidence is not consistent.
    b. may be carried by a gene on the Y chromosome that promotes homosexuality in males, although the evidence is not consistent.
    c. is now known to be controlled by the same genes in male and female homosexuals.
    d. has been disproven, since evolution strongly selects against any genes that would interfere with reproduction.

23. Male homosexuality
    a. is highly correlated with low levels of testosterone in adulthood.
    b. is highly correlated with high levels of estrogen in adulthood.
    c. may be associated with increased stress during prenatal development.
    d. may be redirected to heterosexuality by injections of testosterone in adulthood.

24. Diethylstilbestrol (DES)
    a. can be used in adulthood to change the sexual orientation of homosexual men.
    b. can be used in adulthood to change the sexual orientation of homosexual women.
    c. administered to mothers during pregnancy may slightly increase the likelihood of bisexuality or homosexuality in their sons.
    d. administered to mothers during pregnancy may slightly increase the likelihood of bisexuality or homosexuality in their daughters.

25. The interstitial nucleus 3 of the anterior hypothalamus
    a. is larger in women and homosexual men than in heterosexual men.
    b. is smaller in women and homosexual men than in heterosexual men.
    c. is smaller in homosexual men than in either women or heterosexual men, primarily because the AIDS virus is known to kill neurons in that site more than in the rest of the brain.
    d. is now known to be the primary brain center that determines sexual orientation.

Answers to Multiple-Choice Questions

1. b	6. d	11. c	16. d	21. a
2. b	7. d	12. a	17. a	22. a
3. c	8. a	13. c	18. c	23. c
4. a	9. b	14. d	19. b	24. d
5. c	10. d	15. b	20. d	25. b

Heat, Sex, and Gluttony

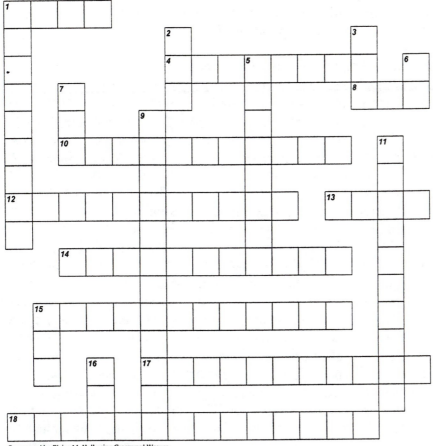

Constructed by Elaine M. Hull using Crossword Weaver

ACROSS

1 *Brain area important for temperature regulation, sexual behavior, and parental behavior*

4 *Initial segment of small intestine*

8 *Gene on Y chromosome that initiates formation of testes (abbr.)*

10 Tendency to maintain a variable within a set range

12 *Hormone produced by renin that signals hypovolemia*

13 *Brain area sensitive to osmotic stimuli (abbr.)*

14 *Type of thirst caused by loss of body fluids*

15 *Hormone produced by corpus luteum*

17 *Chemical produced by leukocytes that elicits a fever*

18 *Body temperature*

MPOA that controls sexual behavior

6 *Chromosomal male*

7 *Hormone from anterior pituitary that stimulates egg to mature and follicle to produce estrogen (abbr.)*

9 *Area of hypothalamus, lesion of which leads to obesity*

11 *Nerve sensitive to nutritive content of stomach*

15 *Brain area that produces vasopressin and that helps end a meal (abbr.)*

16 *Hormone secreted by structure in 4 Across in response to the presence of food (abbr.)*

matching the environment

DOWN

1 *Tract that differentiates into female internal genitals*

2 *Hormone from posterior pituitary that conserves water (abbr.)*

3 *Syndrome characterized by irritability before menstruation (abbr.)*

5 *Transmitter in*

12

EMOTIONAL BEHAVIORS

INTRODUCTION

Emotions require some level of consciousness; however, we can have an emotion without being aware of what caused it. Although strong emotions can impair reasoning, inability to feel emotions can result in a lack of moral behavior and a series of stupid decisions. Activity of the autonomic nervous system, composed of the sympathetic and parasympathetic divisions, has been associated with certain emotional states. For example, sympathetic activity prepares for vigorous or emergency activity. The parasympathetic system promotes digestion and conserves energy. Each situation can be associated with a different combination of sympathetic and parasympathetic activity. There are several theories about the role of autonomic arousal in emotions. The James-Lange theory proposes that autonomic and skeletal activity occurs first, and emotions result from our perception of those responses. The Cannon-Bard theory holds that emotions occur simultaneously with, but independent of, physical arousal. The Schachter-Singer theory suggests that physiological changes determine the strength of emotions, but cognitive appraisal is needed to identify the emotion. There is evidence for the importance of physiological responses in determining the intensity of emotions; however, it is possible to feel some blunted emotions, even after injuries that prevent autonomic responses.

Stress was defined by Hans Selye as the nonspecific response of the body to any demand made upon it. Vulnerability to certain diseases is affected by our behaviors and by stress and emotions. Excessive parasympathetic activity, after a period of intense stress, may cause some cases of ulcers and of voodoo death. Excessive sympathetic activity may contribute to heart disease, whereas social support may decrease sympathetic activity and protect against heart disease. During stress, the hypothalamus directs the anterior pituitary to secrete ACTH (adrenocorticotropic hormone), which in turn stimulates the adrenal gland to secrete cortisol. Cortisol shifts energy metabolism to increase blood sugar and decrease synthesis of proteins, including the proteins necessary for immune function. Two important elements of the immune system are the B cells, which produce antibodies that attach to and inactivate specific antigens, and the T cells, which attack specific "foreign" cells or stimulate responses from other immune cells. Natural killer cells kill tumor cells and cells infected with viruses; their attacks are relatively nonspecific. Although brief stressors activate the immune system, chronic, uncontrollable stressors may depress its functioning and leave an individual more vulnerable to disease. Active coping and a sense of control may help strengthen the immune response. Prolonged stress, with its high cortisol levels, can also increase the vulnerability of hippocampal neurons. Furthermore, a vicious cycle develops, with hippocampal damage resulting in higher cortisol levels, which further damage the hippocampus. Post-traumatic stress disorder (PTSD) occurs in some people who have had traumatic experiences. They have flashbacks, nightmares, and exaggerated arousal to noises and other stimuli. We do not know why some people do, and others do not, succumb to PTSD. Those who do have been found to have a smaller hippocampus and low cortisol levels; however, a cause and effect relationship has not been established.

Aggression is complex and difficult to study. Increased aggressiveness is influenced by heredity and by prenatal influences, including maternal smoking during pregnancy. Men display more unprovoked aggression than do women, although both sexes respond similarly under provocation. Testosterone is correlated with aggressiveness, although its effect is relatively weak. Stimulation of the ventromedial hypothalamus or the amygdala can promote aggressive responses, whereas lesions of the amygdala usually decrease aggressiveness and also impair the interpretation of visual information. Some people with temporal-lobe epilepsy have violent outbursts as a result of seizures that involve the amygdala. Antiepileptic drugs frequently control the epilepsy and the violence; however, for extremely violent individuals who were not helped by drugs, lesions of the amygdala have sometimes reduced the violence and/or the epilepsy. Low serotonin turnover may also be associated with aggressiveness in both animals and people. Turnover is inferred from levels of 5-HIAA, a serotonin metabolite. Low serotonin turnover was observed in mice that showed isolation-induced aggression and in monkeys that were naturally aggressive. Furthermore, the lack of serotonin 5-HT$_{1B}$ receptors was associated with excessive attack behaviors in mice. Low serotonin turnover in humans may be associated with impulsiveness, violent crimes, and suicide. These findings suggest that violence might be controlled by a diet high in tryptophan, the precursor to serotonin, or by drugs that increase serotonin; however, such attempts have met with limited success.

Fear is a temporary experience, whereas anxiety is longer lasting. The amygdala, especially its basolateral and central nuclei, is important for learned fear responses, including enhancement of the startle reflex. Its output to the hypothalamus controls autonomic responses; its output to prefrontal cortex influences interpretation of threat; and its connections to the central gray in the midbrain elicit the startle response. Damage to the amygdala, or infusion of an anesthetic into it, reduces or eliminates learned or enhanced fears. People with Urbach-Wiethe disease suffer atrophy of the amygdala and have a resultant loss of the experience or perception of fear. Anxiety is commonly treated with benzodiazepine tranquilizers. These drugs exert their effect at the "benzodiazepine receptor" on the GABA$_A$ receptor complex, thereby facilitating the binding of GABA to its own receptor at the complex. The binding of GABA increases the flow of chloride ions across the membrane. Alcohol also binds to the GABA$_A$ complex, thereby facilitating GABA binding. Diazepam-binding inhibitor (DBI) is an endozepine (endogenous antibenzodiazepine); it blocks the effects of diazepam and other benzodiazepines, thereby increasing anxiety.

KEY TERMS AND CONCEPTS

Module 12.1 What Is Emotion, Anyway? And What Good Is It?
1. Introduction
   Emotions as observable behaviors vs. feelings as private experiences
       Operational definition
       Require consciousness
           Absence seizure
   Limbic system (border around brainstem)

2. Are emotions useful?
   Extreme emotions: impair reasoning
   Prefrontal cortex damage: lack of emotions
       Stupid decisions, despite predicting outcomes
       No moral behavior

3. Emotions and readiness for action
   Autonomic nervous system arousal
       Sympathetic nervous system: vigorous, emergency activity
       Parasympathetic nervous system: digestion, conservation of energy
       Each situation: mixture of sympathetic and parasympathetic activity
   James-Lange theory: autonomic arousal and actions before emotions
       Each emotion → different bodily response
   Cannon-Bard theory: emotions simultaneous but independent from physical arousal
       Sympathetic nervous system (SNS) too slow to → emotion

239

SNS: operates as a unit
Schachter-Singer theory
    Physiological changes → strength of emotion
    Cognitive appraisal → identify emotion
Spinal cord injuries → decreased emotional intensity, but not absence
Locked-in syndrome
    Ventral brainstem damage → sensory input but no motor output
    Usually tranquil
Brain stimulation during surgery → laughter interpreted as emotion

Module 12.2 Stress and Health

1.   Stress and the autonomic nervous system
    Behavioral medicine
    Stress: nonspecific response of body to any demand made upon it
        Hans Selye
    Psychosomatic illnesses
        Ulcers
            More in rats **without** control of stressor
                Prefrontal cortex damage → no ulcers in similar conditions
            More in monkeys **with** control of stressor
                Monkeys better at avoiding shocks → passive monkey: few shocks
            Develop during rest periods between shock sessions
                Rebound parasympathetic activation of stomach
            Bacterium: increases risk, not major cause
        Heart disease
            Weak link to hostile emotions
            Social support: decreased heart rate and blood pressure
        Voodoo death and related phenomena
            Curt Richter's swimming rats
                Excessive parasympathetic activity
            Most heart attacks: excessive sympathetic arousal

2.   Stress and the hypothalamus-pituitary-adrenal cortex axis
    Slower than autonomic nervous system
    Hypothalamus → anterior pituitary: adrenocorticotropic hormone (ACTH) →
        Human adrenal cortex: cortisol (rat adrenal cortex: corticosterone) →
        Increased blood sugar and metabolism
        Decreased protein synthesis, including immune system proteins
        Useful in short term, harmful if prolonged
    The immune system
        Autoimmune disease
        Leukocytes
        Bone marrow, thymus, spleen, lymph nodes
        "Self" proteins
        Antigens
        Macrophages
        B cells
            Plasma cells → antibodies
            B memory cells

T cells
    Cytotoxic T cells: directly attack intruder
    Helper T cells: stimulate response from other immune cells
Natural killer cells: relatively nonspecific in their targets
Cytokines
    Example: interleukin-1 (IL-1)
    Attack infections
    Peripheral cytokines → vagus nerve → hypothalamus and hippocampus →
        Release cytokines in brain → anti-illness behaviors
Effects of stress on the immune system
    Psychoneuroimmunology
    Inescapable, temporary stressors → response similar to illness
    Brief stressors → brief activation of immune system
    Long-term stressors → decreased protein synthesis, including immune system
        Sense of control helps
        High cortisol → hippocampal damage
            Decreased learning and memory
            Increased cortisol

3. Post-traumatic stress disorder (PTSD)
    Symptoms
        Flashbacks and nightmares
        Avoidance of reminders
        Exaggerated arousal in response to noises and other stimuli
    Vulnerability
        Small hippocampus (cause or effect?)
        Low cortisol levels

4. In closing: Emotions and body reactions
    Which changes are symptoms and which are coping mechanisms?
    Social support: physiological effects or better care of themselves?

Module 12.3 Attack and Escape Behaviors
1. Attack behaviors
    "Play": Attack, escape
    Affective attack
    Corticomedial amygdala
        Prining for further attacks
    Heredity and environment in human violence
        Similarity: monozygotic > dizygotic
        Maternal smoking during pregnancy
        Body size at age 3
        Genetic factors better predictors of adult than juvenile crime
    Hormones
        Male-female differences
            Smaller differences in self-reported than in observed aggression
            Little difference in response to serious provocation
            Men: more unprovoked aggression than women

Testosterone
    Within age groups or prison populations: modest correlation between aggressiveness
        and testosterone
Temporal lobe and violence
    Corticomedial amygdala
    Ventromedial nucleus of hypothalamus
        A site of testosterone's effects
        Output to brainstem
    Amygdala
        Stimulation or epileptic focus → attacks
        Rabies
        Removal: tameness
            Kluver-Bucy syndrome
            Difficulty interpreting visual stimuli
            Impairment of emotional response
        Temporal lobe epilepsy
            Symptoms: hallucinations, lip smacking, repetitive acts, in some cases aggressive
                behaviors
            Antiepileptic drugs
            Surgical destruction of amygdala
    Prefrontal cortex damage → general loss of inhibitions
Serotonin synapses and aggressive behavior
    Nonhuman animals
        Social isolation of male mice → lower serotonin turnover, correlated with aggression
        5-HIAA (5-hydroxyindoleacetic acid): measure of serotonin turnover
        Social isolation of female mice → no change in serotonin turnover or aggression
        Genetically aggressive mice: lack of 5-HT$_{1B}$ receptors
            Also develop cocaine addiction faster
            Impulsive
        Male monkeys: low serotonin turnover correlated with high aggression
    Humans
        Low serotonin turnover: correlation with violent crimes or suicide
        Low tryptophan diet → increase in aggressiveness
        Drugs that increase serotonin → slight decrease in aggressiveness
        Low serotonin also linked to depression
        Serotonin: suppress unwelcome behaviors
            Individual differences in unwelcome behaviors

2. Escape behaviors
    Fear and anxiety
    Fear, enhanced fears, and the amygdala
        Startle reflex
        Auditory input to cochlear nucleus of medulla, then to pons: tense muscles
        Modified by experience: basolateral and central nuclei of amygdala
            Output to hypothalamus: autonomic responses
            Output to prefrontal cortex: interpretation
            Output to midbrain central gray, then to pons: skeletal responses
            Larger effect of anesthetic in right amygdala than in left
    The human amygdala
        Greater response to fearful expressions

Removal: loss of learned emotional response
Urbach-Wiethe disease: atrophy of amygdala, decreased fear
Anxiety-reducing drugs
Transmitters in amygdala: CCK, excitatory; GABA, inhibitory
Barbiturates: habit forming, easy to take fatal overdose
Benzodiazepines
Diazepam (Valium)
Chlordiazepoxide (Librium)
Alprazolam (Xanax)
$GABA_A$ receptor complex
Chloride channel: hyperpolarizes
Benzodiazepines, barbiturates, and alcohol: enhance GABA binding
Diazepam-binding inhibitor (DBI), an endozepine: endogenous antibenzodiazepine
Panic disorder
Occasional attacks of extreme fear, breathlessness, heart palpitations, fatigue, dizziness
Only moderate activation of sympathetic nervous system during attack
Misinterpretation of respiratory signals: suffocation
Increased blood lactate and carbon dioxide (CO_2)
Cigarette smoking → increased risk of panic disorder
Hyperventilating → decreased CO_2 and phosphates →
Decreased vagus nerve activity
Any increase in CO_2 → large percentage increase → increase in heart rate
Treatment with antidepressants and/or psychotherapy
The relationship between alcohol and tranquilizers
Cross-tolerance of alcohol, benzodiazepines, and alcohol
Alcohol → increased flow of chloride ions through $GABA_A$ receptor complex
Ro15-4513: blocks alcohol's effects on $GABA_A$ receptors and behavior
Not marketed because of potential for misuse

SHORT-ANSWER QUESTIONS

Module 12.1 What Is Emotion, Anyway? And What Good Is It?
1. *Are emotions useful?*
   a. What is the effect of extreme emotions? Describe the behavior of people with damage to the prefrontal cortex.

2. *Emotions and readiness for action*
   a. What are the roles of the sympathetic and parasympathetic nervous systems?

b. Describe the James-Lange theory of emotions.

c. What is the Cannon-Bard theory of emotions?

d. What are the two major components of the Schachter-Singer theory?

e. Describe three pieces of evidence concerning the importance of the autonomic nervous system for emotions.

Module 12.2 Stress and Health
1. *Stress and the autonomic nervous system*
   a. What are the assumptions of behavioral medicine? What is a psychosomatic illness?

   b. What was Hans Selye's definition of stress?

c. Describe the different findings regarding the importance of control of the stressor in producing ulcers in rats, compared to monkeys.

d. When do ulcers form, relative to a period of stress?

e. What may be the relative contributions of stress and a bacterium to the onset of ulcers?

f. How important are hostile emotions and social support to heart disease?

g. Describe Richter's experiment with swimming rats.

h. What was the cause of death in Richter's rats? Were wild or domesticated rats more likely to die? What procedure averted death of the dewhiskered rats?

2. *Stress and the hypothalamus-pituitary-adrenal cortex axis*
   a. Describe the steps in the control of cortisol secretion from the adrenal cortex.

   b. What are cortisol's major effects on blood sugar and metabolism? How does this affect the immune system?

   c. What are the most important cells of the immune system? Where are these cells produced?

   d. What are antigens? How was the name "antigen" derived?

   e. What are the roles of B cells and of T cells?

   f. What is the role of macrophages? Of natural killer cells?

g. In what ways does the body react to temporary stressors similarly to illnesses?

h. What is the effect of short-term stress on the immune system? How is this effect mediated?

i. Describe the evidence suggesting that long-term stress impairs the function of the immune system.

j. Describe the vicious cycle that develops with high cortisol levels and the hippocampus.

k. What are the symptoms of posttraumatic stress disorder? What is the evidence that PTSD is not just a prolongation of the stress response?

Module 12.3 Attack and Escape Behaviors
1. *Attack behaviors*
    a. What is one explanation of a cat's "play" behavior with its prey?

b. Describe the behavioral characteristics of affective attack and "cold-blooded" attacks.

c. What are the effects of stimulation of the amygdala on aggressive behavior? Which area of the amygdala is especially important for this effect?

d. What conclusions can be drawn from studies of adopted children and of twins concerning the relative roles of genes and environment in promoting aggressive behavior and crimes?

e. How strong is the correlation between testosterone levels and aggressive behavior?

f. Stimulation of which two brain areas can elicit attack?

g. How does rabies lead to violent behavior?

h.   What are the usual effects of amygdala damage? Describe the Kluver-Bucy syndrome.

i..   What happens in the brain during an epileptic seizure?

j.   What are some behavioral symptoms of temporal lobe epilepsy?

k.   What are two forms of medical or surgical treatment for frequent unprovoked violence?

l.   What transmitter abnormality appears to be associated with aggressive behavior? How can it be measured?

m.   Describe the experimental evidence in mice for this relationship.

n. How was serotonin turnover related to behavior in male monkeys in a natural-environment study?

o. What evidence implicates low serotonin turnover in humans as a factor in aggressive behavior?

2. *Escape behaviors*
    a. Why should researchers be interested in the startle response?

    b. What is a key brain area for learned fears? Which of its nuclei receive sensory input?

    c. What are the main output connections of the amygdala? What does each control?

    d. Damage to which nucleus of the amygdala abolishes the enhancement of the startle reflex?

e. What causes Urbach-Wiethe disease? What are its symptoms?

f. What are one excitatory and one inhibitory transmitter in the amygdala that have been implicated in the control of anxiety?

g. What two types of drugs have been used to reduce anxiety? What are the relative advantages and disadvantages of the two types?

h. When a benzodiazepine molecule attaches to its binding site on the $GABA_A$ receptor, how is the binding of GABA affected? What effect does this have on the flow of chloride ions across the cell membrane?

i. How do alcohol and barbiturates affect this process?

j. What is one endogenous chemical that affects the benzodiazepine receptors? Why is the term endozepine confusing?

k. Increases in blood levels of what two molecules can trigger panic attacks? Under what conditions do these chemicals normally increase?

l. Explain the role of hyperventilating in panic disorder.

m. What are the advantages and disadvantages of a drug that blocks alcohol's effects on the $GABA_A$ receptor? What is your opinion of the decision not to market the drug?

POSTTEST

Multiple-Choice Questions

1. The limbic system
    a. gets its name from the fact that it has many limbs branching in all directions.
    b. includes forebrain areas regarded as critical for emotion, which form a border around the brainstem.
    c. is especially important for higher cognitive functions that differentiate humans from other mammals.
    d. all of the above.

2. Which of the following is true?
   a. A lack of emotions, as in people with prefrontal cortex damage, promotes rational decision making.
   b. The James-Lange theory proposed that emotional experience and autonomic arousal are evoked independently.
   (c.) The Schachter-Singer theory proposed that physiological changes determined the strength of emotion, whereas cognitive appraisal was needed to identify the emotion.
   d. Sympathetic nervous system activity prepares the body for digestion and relaxation.

3. Ulcers
   a. occurred more frequently in rats **without** control of the stressor.
   b. occurred more frequently in monkeys **with** control of the stressor
   c. developed during rest periods between shock.
   (d) all of the above.

4. Voodoo death occurs only
   a. if a witch doctor has special powers.
   b. in very primitive societies.
   (c.) if the victim expects to die.
   d. in people with underactive parasympathetic nervous systems.

5. Curt Richter found that
   (a) cutting off a rat's whiskers immediately before putting it into a tank of water resulted in its struggling frantically and then sinking suddenly to the bottom, dead.
   b. laboratory rats, but not the stronger wild ones, were most susceptible to the sudden death phenomenon.
   c. rats' whiskers are necessary for swimming, since removing them negated the otherwise helpful procedure of rescue training.
   d. all of the above are true.

6. Cortisol
   a. is secreted by the anterior pituitary gland.
   b. serves primarily to activate a sudden burst of "fight or flight" activity.
   c. serves primarily to decrease metabolic activity in order to save energy for later stresses.
   d. shifts energy away from synthesis of proteins, including those necessary for the immune system, and towards increasing blood sugar.

7. T cells
   a. are specialized to produce antibodies.
   (b) mature in the thymus and either attack intruder cells or stimulate other immune system cells.
   c. engulf microorganisms and display antigen of the microorganism.
   d. are useless until they are activated by B cells.

8. Cytokines
   (a) in the periphery activate receptors on the vagus nerve, which relays input to the hypothalamus and hippocampus, which then release cytokines themselves.
   b. help overcome typical illness symptoms, such as fever and sleepiness, after illness is over.
   c. increase appetite to urge the body to acquire more nutrients for fighting the illness.
   d. easily cross the blood-brain barrier, in order to coordinate peripheral and central effects.

9. Stress
    a. is by far the major factor in the success of nonhuman animals' immune response; however, humans are not susceptible to stress effects.
    b. impairs the immune system from the first moments of the stressor's presence.
    c. produces a brief activation of the immune system, followed by inhibition of immune response if the stressor continues for a long time and is sufficiently intense.
    d. all of the above.

10. Prolonged high levels of cortisol
    a. make hippocampal neurons vulnerable to damage, which results in decreased learning and memory and also increased cortisol levels.
    b. lead to an increase in protein synthesis, which helps the immune system during long-term stressors.
    c. are found in almost all people with PTSD.
    d. all of the above.

11. PTSD
    a. occurs in almost all people who are subjected to traumatic experiences.
    b. includes symptoms of flashbacks, nightmares, avoidance of reminders, and exaggerated response to noises or other stimuli.
    c. is usually accompanied by a larger than usual hippocampus, because the memory of the trauma is so firmly established.
    d. all of the above.

12. Affective attack
    a. is described as a "cold-blooded" attack.
    b. is the type of attack in which an animal "plays" with its prey.
    c. is characterized by intense parasympathetic activity during the attack.
    d. can be elicited by stimulation of the corticomedial amygdala.

13. Which of the following is true?
    a. The correlation between testosterone and aggression in humans is real, but of modest size.
    b. Both genetics and environmental factors contribute to the predisposition to commit crimes and aggressive behaviors.
    c. Stimulation of the ventromedial hypothalamus can increase the likelihood of an attack against an intruder.
    d. All of the above are true.

14. Lesions of the amygdala
    a. usually produce difficulty in interpreting visual information as well as decreased aggressiveness.
    b. usually cause temporal lobe epilepsy.
    c. lead to a state that resembles panic disorder.
    d. usually decrease the frequency of predatory attacks, but increase affective attacks.

15. Which of the following has **not** been implicated in aggressiveness?
    a. the corticomedial nucleus of the amygdala
    b. the ventromedial nucleus of the hypothalamus
    c. the entire hippocampus
    d. maternal smoking during pregnancy

16. Temporal-lobe epilepsy
    a. is invariably associated with violence.
    b. is generally untreatable except by surgery.
    c. symptoms include hallucinations, lip smacking or other repetitive acts, and, in some cases, violence.
    d. can frequently be improved with antidepressant drugs.

17. Which of the following is true?
    a. Mice with low levels of serotonin turnover are abnormally placid.
    b. Serotonin turnover has been found to be lower than normal in impulsive, aggressive humans.
    c. 5-HIAA is a drug that has been used successfully to treat uncontrollable violence.
    d. All of the above are true.

18. Output from the amygdala to the hypothalamus controls
    a. the intensity of sensory input to the organism.
    b. the interpretation of potentially frightening stimuli.
    c. skeletal movements of the startle response.
    d. autonomic fear responses, such as increased blood pressure.

19. After damage, inactivation, or atrophy of the amygdala
    a. a person has difficulty recognizing or portraying fearful expressions.
    b. a rat no longer shows any startle reflex.
    c. a rat shows greater deficits in remembering unpleasant experiences if the left side is damaged, compared to the right.
    d. a person shows enhanced reactions to fear-provoking stimuli.

20. Librium, Valium, and Xanax
    a. are more habit-forming than barbiturates and more likely to lead to a fatal overdose.
    b. are benzodiazepines.
    c. act exclusively on CCK synapses.
    d. all of the above.

21. The benzodiazepines
    a. directly stimulate the same receptor sites that GABA stimulates.
    b. decrease the membrane's permeability to chloride ions.
    c. attach to binding sites on the $GABA_A$ receptor complex, thereby facilitating GABA binding.
    d. block $GABA_A$ synapses.

22. Which of the following is true?
    a. Alcohol displaces benzodiazepines from their binding sites, thereby disrupting GABA transmission.
    b. Endozepines, including diazepam-binding inhibitor (DBI), are actually endogenous antibenzodiazepines, which inhibit GABA transmission.
    c. The most effective anti-anxiety drugs are CCK receptor blockers.
    d. Alcohol produces its antianxiety effects by blocking chloride channels.

23. Which of the following is true of people who are prone to panic attacks?
   a. Their brain may misinterpret increases in blood lactate and carbon dioxide as signs of suffocation.
   b. They may have an overresponsive parasympathetic nervous system.
   c. They should hyperventilate at the first sign of panic, in order to avert a full-blown attack.
   d. They are helped only by drug therapy; psychotherapy has no added benefit.

Answers to Multiple-Choice Questions

1. b	6. d	11. b	16. c	21. c
2. c	7. b	12. d	17. b	22. b
3. d	8. a	13. d	18. d	23. a
4. c	9. c	14. a	19. a	
5. a	10. a	15. c	20. b	

13

THE BIOLOGY OF
LEARNING AND MEMORY

INTRODUCTION

Learning depends upon changes within single cells, which then work together as a system to produce adaptive behavior. Different kinds of learning and memory may rely on different neural mechanisms. Classical conditioning establishes a learned association between a neutral (conditioned) stimulus (CS) and an unconditioned stimulus (UCS) that evokes a reflexive response (UCR). As a result, the previously neutral stimulus comes to evoke a response (CR) similar to the reflexive response. Operant conditioning is the increase or decrease in a behavior as a result of reinforcement or punishment. Other forms of learning, such as bird song learning, may fall outside the categories of classical or operant conditioning.

Ivan Pavlov hypothesized that all learning is based on simple neural connections formed between two brain areas active at the same time. Karl Lashley tested this hypothesis by making various cuts that disconnected brain areas from each other and by removing varying amounts of cerebral cortex after rats had learned mazes or discrimination tasks. To his surprise, he found that no particular connection or part of the cortex was critical for any task. Lashley assumed that all learning occurred in the cortex and that all types of learning relied on the same physiological mechanism. Recent evidence suggests that certain subcortical nuclei may be important for specific types of learning and that several different neural mechanisms underlie different types of learning. For example, one simple type of conditioning, the eye-blink response, relies on the lateral interpositus nucleus of the cerebellum. The red nucleus, a midbrain motor center, is necessary for the motor expression of the eye-blink response, but not formation of the memory. Similar mechanisms appear to underlie eye-blink conditioning in rats and in humans.

Memory can be divided into several types: short-term vs. long-term, explicit vs. implicit, and declarative vs. procedural. Some short-term memories are consolidated rapidly into long-term memory; others are consolidated more slowly; most are not consolidated at all. Highly emotional events, which activate the sympathetic nervous system, are easily remembered. A major reason is that epinephrine in the periphery activates the vagus nerve, which relays activation to the brain stem, which in turn activates the amygdala. Cortisol is also released during stressful or exciting experiences; it, too, activates the amygdala, which enhances storage of emotional memories. However, prolonged or excessive stress, and its accompanying high cortisol level, impairs memory. Working memory is the temporary storage of information while we are using it. We may have separate neural mechanisms for storing auditory memory (a "phonological loop") and visual memory (a "visuospatial sketchpad"), as well as a "central executive" that directs attention and determines which items will be stored. The prefrontal cortex seems to be especially important for working memory. A common test of working memory is the delayed response task, in which one must respond to a stimulus presented a short time earlier. Neurons in the prefrontal cortex are active during the delay, and prefrontal damage impairs performance on delayed response tasks.

Information about memory has been obtained from studies of three major syndromes involving amnesia in humans. A main cognitive deficit in all three syndromes is the inability to form new long-term declarative or explicit memories. Declarative memory is memory that people can state in words, whereas procedural memory consists of motor skills. Explicit memory is deliberate recall of information that one recognizes as a memory; implicit memories can be detected as indirect influences on behavior, and do not require recollection of specific information. One syndrome

257

results from hippocampal damage and is exemplified by the patient H. M., who had bilateral removal of the hippocampus to relieve incapacitating epilepsy. Following surgery, H. M. has suffered extensive anterograde amnesia and moderate retrograde amnesia; however, his working memory remains intact. The hippocampus is not the storage site for memories, since previously consolidated memories can still be retrieved; such memories depend on the cerebral cortex. The cases of H. M. and other patients with hippocampal damage suggest that the primary function of the hippocampus is to promote storage of declarative, explicit memory. Nonhuman animals with hippocampal damage show memory impairments on delayed matching tasks, which are somewhat similar to human declarative memory. In addition, they are impaired on tasks that measure spatial memory, suggesting a second hypothesis, that a major function of the hippocampus is spatial memory. Rats with hippocampal damage forget which arms of a radial arm maze they have already entered in search of food; they also forget the location of a platform submerged in murky water. Among related species of birds that live in different habitats, those that are most dependent on finding previously hidden food have the largest hippocampus. Humans also use their hippocampus to solve spatial problems. Apparently, some portions of the hippocampus code spatial information and others code nonspatial aspects. A third hypothesis is that the hippocampus is important for configural learning, in which the meaning of a stimulus depends upon other stimuli that are paired with it. However, hippocampal damage may also impair nonconfigural learning if it is complicated and difficult. A final theory of hippocampal function is that it binds together the various sites in the cortex that form a memory.

The second human disorder, Korsakoff's syndrome, occurs almost exclusively in severe alcoholics and is characterized by apathy, confusion, and both retrograde and anterograde amnesia. It is caused by prolonged thiamine deficiency, which results in loss of neurons throughout the brain, especially in the mamillary bodies of the hypothalamus and the dorsomedial thalamus, which projects to prefrontal cortex. In addition to their deficit in explicit memory, Korsakoff's patients have difficulty recalling the temporal order of events, and they confabulate (accept guesses as if they were memories).

The third human memory disorder is Alzheimer's disease, which is characterized by progressive forgetfulness, leading to disorientation, depression, restlessness, hallucinations, delusions, and loss of sleep and appetite. People with Down syndrome, who have three copies of chromosome 21, almost always get Alzheimer's disease if they survive into middle age. Mutations of genes on chromosome 14 or on chromosome 1 also result in early-onset Alzheimer's disease. Mutation of yet another gene, on chromosome 19, results in later-onset Alzheimer's disease. All of these mutations lead to the accumulation of amyloid deposits in the brain. Amyloid precursor protein is normally cleaved to form a smaller protein of 40 amino acids, amyloid beta protein 40 ($A\beta_{40}$), which probably has a useful function. In people with Alzheimer's disease, the precursor is cleaved to form a slightly larger protein consisting of 42 amino acids ($A\beta_{42}$), which accumulates and impairs the functions of neurons and glia. An abnormal form of tau protein, which forms part of the intracellular support structure of neurons, also accumulates in Alzheimer's patients. Plaques and tangles of dying neurons form in areas of degeneration caused by amyloid deposits. The brains of Alzheimer's victims reveal widespread neural degeneration, especially in the cerebral cortex and hippocampus and in basal forebrain neurons that release acetylcholine. The most heavily damaged area is the entorhinal cortex, which communicates with the hippocampus. Alzheimer's disease can be temporarily alleviated by increasing levels of glucose, which not only supplies nutrition, but also increases insulin secretion, which somehow increases memory. Drugs that stimulate acetylcholine receptors or prolong acetylcholine release may also help. Antioxidants may guard against brain degeneration, and vaccination against $A\beta_{42}$ may someday be used to avoid Alzheimer's disease.

Infant amnesia, the lack of memory for events that occurred in the earliest years of life, may result from the slow rate of maturation of the hippocampus. We have learned from various types of amnesia that people have several kinds of memory that depend on different brain areas.

Donald Hebb suggested that the cellular basis for memory storage is increased effectiveness of specific synapses, brought about by simultaneous activity in pre- and postsynaptic neurons. Many researchers have studied the cellular mechanisms of learning in invertebrates, which have simple, well-defined nervous systems. Studies using Aplysia have demonstrated changes in identified synapses during habituation and sensitization. Long-term potentiation (LTP) is an increased synaptic responsiveness in cells of the mammalian hippocampus and other brain areas. LTP shows specificity, in that only the active synapses become strengthened. It also shows cooperativity, in which near simultaneous stimulation by two or more axons increases LTP. A third characteristic is associativity, which refers to the increased responsiveness to a weak stimulus as a result of its being paired with a strong stimulus. The opposite change, long term depression (LTD), occurs in both the hippocampus and cerebellum. It is a decreased responsiveness to a synaptic input that has been repeatedly paired with another input at low frequency. LTP depends on stimulation of two types of glutamate receptors. Stimulation of AMPA receptors depolarizes the neuron, thereby displacing the magnesium ions that normally block the ion channels of nearby NMDA receptors. As a result, the NMDA receptors are able to respond to glutamate, allowing both sodium and calcium ions to enter the cell. The calcium, in turn, activates certain chemicals and genes inside the postsynaptic neuron. These changes result in either altered structure or increased numbers of AMPA receptors and increased dendritic branches. Incoming axons may also be altered. Although stimulation of NMDA receptors is necessary for the establishment of LTP, activity of these receptors is not required for its maintenance. LTP and NMDA receptors may underlie the consolidation of memories and other forms of brain plasticity in the intact organism. For example, LTP may be important in the development of connections during early critical periods. During training LTP can be detected first in the hippocampus, and then 90 to 180 minutes later, it is detectable in parts of the cortex. Genetic alterations producing abnormal NMDA receptors result in impaired learning in mice, whereas alterations producing excess NMDA receptors result in better than normal memory. Finally, memory impairment in aged mammals may result from "leaky" NMDA receptors that let in too much calcium.

KEY TERMS AND CONCEPTS

Module 13.1 Learning, Memory, Amnesia, and Brain Functioning
1. Localized representations of memory
    Classical conditioning
        Ivan Pavlov
        Conditioned stimulus (CS)
        Unconditioned stimulus (UCS)
        Unconditioned response (UCR)
        Conditioned response (CR)
    Operant conditioning
        Reinforcement
        Punishment
    Bird-song learning
    Lashley's search for the engram
        Engram: physical representation of what has been learned
        Amount of damage, not location
            Equipotentiality: All parts of cortex contribute equally to complex behaviors
            Mass action: Cortex works as a whole
        Unnecessary assumptions:
            Cerebral cortex is the site of the engram.

All kinds of memory are the same.
The modern search for the engram
    Richard F. Thompson
        Rabbit eye-blink response
        Lateral interpositus nucleus of cerebellum: site of conditioning
        Red nucleus: motor expression
    Classical conditioning of eye-blink in humans
        PET scans: increased activity in cerebellum, red nucleus, and other areas
        Damage to cerebellum: impaired eye-blink conditioning

2.   Types of memory
Short-term and long-term memory
    Donald Hebb
Consolidation of long-term memories
    Reverberating circuit
    Epinephrine → vagus nerve → brain stem → amygdala
    Cortisol → amygdala
    Amygdala → hippocampus → cerebral cortex → memory storage
    Excessive or prolonged stress or cortisol → memory impairment
    Damage amygdala: emotional arousal does not enhance storage
A modified theory: Working memory
    Phonological loop: stores auditory information
    Visuospatial sketchpad: stores visual information
    Central executive: directs attention and picks items for storage
    Delayed response task
        Cells in prefrontal cortex: specific locations or stimuli
    Central executive: divided attention
        Activity in prefrontal cortex

3.   The hippocampus and amnesia
Amnesia: memory loss
Memory loss after hippocampal damage
    H. M.: surgery for severe epilepsy
        Severe anterograde amnesia (declarative memory for events after surgery)
        Moderate retrograde amnesia (events shortly before surgery)
        Normal short-term or working memory
        Impaired declarative memory
        Intact procedural memory
        Better implicit than explicit memory
Theories of the function of the hippocampus
    Important for consolidation
        Well-consolidated memories stored in cortex
    The hippocampus and declarative memory
        Damage to the hippocampus in monkeys
            Delayed matching-to-sample test: impaired
            Delayed nonmatching-to-sample test: impaired
            Minor procedural changes: variable results
    The hippocampus and spatial memory
        Rats: hippocampal neurons tuned to spatial locations
        London taxi drivers: hippocampus activated by answering spatial questions

Damage to the hippocampus in rats
    Radial maze: forget which arms they already tried
    Morris search task: forget location of platform
Closely related species that differ in spatial memory
    Clark's nutcracker: most dependent on buried food
        Largest hippocampus
        Best performance on spatial tasks
    Pinyon jays: moderately dependent on buried food
        Second largest hippocampus
        Second best performance on spatial tasks
    Scrub jay and Mexican jay: least dependent on buried food
        Smallest hippocampus
        Worst performance on spatial tasks
Some parts of hippocampus: nonspatial aspects of task
The hippocampus and configural learning
    Configural learning: meaning of a stimulus depends on other stimuli
    Hippocampal damage: impaired performance
        Complicated nonconfigural learning: also impaired
The hippocampus and binding memories
    Input from secondary and tertiary areas of sensory cortex
    Output to diverse areas
    Hippocampus: holds together sites that constitute memory

4. Other types of brain damage and amnesia
Korsakoff's syndrome and other prefrontal damage
    Wernicke-Korsakoff syndrome
    Thiamine deficiency
        Chronic alcoholics
    Widespread loss of neurons, especially in:
        Mamillary bodies of hypothalamus and
        Dorsomedial thalamus (projects to prefrontal cortex)
    Both anterograde and retrograde amnesia, apathy, confusion
    Better implicit than explicit memory
        Priming
    Poor recall of temporal order of events
    Confabulation
Alzheimer's disease
    Memory loss, confusion, depression, restlessness, hallucinations, delusions, sleeplessness,
        loss of appetite
    Better procedural than declarative memory
    Better implicit than explicit memory
    Genetic and nongenetic causes
        Relationship to Down syndrome (3 copies of chromosome 21)
        Mutations on chromosome 14: 70% of early-onset Alzheimer's disease
        Mutations on chromosome 1: additional cases of early-onset disease
        Mutations on chromosome 19: late-onset disease
        Amyloid precursor protein $\rightarrow$ amyloid beta protein 40 ($A\beta_{40}$)
            Alzheimer's patients: amyloid beta protein 42 ($A\beta_{42}$, longer form, impairs
            function)
        Tau protein: part of intracellular support

Tangles: degenerating cell bodies

Plaques: degenerating axons and dendrites

Widespread atrophy

Entorhinal cortex: communicates with hippocampus

Loss of acetylcholine neurons in basal forebrain → impaired attention

Prevention or alleviation

Increase glucose → insulin secretion → enhance memory

Stimulate acetylcholine receptors

Block formation of $A\beta_{42}$

Antioxidants

"Vaccinate" with $A\beta_{42}$

PDAPP mouse: overproduce $A\beta_{42}$

Inject young mice with a little $A\beta_{42}$ → immune attack → no Alzheimer's

What amnesic patients teach us

Somewhat independent kinds of memory: dependent on different brain areas

5. Infant amnesia

Poor declarative memory for events early in life

Hippocampus slow to mature

Human version of Morris search task

Poorer performance of children less than seven years old

6. In closing: Different types of memory

"Overall intelligence" as measured by IQ tests: convenient fiction

Different abilities: different brain processes

Module 13.2 Storing Information in the Nervous System

1. Learning and the Hebbian synapse

Simultaneous pre- and postsynaptic activity → increased synaptic efficiency

2. Single-cell mechanisms of invertebrate behavior change

Aplysia as an experimental animal

Plasticity

Siphon, mantle, or gill withdrawal response

Habituation in Aplysia

Decreased ability of sensory neuron to activate motor neuron

Sensitization in Aplysia

Increase in response to mild stimuli after more intense stimuli

Facilitating interneuron

Serotonin (5-HT)

Presynaptic receptors → closing of potassium channels → prolonged action potential →
more transmitter release

Protein synthesis → long-term sensitization

3. Long-term potentiation in mammals (LTP)

Brief but rapid series of stimuli → increased responsiveness for minutes, days, or weeks

Characteristics

Specificity: only active synapses strengthened

Cooperativity: nearly simultaneous stimuli more effective than single stimuli

Associativity: pairing weak and strong inputs → enhanced later response to weaker one

Long term depression (LTD) in hippocampus and cerebellum
  LTD: prolonged decrease in response to input that was paired with other input at low
    frequency
Biochemical mechanisms
  AMPA glutamate receptors
    Open sodium channels
  NMDA glutamate receptors
    Magnesium blockade of ion channel
    Removal of magnesium by depolarization
    Sodium and calcium influx into postsynaptic neuron
    Calcium → activation of genes and many chemicals →
    Increase in later responsiveness to glutamate
      CaMKII (α-calcium-calmodulin-dependent protein kinase II) activation →
      AMPA receptor structure change → more responsive to glutamate
      NMDA receptors change into AMPA receptors
      New AMPA receptors or old ones moved to better location
      Dendrite: new branches
    Possible presynaptic changes
    NMDA receptors: establish, not maintain, LTP
LTP and behavior
  Modification of synapses during developmental critical period
  LTP first in hippocampus, then in cortex
  Mutation of gene that controls NMDA receptors → impaired LTP and spatial memory
  Genes that → extra NMDA receptors → better than normal memory
  Similar effects of drugs on LTP and on memory
  "Leaky" calcium channels in old age
Blind alleys and abandoned mines in research
  Wilder Penfield: suggestion that each neuron stores one memory
    "Memories" not accurate
  G. A. Horridge: report that decapitated cockroaches learn
    Slow learning and variable results
  James McConnell and others: transfer of memories by feeding or injecting "trained" RNA
    Variable results

4. In closing: The physiology of memory
    Complex behaviors: large interacting network
    Requirement of memory: record what we need to remember, not everything

SHORT-ANSWER QUESTIONS

Module 13.1 Learning, Memory, Amnesia, and Brain Functioning
1. *Localized representations of memory*
    a. Describe the relationships among the conditioned and unconditioned stimuli and the
        unconditioned and conditioned responses in classical conditioning.

b. Who discovered classical conditioning? What were the conditioned and unconditioned stimuli in his experiments? What was the unconditioned, and eventually the conditioned, response?

c. What is the fundamental difference between classical and operant conditioning? Define reinforcement and punishment in terms of operant conditioning.

d. Why is bird-song learning difficult to classify?

e. What is an engram? What did Lashley discover in his search for the engram?

f. What two assumptions did Lashley make, that later investigators rejected?

g. What brain area was found by Richard F. Thompson to be important for classical conditioning of the eye-blink response in rabbits?

h. What area was important for the expression of the motor response, but not for the initial conditioning?

i. Which areas showed increased activity on PET scans during eye-blink conditioning in humans?

2. *Types of memory*
    a. Define short-term memory and long-term memory.

    b. How did Donald Hebb explain consolidation?

    c. In what two ways do exciting experiences enhance memory consolidation?

    d. What brain areas are stimulated by the amygdala after an emotional experience? What is the effect of long term or excessive stress?

e. What is working memory? What are its three hypothesized components?

f.. What brain area seems to be especially important for working memory? What is a common test of working memory?

3. *The hippocampus and amnesia*
    a. Why was H. M.'s hippocampus removed bilaterally? How successful was this treatment at relieving epilepsy? What were the other effects of the surgery?

    b. What is the difference between retrograde and anterograde amnesia? Which is more evident in H. M.?

    c. Distinguish between declarative and procedural memory. Which is impaired in H. M.?

    d. Distinguish between explicit memory and implicit memory.

e. What is priming? Is it used to test explicit or implicit memory?

f. What seems to be the major function of the hippocampus? Why can we conclude that memories are not stored in the hippocampus itself? Where are well-consolidated memories stored?

g. For what three types of memory is the hippocampus hypothesized to be important?

h. Describe the delayed matching-to-sample and delayed nonmatching-to-sample tasks. Which type of memory is tested by these tasks?

i. Under what conditions does hippocampal damage impair performance on matching- or nonmatching-to-sample tasks? What other brain area is important for these tasks?

j.   What type of memory is tested by the radial maze and the Morris search task? What two kinds of errors can rats make in the radial maze? Which type of error do rats make after damage to the hippocampus?

k.   Describe the Morris search task. What deficits on this task are seen in hippocampally damaged rats?

l.   Describe the relationship between birds' dependence on finding previously hidden food and the size of their hippocampus.

m.   What is configural learning? What is one explanation for why hippocampal damage impairs configural learning?

n.   What is Larry Squire's view of the role of the hippocampus in memory? From what kinds of brain areas does the hippocampus receive input?

4. *Other types of brain damage and amnesia*
    a. What is the immediate cause of Korsakoff's syndrome? What are its symptoms? In what group of people does it usually occur?

    b. Which brain areas show neuronal loss in Korsakoff's syndrome?

    c. Describe the symptoms of Korsakoff's syndrome in terms of anterograde vs. retrograde amnesia and explicit vs. implicit memory. What is one test for implicit memory?

    d. What symptom do Korsakoff's patients have in common with patients with frontal-lobe damage? What additional symptom do Korsakoff's patients have?

    e. Describe the symptoms of Alzheimer's disease.

f.   Why are some cases of Alzheimer's disease thought to be related to a gene on chromosome 21? How does the chromosomal abnormality differ from that in Down syndrome?

g.   What other chromosomes contain genes that have been linked to early-onset Alzheimer's disease? To late-onset Alzheimer's disease?

h.   What is amyloid precursor protein? What are the two forms of amyloid beta protein? Which form is implicated in the formation of amyloid deposits?

i.   What other protein is implicated in Alzheimer's disease? What is its normal function?

j.   Which brain areas are atrophied in Alzheimer's disease? Basal forebrain neurons containing which neurotransmitter degenerate? What physical signs are present in areas of atrophy?

k. What are two temporary means of alleviating Alzheimer's disease? What dietary factors may guard against Alzheimer's disease?

l. Describe the research on PDAPP mice.

m. What have we learned about memory from amnesic patients?

5. *Infant amnesia*
    a. What is infant amnesia? Is there greater loss of declarative or procedural memories?

    b. Give one physiological explanation for infant amnesia.

    c. What was the major finding of an experiment using a human version of the Morris search task?

Module 13.2 Storing Information in the Nervous System

1. *Learning and the Hebbian synapse*
    a.   What is a Hebbian synapse? How is it related to classical conditioning?

2. *Single-cell mechanisms of invertebrate behavior change*
    a.   Why should anyone be interested in the cellular mechanisms of habituation or sensitization in the lowly Aplysia?

    b.   What possible mechanisms of habituation were ruled out? What mechanism does seem to account for habituation in Aplysia?

    c.   How is sensitization produced experimentally in Aplysia?

    d.   Describe the cellular events that explain sensitization in Aplysia. How does a decrease in potassium outflow increase transmitter release?

e. How does long-term sensitization differ from the short-term variety?

3. *Long-term potentiation in mammals*
    a. How is long-term potentiation (LTP) produced? How long does it last? In what brain area was it first discovered?

    b. What is meant by specificity? Cooperativity? Associativity?

    c. What is long term depression (LTD)? Where has it been observed?

    d. Which transmitter stimulates both NMDA and AMPA receptors? Why must AMPA receptors be stimulated, in addition to NMDA receptors, in order to produce LTP?

    e. Describe the sequence of events that follows the successful activation of NMDA receptors.

f. What is CaMKII?

g. List four changes that help produce LTP.

h. Are NMDA receptors important for the establishment or maintenance of LTP?

i. What type of developmental brain plasticity also depends on stimulation of NMDA receptors?

j. What kinds of experiments have shown the relevance of NMDA receptors for establishing memories in intact organisms?

k. How may "leaky" calcium channels impair memory in aged mammals?

POSTTEST

Multiple-Choice Questions

1. In classical conditioning
   a. the meat used by Pavlov was the conditioned stimulus.
   b. the learner's behavior controls the presentation of reinforcements and punishments.
   c. a stimulus comes to elicit a response that may be similar to the response elicited by another stimulus.
   d. bird-song learning can be fully explained in terms of CS and UCS.

2. Ivan Pavlov believed that learning occurs when
   a. the connection between the CS center and the UCS center is strengthened.
   b. the connection between the CS center and the CR center is strengthened.
   c. the CS center takes over the UCS center's ability to elicit a UCR.
   d. cells in the UCS center degenerate and cells in the CS center branch diffusely.

3. Lashley successfully demonstrated that
   a. the lateral interpositus nucleus is the site of all engrams.
   b. all learning takes place in the cerebral cortex.
   c. the same neural mechanisms underlie all types of learning.
   d. none of the above.

4. The lateral interpositus nucleus of the cerebellum
   a. is important for the motor expression of eye-blink conditioning in rabbits, but not the actual conditioning.
   b. is important for the actual conditioning of the eyelid response.
   c. is more important for explicit than implicit memory formation.
   d. is an area that shows a great deal of damage in Korsakoff's syndrome.

5. Hebb's distinction between short-term and long-term memory
   a. is supported by data showing that certain kinds of brain damage can disrupt formation of new long-term memories, despite normal short-term, memory.
   b. is supported by data showing that short-term memories are stored in the hippocampus and long-term memories are stored in the lateral interpositus nucleus of the cerebellum.
   c. has been rejected by researchers because short-term and long-term memory merge so gradually that they are considered to be a single type of memory.
   d. has recently been attributed to Pavlov, instead of Hebb.

6. Experiments on consolidation have shown that
   a. the most important factor promoting consolidation is the amount of time allowed for reverberating circuits to operate.
   b. emotional stimuli activate the amygdala, which in turn stimulates the hippocampus and cerebral cortex, which are both important for memory storage.
   c. prolonged high elevations of cortisol levels are even more effective than brief moderate elevations for promoting memory storage.
   d. all of the above are true.

275

7. Epinephrine in the blood facilitates memory consolidation by
    a. causing circuits to reverberate.
    b. crossing the blood-brain barrier and activating epinephrine synapses in the hippocampus.
    c. stimulating the vagus nerve, which activates neurons in the brain stem, which in turn stimulates the amygdala.
    d. being converted into norepinephrine and then crossing the blood-brain barrier to activate synapses.

8. Working memory consists of
    a. a phonological loop.
    b. a visuospatial sketchpad.
    c. a central executive.
    d. all of the above.

9. The delayed response task for monkeys was used to show that
    a. visual memories are stored in primary visual cortex.
    b. each location of the to-be-remembered light activated a different group of cells in the prefrontal cortex.
    c. cells in the prefrontal cortex are more important for initiating movement than for storing information about the stimulus.
    d. damage to the prefrontal cortex produced severe deficits on tasks that required eye movements without delay, as well as with delay.

10. H. M.
    a. had his hippocampus removed because of his uncontrollable violence.
    b. acquired severe epilepsy as a result of the surgery.
    c. has a terrific memory for numbers but can learn no new skills.
    d. has more severe problems with declarative than with procedural memory.

11. Which of the following statements applies to H. M.?
    a. He has more severe anterograde than retrograde amnesia.
    b. He has more trouble with implicit than with explicit memory.
    c. His deficits show conclusively that the hippocampus is the storage site for all factual memories.
    d. All of the above are true.

12. Your memory of what you had for dinner last night is an example of
    a. explicit memory.
    b. implicit memory.
    c. procedural memory.
    d. short-term memory.

13. Priming is useful for
    a. producing memory consolidation.
    b. testing short-term memory.
    c. testing implicit memory.
    d. testing explicit memory.

14. Damage to the hippocampus produces impairment on tasks requiring
    a. declarative, explicit memory.
    b. configural learning and complicated nonconfigural learning.
    c. spatial memory.
    d. all of the above.

15. Damage to the hippocampus results in
    a. rats going down a never-correct arm of the radial maze.
    b. rats forgetting which arms they have already explored.
    c. inability to climb onto a platform in the Morris search task because of motor impairment.
    d. monkeys that cannot choose a nonmatching stimulus under any conditions.

16. Which of the following is true?
    a. Clark's nutcracker birds are very dependent on previously hidden food and have a large hippocampus.
    b. Mexican jays are also dependent on previously hidden food, but have a small hippocampus.
    c. The use of color in solving problems is a better predictor of hippocampal size than is dependence on previously hidden food.
    d. Hippocampal damage impairs performance on all tasks that use spatial memory, but does not impair any other tasks.

17. Korsakoff's syndrome
    a. occurs because alcohol dissolves proteins in the brain, thereby shrinking presynaptic endings.
    b. is caused by prolonged thiamine deficiency.
    c. results from damage primarily to the hippocampus.
    d. all of the above.

18. Patients with Korsakoff's syndrome
    a. have damage in the mamillary bodies of the hypothalamus and the dorsomedial nucleus of the thalamus, which projects to prefrontal cortex.
    b. have symptoms somewhat similar to those of patients with damage to the prefrontal cortex.
    c. have better implicit memory than explicit memory.
    d. all of the above.

19. Alzheimer's disease
    a. results from three copies of chromosome 21.
    b. results from a long history of excessive alcohol consumption.
    c. is characterized by widespread atrophy of the cerebral cortex (especially the entorhinal cortex), the hippocampus, and neurons that release acetylcholine.
    d. is characterized by severe atrophy of the prefrontal cortex, amygdala, and neurons that release enkephalins, but sparing of the rest of the brain.

20. Patients with Alzheimer's disease
    a. have plaques and tangles in damaged areas of their brains.
    b. unlike H. M. and Korsakoff's patients, have more problems with implicit than explicit memory.
    c. have a nearly 100% probability of passing the disease on to their offspring.
    d. all of the above.

21. Which of the following is true concerning Alzheimer's disease?
    a. Amyloid precursor protein can be cleaved to produce amyloid beta protein 42 ($A\beta_{42}$), which accumulates in the brain and impairs the function of neurons and glia cells.
    b. An abnormal form of the tau protein, which forms part of the intracellular support structure in neurons, also accumulates in Alzheimer's patients.
    c. Genes on chromosomes 21, 14, 1, and 19 all lead to accumulation of amyloid deposits in the brain.
    d. All of the above are true.

22. Techniques for alleviating or preventing Alzheimer's disease include
    a. maintaining low levels of blood glucose, in order to decrease levels of insulin, which is destructive of neurons.
    b. eating a diet rich in antioxidants.
    c. giving drugs that block acetylcholine receptors or decrease acetylcholine release.
    d. injecting large amounts of $A\beta_{42}$ into the brains of aging people.

23. Infant amnesia
    a. shows a greater loss of implicit than explicit memories.
    b. may result from low levels of blood glucose.
    c. may result from the slow development of the hippocampus.
    d. is characterized by symptoms that are essentially the opposite of those seen in old age.

24. Donald Hebb proposed that
    a. a cellular basis of memory is the strengthening of synapses by simultaneous activity in the pre- and postsynaptic neurons.
    b. having two different axons stimulating a given dendrite at the same time is confusing to the dendrite and leads to long-term depression.
    c. short-term and long-term memory are the same thing.
    d. Hebbian synapses can explain operant, but not classical, conditioning.

25. Aplysia are studied because
    a. they are the intellectual giants of the ocean.
    b. they have simple nervous systems with large neurons that are virtually identical among individuals.
    c. they have the most complex brains of all invertebrates.
    d. we can automatically infer the principles of learning in complex vertebrates.

26. Habituation in Aplysia is the result of
    a. a decrease in the firing rate of a facilitating interneuron.
    b. a decrease in the firing rate of the sensory neuron.
    c. a change in the synapse between the sensory neuron and the motor neuron.
    d. muscle fatigue.

27. The mechanism mediating sensitization in Aplysia includes
    a. the release of dopamine from the sensory neuron onto the facilitating interneuron.
    b. the release of serotonin by the sensory neuron onto the motor neuron.
    c. release of serotonin by the facilitating interneuron onto the presynaptic terminals of sensory neurons, resulting in decreased outflow of potassium in the sensory neurons and a resulting prolongation of transmitter release.
    d. synthesis of new proteins in short-term, but not long-term sensitization.

28. Long-term potentiation (LTP)
    a. was first discovered in Aplysia.
    b. results from increased inflow of magnesium through AMPA receptors.
    c. requires depolarization via NMDA receptors in order to allow calcium outflow through AMPA receptors.
    d. requires depolarization via AMPA receptors in order to dislodge magnesium ions from NMDA receptors.

29. LTP
    a. is very powerful but lasts only a few seconds.
    b. may result from structural changes in AMPA receptors, increased numbers of AMPA receptors, and/or increased dendritic branching.
    c. depends on NMDA receptors for its maintenance, but not for its establishment.
    d. may result from decreased sensitivity of the postsynaptic cell to the inhibitory transmitter glutamate.

30. Which of the following is true?
    a. Modification of synapses during the critical period in early development may depend on NMDA receptors.
    b. LTP occurs first in the entorhinal cortex and then in the hippocampus.
    c. Cooperativity refers to the strengthening of all synapses throughout an area of the brain by the activity of only one or two of them.
    d. A problem in aged mammals is the near total closing down of calcium channels, so that NMDA receptors can no longer let calcium flow in.

Answers to Multiple-Choice Questions

1. c	6. b	11. a	16. a	21. d	26. c
2. a	7. c	12. a	17. b	22. b	27. c
3. d	8. d	13. c	18. d	23. c	28. d
4. b	9. b	14. d	19. c	24. a	29. b
5. a	10. d	15. b	20. a	25. b	30. a

Emotions and Memories

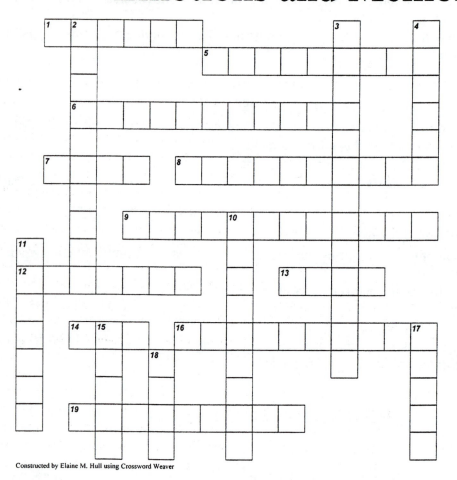

Constructed by Elaine M. Hull using Crossword Weaver

ACROSS

1 Researcher who studied type of learning in 19 Across

5 Transmitter that may inhibit aggressiveness

6 Brain structure that regulates cortisol and memory formation

7 5-____: Major metabolite of serotonin, a measure of serotonin turnover (abbr.)

8 Site of neurons in interpositus nucleus that mediate eyeblink conditioning

9 Nucleus in hypothalamus on which testosterone acts to promote aggression

12 Researcher who searched for the engram

13 Hormone from anterior pituitary that stimulates the adrenal cortex (abbr.)

14 Endozapine that increases anxiety (abbr.)

16 Syndrome found in alcoholics in which memory consolidation is impaired

19 Type of conditioning based on stimulus-stimulus associations

DOWN

2 Disease with symptoms of impaired memory formation, plaques and tangles, and general neural degeneration

3 Formation of long-term memories

4 Anatomical locus of memory, studied by researcher in 12 Across

10 Type of memory that does not change from time to time

11 Nutrient that promotes memory formation

15 Type of leukocyte that produces antibodies

17 Pioneed or stress research

18 Disorder produced by trauma, characterized by nightmares, avoidance, and flashbacks (abbr.)

280

14

LATERALIZATION AND LANGUAGE

INTRODUCTION

Each hemisphere of the brain receives sensory input primarily from the opposite side of the body and controls motor output to that side as well. The hemispheres are connected by a large bundle of fibers, the corpus callosum, as well as several smaller bundles. In humans, the eyes are connected with the brain in such a way that the left half of each retina supplies input to the left hemisphere, and vice versa. Furthermore, the left half of each retina receives input from the right half of the visual field. Therefore, the right half of the visual field projects to the left hemisphere, and vice versa. The auditory system projects bilaterally, although the projection to the opposite side is stronger. This relationship has allowed researchers to test the roles of the two hemispheres in people whose corpus callosum had been severed in order to relieve epilepsy. Such studies have shown that the left hemisphere is specialized for language, analytic music perception, and details, whereas the right hemisphere is particularly adept at emotional expression and perception, complex spatial problems, music perception by nonmusicians, and overall patterns. In addition, happy emotions are more localized in the left hemisphere, and fear and anger, in the right. Split-brain people sometimes seem to have two "selves" occupying the same body. In these people each half of the brain processes information and solves problems more or less independently of the other, although cooperation can be learned, thanks to enhanced function of subcortical connections. Even in intact people, evidence for hemispheric specialization can be seen. One possible basis for the lateralization of language functions in the left hemisphere is that in 65 percent of people a portion of the left temporal lobe, the planum temporale, is larger on the left side than on the right. The size difference is apparent even shortly after birth, and is correlated with performance on language tests.

The corpus callosum matures gradually, and experience determines the survival of the axons that make the best functional connections through the corpus callosum. People born without a corpus callosum are different from those who had split-brain surgery in adulthood. They can verbally describe sensory input from either hand and from either visual field. They may rely on greater development of the anterior commissure and hippocampal commissure to convey information from one hemisphere to the other. In addition, each hemisphere develops connections to both sides of the body. About 10% of people are either left-handed or ambidextrous; most of them have mixed hemispheric control of speech, though the left is usually dominant. The corpus callosum is thicker in left-handers, especially those with left hemisphere dominance for speech. Although there may be hemisphere specialization, almost all tasks require cooperation by both hemispheres.

Because new features evolve from older ones that may have served similar functions, researchers have studied the language abilities of our nearest relatives, the chimpanzees. A number of chimpanzees have been taught to communicate with their trainers, a computer, or each other using various nonspoken language systems. However, even after years of training, their linguistic abilities fall far short of those of young children. Bonobos (Pan paniscus, or pygmy chimpanzees) have shown the most impressive linguistic abilities among our primate relatives. They have learned by imitation, have used words to describe objects (as opposed to making a request) or to refer to a past event, and have created original sentences. In addition, some have learned to understand spoken English sentences. Dolphins and parrots also show some language-like abilities. Studies of nonhuman language abilities may provide insights about how best to teach language to brain-damaged or autistic people; they may also stimulate consideration of the unique versus shared abilities of humans and of the nature of language. Language may have evolved as a by-product of larger brains and increasing intelligence. However, neither absolute brain size nor brain to body ratio provides a reliable prediction of intelligence. Furthermore, some people with normal brains and intelligence have severely impaired language. Conversely, people with Williams syndrome have severe mental retardation and abnormally developed brains, but nearly normal language, social, and musical abilities. On some tests they even have better than average abilities. An alternative view is that language arose as an extra brain module. This view is supported by the ease with which children develop language. Indeed, if children do not learn some language when they are young, they will always be disadvantaged. However, much of the brain is involved in language processing, not just one or two new modules. Therefore, increasing intelligence may have occurred because of the growing importance of language for social interaction.

Paul Broca discovered that damage to an area of the left frontal lobe results in difficulties with language production and with the use of grammatical connectives and other closed-class grammatical forms. People with such damage can usually understand both written and spoken language better than they can produce it, although they do have difficulty understanding the closed class words that they have most trouble producing. Carl Wernicke, on the other hand, described a pattern of deficits almost the opposite of the pattern Broca discovered: poor language comprehension, anomia (difficulty finding the right word), but articulate (though frequently meaningless) speech. This syndrome results from destruction of an area in the left temporal lobe near the primary auditory cortex. PET scans and functional MRI studies in intact adults have shown that speaking increases activity in much of the left frontal, temporal, and parietal cortex and in parts of the left thalamus and basal ganglia. Reading aloud increases activity in Broca's and Wernicke's areas and surrounding areas, in addition to lesser increases in corresponding areas of the right hemisphere. Naming objects activated Wernicke's area and other areas, depending on the particular object.

Dyslexia, a reading disorder in otherwise normal people, may result from incomplete specialization of the hemispheres for language or from deficits in the magnocellular visual pathways. There are many kinds of dyslexia, which have different underlying causes. Some dyslexics' reading ability may be improved by focusing on one word at a time.

KEY TERMS AND CONCEPTS

Module 14.1 Lateralization of Function
1. Connections
        Corpus callosum
        Anterior commissure
        Hippocampal commisure
    Lateralization

2. Visual connections to the hemispheres
    Right visual field → left half of both retinas → left hemisphere (and vice versa)
        Optic chiasm
        Small vertical strip in center of retina → both hemispheres
    Both ears → both hemispheres
        Opposite side stronger

3. Cutting the corpus callosum
    Decreases frequency of epileptic seizures
    Epilepsy: repeated episodes of excessive neural activity
        Decreased release of GABA
        Generalized seizures: spread quickly over a large portion of the brain

Grand mal seizures: sudden repetitive jerking movements followed by exhaustion
Petit mal seizures (absence seizures): unresponsive for 15 – 20 seconds
Partial seizures: begin in a focus, spread to nearby areas
Partial seizure with complex symptomatology (temporal lobe, or psychomotor, seizure)
Slight movements, complex psychological states
Antiepileptic drugs
Block sodium flow across membrane
Enhance effects of GABA
Split-brain people or animals
Independent control of two sides of body
Abnormal behavior only if input is restricted to one side
Left hemisphere: speech
Methods 14.1: Testing hemispheric dominance for speech
Wada test: sodium amytal injected into carotid artery on one side of head
Dichotic listening task: earphones → different words to the two ears at same time
Split hemispheres: competition and cooperation
Hands do competing tasks
Learning to cooperate
Use of subcortical connections
Verbal task: one word to each hemisphere
Right hand drew input to left hemisphere
Left hand drew two pictures, but not combined concept
The right hemisphere
Understands simple speech
Emotional content of speech and facial expression, humor, and sarcasm
Left hemisphere: happiness
Right hemisphere: fear and anger
Complex visual patterns, spatial relationships
Stronger magnocellular visual projection to right hemisphere
Stronger parvocellular visual projection to left hemisphere
"Big picture" of language, as well as vision
Left hemisphere: details
Music perception by nonmusicians
Left: music perception by musicians
"Tonal" languages
Native speaker: left hemisphere
English speaker: both hemispheres
Hemispheric specializations in intact brains
Small differences
Difficulty doing two things at once when both depend on same hemisphere

4. Development of lateralization and handedness
Anatomical differences between the hemispheres
Innate tendency to attend to language sounds
Planum temporale: larger in left hemisphere
Left to right ratio: correlation with language skills
Less ability to acquire language after early damage to left than to right
Maturation of the corpus callosum
Survival of functional connections
Matures between ages 3 and 5

Development without a corpus callosum
- Each hemisphere: connections to both sides of body
- Anterior commissure
- Hippocampal commissure
- Posterior commissure

Handedness and language dominance
- 10% of people: left-handed or ambidextrous
- 99% of right-handed: left hemisphere for speech
- Most left-handers: left hemisphere for speech, though some mixed control
- Left-handers: thicker corpus callosum

5. Avoiding overstatements
   Complicated tasks: both hemispheres

Module 14.2 Evolution and Physiology of Language
1. Nonhuman precursors to language
   Productivity: ability to produce new signals to represent new ideas
   Common chimpanzees
   - Inability to speak
   - Ability to use visual symbols
   - Few original sentences
   - Symbols used to request, not describe
   - Limited comprehension of others' communications

   Bonobos
   - Pan paniscus (pygmy chimpanzees)
   - Language ability of 2- to 2 ½-year-old child
   - Understand more than they produce
   - Name and describe without request
   - Request what they do not see
   - Refer to past
   - Creative requests
   - Early training by observation and imitation

   Nonprimates
   - Dolphins
     - Respond to new combinations of words, if meaningful
   - Parrots
     - Speak, name, count, form concepts

   Implications
   - How to teach brain-damaged or autistic people
   - Difficulty of defining language

2. How did humans evolve language?
   Language as a product of overall intelligence
   - First problem: unclear relationship between brain and intelligence
     - Brain-to-body ratio
       - Humans' not highest
       - The chihuahua problem
   - Second problem: people with full-sized brains and impaired language
   - Third problem: Williams syndrome

Mental retardation, skillful use of language
Genes deleted from chromosome 7
Abnormal development of posterior cerebral cortex, some subcortical areas
Severe impairment in skills of living
Normal abilities:
    Interpretation of facial expressions
    Social behavior
    Music
- Language: variable, from near normal to spectacular
    Slow development
    Sometimes odd grammar
Language as a special module
    Language acquisition device
    Ease of language development in most children
    Poverty of the stimulus argument:
        Children hear few examples of some grammatical structures they acquire
        But: thousands of languages; can't be born knowing all
    Intelligence as a byproduct of language
Is there a critical period for language learning?
    Adults: better at memorizing vocabulary
    Children: better at pronunciation and unfamiliar grammar
    No age cutoff
    Second language: if mastered, same language areas as first language
    Some language: the earlier the better

3. Effects of brain damage on language
    Broca's aphasia
        Broca's area: small part of left frontal cortex, near motor cortex
            Serious deficits only with more extensive damage
        Nonfluent aphasia: deficits in production and comprehension if meaning is difficult
        Difficulty in language production
            Articulation, writing, and gestures
            Omission of closed-class grammatical forms (prepositions, conjunctions, etc.)
            Ability to speak open-class forms (nouns and verbs)
        Problems comprehending grammatical words and devices
            Still use normal word order for their language
    Wernicke's aphasia
        Wernicke's area: near auditory cortex
        Fluent aphasia
        Articulate speech
        Anomia: difficulty finding the right word
        Poor language comprehension, especially nouns and verbs
    Beyond Broca and Wernicke
        PET scan and functional MRI studies of language processing
            Speaking: left frontal, temporal, and parietal cortex, thalamus, basal ganglia
            Reading aloud: Broca's and Wernicke's areas, surrounding areas
                Lesser increases in corresponding areas of right hemisphere
                Difficulty of language: determines extent of activation
            Naming object: Wernicke's area and other areas, depending on objects
            Stating use for object: motor or premotor frontal cortex

Reorganization of much of brain for language
Phrenology: relating skull anatomy to behavioral capacities

4. Dyslexia
    Specific impairment of reading
        Adequate vision and other academic skills
    No single abnormality
    Relatively unresponsive magnocellular system
    -   Impaired perception of visual motion
    Altered organization of left and right hemispheres
        More bilaterally symmetrical
    Perceptual abnormalities in several modalities
    Differences in attention or strategy
        Combinations of letters

SHORT-ANSWER QUESTIONS

Module 14.1 Lateralization of Function and the Corpus Callosum
1. *Visual connections to the hemispheres*
    a. To which hemisphere(s) does the right visual field project? To which hemisphere(s) does the right half of both retinas project? To which hemisphere(s) does the right eye project?

    b. To which hemisphere(s) does the right ear project?

2. *Cutting the corpus callosum*
    a. What is the corpus callosum? Why is it sometimes severed in cases of severe epilepsy? What are the effects of such an operation on overall intelligence, motivation, and gross motor coordination?

b. What have we learned from split-brain humans concerning specialization of the two hemispheres? Which tasks are best accomplished by the left hemisphere?

c. What is the basis for learned cooperation between the hemispheres in split-brain people?

d. What did the split-brain person draw with his right hand, when two different words were flashed to his right and left visual fields? What did he sometimes draw with his left hand? Could he combine information from his right and left visual fields to form a new concept?

e. Which functions are best performed by the right hemisphere?

f. What is one task that can show hemispheric specialization in intact people? How large are the hemispheric differences in intact people?

3. *Development of lateralization and handedness*
   a. What is the planum temporale and what is its significance for language?

   b. How early is the size difference in the left vs. right planum temporale apparent?

   c. What happens to the language ability of children who suffer damage to their left hemisphere in infancy?

   d. Compare the ability of 3-year-olds and of 5-year-olds to discriminate fabrics with either one hand or different hands. What can we infer from this about the development of the corpus callosum?

   e. In what ways are people who never had a corpus callosum different from split-brain people?

f. Which other major axonal connections between the two hemispheres may compensate for the lack of a corpus callosum in people born without one?

g. What percentage of right-handed people have left-hemisphere dominance for language? Describe the control of language in left-handed people.

h. Is the corpus callosum thicker in right- or left-handed people? What is the functional correlate of this increased thickness?

i. How valid is the assumption that a given individual relies consistently on one hemisphere or the other?

Module 14.2 Evolution and Physiology of Language

1. *Nonhuman precursors of language*
    a. What are some differences between the abilities of common chimpanzees and of humans to use symbols?

b. What was unusual about the ability of some bonobos to learn language?

c. In what ways do bonobos resemble humans more than common chimpanzees in language abilities?

d. What are three possible explanations for why bonobos have been more successful than other chimps at learning language?

e. What evidence is there that nonprimate species can learn language?

2. *How did humans evolve language?*
   a. Briefly discuss the proposal that our language may have developed as a by-product of overall intelligence.

b. How well do the correlations between intelligence and brain size or between intelligence and brain-to-body ratio hold up? How is this a problem for the view that language evolved as a product of large brains and intelligence?

c. Describe the pattern of abilities and disabilities in the family with a genetic mutation that produces language deficits. How is this a problem for the view that language evolved as a product of large brains and intelligence?

d. Describe Williams syndrome. How does this relate to the evolution of language as a product of general intelligence?

e. What is the main argument for the hypothesis that language evolved as an extra brain module? What is a problem with that hypothesis?

f. What is an alternative hypothesis regarding the evolution of language?

g. Is there a critical period for language learning? What are some ways of testing this idea?

3. *Effects of brain damage on language*
   a. Where is Broca's area located?

   b. Describe the effects of damage to Broca's area. What are closed-class words?

   c. Locate Wernicke's area.

   d. Contrast the effects of damage to Wernicke's area with those of damage to Broca's area.

   e. What information about language processing has been gained from PET scans and functional MRI studies?

f.   What is our current understanding of the brain modules that underlie language?

4. *Dyslexia*
   a.   What is dyslexia? How consistent are its symptoms?

   b.   What are two possible biological causes of dyslexia?

   c.   What is one method of improving the ability of dyslexics to read?

POSTTEST

Multiple-Choice Questions

1. Severing the corpus callosum
   a.   usually destroys language abilities.
   b.   usually relieves the symptoms of epilepsy.
   c.   has provided evidence that linguistic abilities reside largely in the right hemisphere.
   d.   none of the above.

2. A person with a bisected brain
   a.   can draw pictures and arrange puzzle pieces better with the left hand than the right.
   b.   develops cooperation between the hemispheres because the corpus callosum grows back.
   c.   performs very poorly on intelligence tests.
   d.   all of the above.

3. The only way to present visual input to only the right hemisphere of a split-brain person is to
    a.   flash it briefly to the left eye while the right eye is closed.
    b.   flash it briefly to the right eye while the left eye is closed.
    c.   flash it briefly in the left visual field while the person is looking straight ahead.
    d.   flash it briefly in the right visual field while the person is looking straight ahead.

4. A split-brain person who sees a picture of an object in his left visual field usually
    a.   will be able both to point to the correct object with his left hand and to name it.
    b.   will not be able to pick out the object or to name it.
    c.   will be able to pick it out with his left hand, but will not be able to name it.
    d.   will be able to name it but not pick it out.

5. A split-brain person sees this picture flashed briefly on a screen while looking at a point in the middle of the screen. He reports seeing
    a.   a woman.
    b.   a bearded man.
    c.   a meaningless hodge podge of lines, since the spatial perception center has been damaged.
    d.   one badly constructed face of two different people.

6. People with right-hemisphere damage
    a.   have trouble producing and understanding emotional facial expressions.
    b.   have trouble speaking with emotional expression and understanding others' vocal emotional expression.
    c.   have trouble with some complex visual and spatial tasks.
    d.   all of the above.

7. Hemispheric specialization in intact people
    a.   has not been demonstrated.
    b.   can be shown but is small and inconsistent.
    c.   is consistent with that observed in split-brain people but is even more dramatic.
    d.   is the reverse of specialization in split-brain people.

8. Which of the following is true of the planum temporale?
    a.   Children with the biggest ratio of left to right planum temporale performed best on language tests.
    b.   It is larger in the right than in the left hemisphere for almost everyone.
    c.   It is equal in size in the two hemispheres at birth, indicating that maturation of language causes the size difference in adults.
    d.   All of the above are true.

9. What did Galin et al. discover when they asked 3-year-old and 5-year-old children to discriminate two fabrics?
    a.   The 3-year-olds were better than the 5-year-olds.
    b.   All children made fewer errors with their right hands than with their left.
    c.   All children made 90 percent more errors using different hands than when using the same hand.
    d.   Three-year-olds made 90 percent more errors using different hands than using the same hand, but 5-year-olds did equally well with one hand or two.

10. People who never had a corpus callosum
    a. are just like split-brain patients.
    b. can read words in either visual field and name objects that they touch with either hand.
    c. are especially fast at tasks requiring coordination of both hands.
    d. all of the above.

11. Which of the following is true of handedness and language dominance?
    a. Humans are the only species that show an arm preference.
    b. Most left-handed people have language dominance in the right hemisphere.
    c. Right-handers have a thicker corpus callosum.
    d. Most left-handed people have a mixture of left- and right-hemisphere control of speech, but dominance by the left side.

12. Productivity
    a. refers to the ability to produce new language signals to represent new ideas.
    b. is a characteristic of communication systems of most mammals.
    c. refers to the ability to translate one signal into another.
    d. is only a means of increasing ones income, and has nothing to do with language.

13. Ordinary chimpanzees
    a. frequently use symbols in new, original combinations.
    b. frequently use symbols to describe scenes and events.
    c. have a social order much like that of humans.
    d. use symbols almost always to request, only rarely to describe.

14. Bonobos
    a. are unable to put symbols together in new ways to express new meanings.
    b. use symbols only to request objects.
    c. can understand spoken English sentences.
    d. have learned to speak English fluently.

15. Which of the following is a problem with the theory that human language evolved as a product of overall intelligence and larger brains?
    a. There is not a clear relationship between either overall brain size or brain-to-body ratio and intelligence.
    b. Some people have full-sized brains and normal overall intelligence, but have impaired language.
    c. Some people are severely retarded and have abnormal brain development, but have near normal language ability.
    d. All of the above are true.

16. People with Williams syndrome
    a. have severe difficulties with even simple grammatical rules.
    b. have good language abilities, but are retarded in nonlinguistic function.
    c. can draw beautifully, but cannot write.
    d. have almost total loss of Wernicke's area.

17. A patient has great difficulty in articulating words and a tendency to omit endings and abstract words, but less difficulty comprehending spoken and written words. The patient probably has damage in
    a. Broca's area.
    b. Wernicke's area.
    c. the corpus callosum.
    d. primary motor cortex controlling muscles of articulation.

18. A second patient has difficulty naming objects and understanding both spoken and written language; speech is fluent but not very meaningful. You suspect that the patient has damage in
    a. Broca's area.
    b. Wernicke's area.
    c. the anterior commissure and hippocampal commisure.
    d. left visual cortex and posterior corpus callosum.

19. PET scans and functional MRI studies of intact humans showed that
    a. speaking increased activity only in Broca's area.
    b. reading a sentence aloud activated only primary visual cortex and Broca's area.
    c. naming objects activated the temporal lobe in the general area of Wernicke's area, as well as other areas, depending on the specific object named.
    d. all of the above.

20. Dyslexic people
    a. all have very similar symptoms, and all of the symptoms are limited to difficulties in visual perception.
    b. are sometimes helped by focusing on whole paragraphs at a time, rather than reading one word at a time.
    c. are more likely than normal readers to have a bilaterally symmetrical cerebral cortex, larger language-related areas in the right hemisphere than in the left, or relatively unresponsive magnocellular visual pathways.
    d. all of the above.

Answers to Multiple-Choice Questions

1. b	6. d	11. d	16. b
2. a	7. b	12. a	17. a
3. c	8. a	13. d	18. b
4. c	9. d	14. c	19. c
5. a	10. b	15. d	20. c

Diagram

Label the following areas related to language processing: Broca's area, Wernicke's area, Sylvian or lateral fissure, visual cortex.

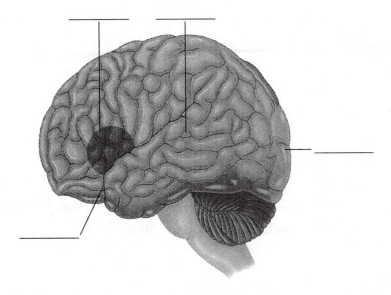

15

ALCOHOLISM, MOOD DISORDERS, AND SCHIZOPHRENIA

INTRODUCTION

Substance abuse is a maladaptive pattern of substance use leading to clinically significant impairment or distress. Alcohol is the most commonly abused drug. There are two major types of alcoholism. Type I alcoholism is less dependent on genetics, develops gradually, and is equally common in women and men. Type II alcholism has a stronger genetic basis, a rapid, early onset, and a great preponderance of men. Type II alcoholics have low serotonin turnover and a history of impulsivity and violence. Antabuse (disulfiram) is used to treat alcoholism; it inactivates acetaldehyde dehydrogenase, the enzyme that converts acetaldehyde (the toxic metabolic product of alcohol) to acetic acid (a source of energy). A person who drinks after taking Antabuse will become sick. However, many persons who use Antabuse never drink, and therefore never become ill; they use Antabuse as a daily reminder not to drink alcohol. Some factors that may mediate the genetic predisposition to alcoholism include less intoxication from small to moderate amounts of alcohol and greater than average relief from tension after drinking alcohol. Gambling and other habitual behaviors have much in common with alcoholism and other forms of substance abuse. Therefore, the addiction is not specific to the drug, but to the user.

Depression is typified by episodic sadness and helplessness, lack of energy, feelings of worthlessness, suicidal ideas, sleep disorders, and lack of pleasure. While the cause of depression is not fully understood, a number of possible factors have been identified. There may be a genetic component to depression, especially for severe, long-lasting depression beginning before age 30. However, no single gene has been found to have a strong link to depression. Women are at greater risk for depression than are men, although hormone levels are not strongly correlated with depression. Traumatic experiences may trigger depression in people who had already suffered some depression; however, they do not cause long-lasting depression in those who were not predisposed. Abnormal hemispheric dominance is sometimes associated with mood disorders. Happiness in normal people is associated with activation of the left prefrontal cortex, whereas depressed people have lower metabolic activity in the left, and increased activity in the right prefrontal cortex. Depression may occasionally be caused by exposure to a virus at some point in life. The Borna virus predisposes people to various psychiatric difficulties, perhaps including depression.

Most drugs that improve affective disorders act in one of three ways: blocking reuptake of monoamines (tricyclics), inhibiting monoamine oxidase (monoamine oxidase inhibitors, or MAOIs), or blocking reuptake of only serotonin (selective serotonin reuptake inhibitors, or SSRIs). Fluoxetine and other SSRIs have fewer side effects than do the tricyclics. A major problem with the transmitter hypothesis is that drugs affect transmitter levels almost immediately but exert noticeable effects on mood only after two or three weeks. Alterations of sensitivity of either autoreceptors or postsynaptic receptors may underlie drug effectiveness; however, the mechanism of action is not understood.

In addition to treatment by drug therapy, mood disorders are sometimes treated with electroconvulsive therapy (ECT), sleep alterations, or bright lights. ECT is particularly useful for patients who are unresponsive to antidepressants or who are suicidal and need rapid relief. Sleep-deprivation therapy is based on observations that depressed persons enter REM sleep much sooner than normal persons, as though their body temperature rhythms were phase-advanced. Earlier bedtimes may allow their activity cycles to become synchronized with their temperature cycles.

Depression can occur as either a unipolar or a bipolar disorder. A unipolar disorder is one in which an individual varies between normal mood and depression. Bipolar disorder, or manic-depressive disorder, is characterized by cycles of depression and mania. During their manic phase, people are restless, uninhibited, excitable, impulsive, self-confident, and apparently happy. Manic-depressive cycles may last a year or only a few days. Bipolar disorder has been linked to genes on several chromosomes; however, the specific genetic influences are not understood. Lithium is effective in treating manic-depressive disorder, and if taken regularly, prevents relapse into either mania or depression. It has complex effects on second-messenger systems and may stabilize fluctuating brain systems. Anticonvulsant drugs are another common treatment for bipolar disorder; they may work by blocking certain second messenger systems. Seasonal affective disorder (SAD) occurs mostly in areas where nights are long in the winter. SAD patients may have phase-delayed sleep and temperature cycles, unlike other depressed people. Exposure to bright lights is usually an effective treatment for SAD.

Schizophrenia is an illness in which emotions are "split off" from the intellect. Its positive symptoms include a psychotic cluster (hallucinations and delusions) and a disorganized cluster (inappropriate emotions, bizarre behaviors, and thought disorder). Negative symptoms include deficits in social interaction, emotional expression, speech, and working memory. Approximately 1.3 percent of the US population will suffer schizophrenia at some point in their lives; another 1 percent will have a milder schizoid condition. Schizophrenia is less common in the Third World, where fewer people live in crowded cities and where their extended families care patiently for schizophrenic relatives. The incidence of schizophrenia appears to be decreasing worldwide, for unknown reasons.

Much evidence favors a genetic predisposition to schizophrenia. It is more common in monozygotic than in dizygotic twins of schizophrenics and is more common in biological relatives than in adopted relatives of schizophrenics. Also, adopted paternal half-siblings of schizophrenics, who did not share even the prenatal environment of the affected child, have a much greater frequency of schizophrenia than is found in the overall population. Genetics cannot completely explain the occurrence of schizophrenia, however, since the concordance rate for monozygotic twins is not 100 percent. Also, there may be greater similarity in the prenatal environment in monozygotic than dizogotic twins, since they usually develop in a single placenta, and in dizygotic twins, compared to non-twin siblings. One confounding factor in many genetics studies is that biological parents of schizophrenics are more likely to engage in unhealthy habits, including smoking and drinking, that could impair prenatal development. Some studies have found genes with possible links to schizophrenia, but no strong link. Perhaps several genes on different chromosomes may predispose people to schizophrenia and may interact with environmental factors.

The neurodevelopmental hypothesis suggests that schizophrenia results from abnormal early development of the brain. Difficulties surrounding birth or during early or middle pregnancy have been linked to increased incidence of schizophrenia. These include complications during delivery, low birth weight, starvation during pregnancy, Rh incompatibility, and fevers due to viral infections during middle pregnancy. A number of minor brain abnormalities have been found in the brains of schizophrenics. Prefrontal and temporal cortex, hippocampus, and amygdala are smaller than usual; the ventricles are larger; the left hemisphere is smaller and less active. The area of most consistent abnormalities is the dorsal prefrontal cortex, one of the latest brain areas to mature. Schizophrenics have fewer synapses there and less activation during working memory tasks. In addition, neurons are smaller and less ordered. Because there is no evidence of brain damage in adulthood, it is thought that the brain abnormalities result from early developmental factors. Since the most affected brain areas are those that mature slowly, the behavioral problems may not emerge until long after the damage occurred.

Antipsychotic drugs, including phenothiazines (chlorpromazine: Thorazine) and butyrophenones (haloperidol: Haldol), block dopamine receptors. Furthermore, some symptoms of schizophrenia can be temporarily experienced by people who are stressed or who take large doses of drugs that stimulate dopamine synapses, although drug-induced hallucinations are typically visual, rather than auditory. On the basis of such observations it has been hypothesized that schizophrenia occurs because of excess activity at dopamine synapses. There are a number of problems with this hypothesis. First, neuroleptic drugs block dopamine receptors almost immediately, but take two or three weeks to produce therapeutic benefits. In addition, there is no consistent evidence of abnormally high levels of dopamine or its metabolites in schizophrenics, although there may be altered ratios of specific types of dopamine receptors. A second hypothesis is that there may be a deficit in glutamate activity, especially in the prefrontal cortex. Schizophrenics release less glutamate in prefrontal cortex and hippocampus than do other people, and glutamate has effects that are frequently opposite to those of dopamine. Therefore, any problem observed could be due either to insufficient glutamate or excess dopamine. Phencyclidine (PCP) inhibits NMDA glutamate receptors, produces both positive and negative symptoms similar to schizophrenia, and impairs prefrontal cortex function. It also produces little psychotic response in preadolescents and produces a long-lasting relapse in recovered schizophrenics. A drug that stimulates one type of metabotropic glutamate receptor blocks the behavioral effects of PCP in rats. Finally, the amino acid glycine stimulates a co-transmitter site on the NMDA receptor and increases the effectiveness of other antipsychotic drugs, especially on negative symptoms.

The decision to administer neuroleptic drugs has been complicated by their potentially severe side effects. The most troublesome effect is tardive dyskinesia, which consists of tremors and other involuntary movements. This condition develops gradually and may result from receptor supersensitivity, although the exact mechanism is not understood. Recent advances in research have led to the use of new atypical antipsychotic drugs (such as clozapine), which appear to control schizophrenia without causing tardive dyskinesia. These drugs block dopamine receptors in the prefrontal cortex, especially those of the D_4 subtype, with little effect on D_2 receptors, which are more common in the basal ganglia. Clozapine also blocks serotonin 5-HT_2 receptors and relieves negative, as well as positive, symptoms. Clozapine's major side effect is a decrease in white blood cells, which leaves the patient vulnerable to infections.

KEY TERMS AND CONCEPTS

Module 15.1 Alcoholism
1. Substance abuse: maladaptive pattern of substance use leading to clinically significant impairment or distress
    Alcoholism (alcohol dependence): cannot quit or control the amount consumed
2. Genetics
    Type I (or Type A) alcoholism
        Less dependence on genetics
        Develops gradually
        Men and women about equally affected
        Generally less severe
    Type II (or Type B) alcoholism
        Stronger genetic basis
        Rapid, early onset
        Overwhelmingly men
        More severe
        More associated with criminality
        Low serotonin turnover: strong genetic basis
            History of impulsive and violent behaviors

Alcohol increases impulsiveness
Monozygotic twins: greater concordance for alcoholism than dizygotic twins
Biological children of alcoholics: greater risk of alcoholism
Possible relation to less responsive forms of dopamine type D_2 and D_4 receptors

3. Alcohol metabolism and Antabuse
Ethyl alcohol → acetaldehyde → acetic acid
     Acetaldehyde dehydrogenase
  - Abnormal gene: metabolize acetaldehyde more slowly → illness after alcohol
Antabuse (disulfiram): antagonizes acetaldehyde dehydrogenase → illness after alcohol
     Moderately effective
     Supplement to alcoholic's commitment to quit

4. Risk factors for alcohol abuse
Genetic predisposition
     Sons of alcoholic fathers
          Less than average intoxication after small to moderate amount of alcohol
          More than average relief from tension after alcohol

5. In closing: Alcoholism and addiction
Similarities among addictions
     Not just the pharmacological properties of the substance
     Addiction not in the drug, but in the user

Module 15.2 Mood Disorders
1. Major depressive disorder
Symptoms
     Sad and helpless for weeks
     No energy, feel worthless, contemplate suicide
     Trouble sleeping
     Little pleasure from sex or food
     Cannot imagine being happy again
Incidence
     Twice as common in women as men
     Any time from adolescence to old age, peaks in 25- to 44-year age range
     19% of all people suffer depression at least once
Genetics
     Adopted children: similar to biological parents
     Severe, long-lasting depression before age 30: greater genetic factor
     Genetic factor stronger in women
          Beginning at puberty: more women have depression
          True in all cultures studied
          Not just more women seeking treatment
          Not strongly correlated with hormone levels
     No single gene
Triggering depressed episodes
     Interaction between heredity and environment
          Traumatic experiences
     Episodic
          Postpartum depression

Abnormalities of hemispheric dominance
    Happy mood: increased activity in left prefrontal cortex
    Depression: decreased activity in left and increased in right prefrontal cortex
Viruses
    Borna disease
Antidepressant drugs
    Tricyclics
        Decrease reuptake of catecholamines or serotonin → longer in synapse
        Imipramine (Tofranil)
        Also block histamine and acetylcholine receptors and some sodium channels → side effects
    MAOIs
        Block monoamine oxidase → monoamines broken down more slowly
        Phenelzine (Nardil)
    Selective serotonin reuptake inhibitors (SSRIs)
        Similar to tricyclics, but selective for serotonin
        Fluoxetine (Prozac), sertraline (Zoloft), fluvoxamine (Luvox), citalopram (Celexa) and paroxetine (Paxil or Seroxat)
        Fewer side effects
    Atypical antidepressants
        Bupropion (Wellbutrin)
            Inhibits reuptake of dopamine and, to some extent, norepinephrine
            Does not affect serotonin reuptake
        Venlaxafine
            Inhibits reuptake mostly of serotonin
            Somewhat inhibits reuptake of norepinephrine, slightly that of dopamine
        Nefazodone
            Specifically blocks serotonin type 2A receptors
            Weakly blocks reuptake of serotonin and norepinephrine
    Delayed effects
        Decrease sensitivity of postsynaptic receptors
        Stimulate autoreceptors → decrease release
Implications for the physiology of depression
    Mood: combination of transmitters
    Different people: different transmitter abnormalities
    Problem of time course
        Rapid effect on synapses
        Effects on behavior: two to three weeks
            Contrast: methylphenidate (Ritalin) for attention deficit disorder
                Effects on synapses and behavior: peak at 60 minutes
    Brain-derived neurotrophic factor
        Increased with repeated use of antidepressants
        Parts of hippocampus and cerebral cortex
            Decrease in size during depression
Other therapies
    Psychotherapy
    Placebo effect
    St. John's wort
        Psychotherapy
            Side effects: gastrointestinal distress, sedation, painful sensitivity to light

Electroconvulsive therapy (ECT)
    Used for patients who do not respond to drug therapy or who are suicidal
    Works faster than drugs
    Administered every other day for two weeks
    Used with muscle relaxants or anesthetics
    Side effect: memory loss; minimized with shock to right hemisphere only
    Half are depressed again within six months
    Increases D_1 and D_2 receptors in nucleus accumbens
    Decreases postsynaptic norepinephrine receptors
    Variety of other effects
    Repetitive transcranial magnetic stimulation
Altered sleep patterns
    Depresssed: REM within 45 minutes, not 80 minutes
    Therapy: earlier bedtime, effective for months

2. Bipolar disorder
Definitions
    Unipolar disorder: one extreme – vary between normal and depression
    Bipolar disorder: manic-depressive disorder
        Mania: restlessness, excitement, laughter, self-confidence, rambling speech, loss of inhibitions
Cycle length: days to a year
Glucose metabolism: higher than normal in mania, lower than normal in depression
Larger than normal amygdala
Genetics
    Greater similarity in monozygotic than dizygotic twins and in biological than adoptive relatives
    Apparent linkage to genes on several chromosomes
Treatments
    Lithium salts
        May have toxic side effects
        Complex effects on second messenger systems
        May stabilize fluctuating systems
    Anticonvulsant drugs
        Valproic acid (Depakene, Depakote)
        Block certain second messenger systems
        High levels of omega-3 fatty acids
        Also block those second messenger systems, help some bipolar patients

3. Accidental discoveries of psychiatric drugs
Disulfiram (Antabuse): helps people avoid alcohol
    Originally used in manufacture of rubber
Iproniazid: antidepressant
    Originally used as rocket fuel, then to treat tuberculosis
Bromides: treatment for epilepsy
    Originally thought to reduce sexual drive
Today: synthesize chemicals similar to other drugs; evaluate in test tubes or tissue samples

4. Seasonal affective disorder (SAD)
Common where nights are long in winter

SAD: phase-delayed sleep and temperature rhythms, unlike other depressed people, who are
   phase-advanced
Bright lights, especially in morning
   May affect serotonin synapses
   May affect circadian rhythms

5. In closing: The biology of mood swings
Brain structure and chemistry: alter reactions to events
Experience alters brain

Module 15.3 Schizophrenia
1. Characteristics
Deteriorating function in everyday life; some combination of hallucinations, delusions, thought
   disorder, movement disorder, and inappropriate emotional expressions
   Dementia praecox
   Not multiple personality
Behavioral symptoms
   Negative symptoms: behaviors that are absent, but should be present
      Deficits in social interaction, emotional expression, speech, and working memory
      More stable, less responsive to treatment
   Positive symptoms: behaviors that are present, but should be absent
      Sporadic occurrence
      Psychotic cluster: delusions and hallucinations
         Increased activity in thalamus, hippocampus, basal ganglia, and prefrontal cortex
      Disorganized cluster: inappropriate emotions, bizarre behaviors and thought disorder
         Difficulty with abstract concepts
   Main problem: disordered thinking
      Abnormal connections between cortex and thalamus and cerebellum
   Acute onset: greater probability of recovery than with chronic onset
Demographic data
   Approximately 1.3 percent of US population: schizophrenia at some time
   Additional 1 percent of population: schizoid condition
      Gradual decline in prevalence
   Reported 10-100 times more often in United States and Europe than in Third World
      More common in crowded cities
         More crowded cities in developed world
      Expressed emotion by care-givers: hostile expressions → aggravation of condition
         More traditional cultures: large extended family; more patience
   Diagnosed at earlier age in men than women, though lifetime prevalence is similar
      Protective effect of estrogen?
   Childhood-onset: much less common
      Identifiable genetic abnormalities
      Gradually increasing and more severe brain damage

2. Genetics
Twin studies
   Greater concordance for monozygotic (50%) than dizygotic (15-20%) twins
      Heredity not the only factor
      Greater similarity of prenatal environment (monozygotic twins: single placenta)
      Dizygotic twins: same genetic resemblance as siblings, but higher concordance

Greater environmental similarity
Adopted children who develop schizophrenia
Greater concordance with biological than adoptive parents
Potentially more decisive evidence: paternal half-siblings
Different mothers: no shared prenatal environment
Higher concordance than for general population
Probably parents had similar smoking, drinking, and other health habits
Children of people with schizophrenia and their twins
- Children of twin without schizophrenia: first reported to have similar risk as children of twin with schizophrenia
Further analysis: twin without schizophrenia: less likely to pass it to children, more likely to have children
No statistically significant difference: small sample size
Efforts to locate a gene: no strong links
Possible problems
Inaccurate diagnoses
Complex combinations of genes
Schizophrenia: not a single-gene disorder

3. The neurodevelopmental hypothesis
Argument for:
Several early brain abnormalities linked to later schizophrenia
People with schizophrenia: numerous small brain abnormalities originating early in life
Plausible that early brain abnormalities → adult behavioral abnormalities
Prenatal and neonatal abnormalities of development
Poor nutrition, premature birth, low birth weight, delivery complications
Rh-positive child of Rh-negative mother: immunological rejection
Several problems, including schizophrenia: worse in later-born children; worse in boys than girls
Season of birth effect
Winter births: higher risk
Only in non-tropical climates
Especially strong effect: people with schizophrenia but no schizophrenic relatives; those born in large cities
Viral epidemics
Influenza in fall → later schizophrenia in babies born in winter
Fever in mother slows cell division
Inconsistent results: poor records of influenza cases
Mild brain abnormalities
Smaller prefrontal cortex, temporal cortex, hippocampus, amygdala
Enlarged ventricles
Most abnormal in those with greatest behavioral deficits and earliest symptoms
Lateralization
Larger right hemisphere
Lower activity in left hemisphere
More likely left-handed
Memory and attention deficits
Similar to those with temporal or prefrontal cortex damage
Most consistent deficits in areas that mature slowly: dorsolateral prefrontal cortex
Fewer synapses in prefrontal cortex

305

        Poor working memory
     Microscopic level
        Smaller cell bodies, especially in hippocampus and prefrontal cortex
        Disorderly cell arrangement
        Abnormal amounts of cell recognition molecules
     Brain damage not progressive
        IQ and brain measurements: similar in older and younger patients
        No glial cell proliferation
   Early development and later psychopathology
     Prefrontal cortex: slow maturing
     Neurodevelopmental hypothesis: plausible, not firmly established

4.   Neurotransmitters and drugs
   The dopamine hypothesis: excess activity at certain dopamine synapses
     Antispychotic (neuroleptic) drugs: block postsynaptic dopamine receptors
        Phenothiazines
            Chlorpromazine (Thorazine)
        Butyrophenones
            Haloperidol (Haldol)
     Drugs that can provoke schizophrenic symptoms
        Substance-induced psychotic disorder
            Hallucinations (usually visual) and delusions
        Amphetamine, methamphetamine, cocaine: increase activity at dopamine synapses
            LSD: effects at serotonin synapses; increases activity at dopamine synapses
     Additional support for the dopamine hypothesis
        Stress: exacerbates schizophrenia
            Increases dopamine release in prefrontal cortex
            Stress-induced impairments: relieved by dopamine-blocking drugs
            Substance-induced psychotic disorder
     Problems with the dopamine hypothesis
        Time course of drugs
            Affect synapses quickly
            Effects on behavior: build up over 2 to 3 weeks
        Approximately normal levels of dopamine and its metabolites
        Dopamine receptors
            Low D_1 receptor density
            High D_3 and D_4 receptor density
            Normal D_2 receptor density
            No apparent relationship between schizophrenia and genes for dopamine receptors
  The glutamate hypothesis
     Deficient activity at certain glutamate synapses, especially in prefrontal cortex
     Relationships between dopamine and glutamate: opposing effects
        Dopamine inhibits glutamate release
        Glutamate excites neurons that inhibit dopamine release
        Glutamate excites neurons that dopamine inhibits
     The effects of phencyclidine (PCP, "angel dust")
        Inhibits NMDA glutamate receptors
        Positive and negative symptoms similar to schizophrenia
        Impairs prefrontal cortex function, including dopamine synapses
        PCP and ketamine → little psychotic effect in preadolescents

PCP → long-lasting relapse in people recovered from schizophrenia

      LSD, amphetamine, and cocaine → only temporary symptoms

         No worse in those recovered from schizophrenia

Measurements of glutamate

    Lower than normal glutamate release in prefrontal cortex and hippocampus

    Deficient expression of genes for glutamate receptors in temporal lobe, hippocampus, and prefrontal cortex

    Deficiency correlates with deterioration of memory and reasoning

Drugs that enhance glutamate activity

    Too much glutamate → toxic effects

    LY 354740: selectively stimulates one type of metabotropic glutamate receptor

        Blocks behavioral effects of PCP in rats

        Prevents PCP's disruption of prefrontal cortex activity

    Glycine: co-transmitter at NMDA glutamate receptors

        Increases effectiveness of glutamate

        Increases effectiveness of antipsychotic drugs, especially for negative symptoms

The search for improved drugs

    Antipsychotic drugs: decrease mesolimbocortical activity → beneficial effects

    Decrease activity of dopamine neurons that control movement → undesired effects

        Tardive dyskinesia: tremors and other involuntary movements

            May result from denervation supersensitivity

            May last for years after quitting drug

    Atypical antipsychotics

        Clozapine

            Blocks dopamine activity in prefrontal cortex, especially at D_4 receptors

            Little effect on D_2 receptors, more abundant in basal ganglia

            Also blocks serotonin $5\text{-}HT_2$ receptors

            Effective on negative, as well as positive, symptoms

            Side effect: decrease white blood cells

In closing: The fascination of schizophrenia

    Search for pattern among many clues and false leads

Differential diagnosis of psychological disorders

    Identification of a condition as distinct from similar conditions

    Conditions that may be similar to schizophrenia

        Mood disorder with psychotic features

        Prolonged substance abuse: amphetamine, methamphetamine, cocaine, LSD, phencyclidine, marijuana

        Brain damage: lesions of temporal or prefrontal cortex

        Undetected hearing deficits

Methods 15.1: The Wisconsin Card Sorting Task

    Sort cards by one rule, and then switch to another

Chapter closing: The biology of psychological disorders

    Interaction of biological dispositions and life events

Module 15.1 Alcoholism
1. *Genetics*
    a. List the differences between Type I and Type II alcoholism.

    b. Turnover of what neurotransmitter has been linked to Type II alcoholism? What other behavioral characteristic is associated with low turnover of that neurotransmitter?

    c. Describe the evidence for a genetic risk factor for alcoholism. How strong is that evidence?

2. *Alcohol metabolism and Antabuse*
    a. Describe the metabolism of alcohol.

    b. What is the biochemical effect of Antabuse? What is its physiological effect when combined with alcohol use?

c   How may Antabuse work, in addition to its physiological effect?

3. *Risk factors for alcohol abuse*
    a.   What are two characteristics of sons of alcoholics that may predispose them to alcoholism?

Module 15. 2 Mood Disorders
1. Major depressive disorder
    a.   List the symptoms of major depression.

    b.   What is the evidence for a genetic predisposition for depression?

    c.   Are men or women more vulnerable to depression? What factors can be ruled out as significant causes of that excess vulnerability?

    d.   What seems to be the role of traumatic experiences in the onset of episodes of depression?

e. What patterns of hemispheric dominance have been associated with happy moods in normal people? With depression?

f. What is Borna disease? What evidence links it to depression?

g. Name three groups of antidepressant drugs and explain how each exerts its effects.

h. Why is fluoxetine (Prozac) preferred over the tricyclics and the monoamine oxidase inhibitors?

i. What are atypical antidepressants? For whom are they used?

j. What is a major delayed effect of most antidepressants?

k. What is an autoreceptor? What is an effect of antidepressants on autoreceptors?

l. Explain the problem of the time course of drugs' effects on neurotransmitters and their effects on depressive symptoms.

m. What neurotrophin is produced as a result of repeated use of antidepressants? In which brain areas is it produced?

n. What is a placebo effect?

o. How is electroconvulsive therapy (ECT) applied today? How is this an improvement over practices in the 1950s?

p. For which two groups of patients is ECT most often used?

q. What are the advantages and disadvantages of ECT?

r. What newer treatment is similar to ECT?

s. How does the onset of REM sleep differ in depressed people, compared to nondepressed individuals? How may this be related to body temperature cycles?

t. What change in sleeping schedules has been found to alleviate depression? How long do the benefits last?

2. *Bipolar disorder*
   a. What is the difference between unipolar and bipolar disorder? What is another term for bipolar disorder?

   b. Describe the symptoms of mania.

c. Describe the pattern of glucose use in the two extreme conditions of bipolar disorder. What additional brain abnormality has been reported?

d. What can we say about genetic factors in bipolar disorder?

e. What is the most effective therapy for bipolar disorder? What can we say about its mode of action?

f. What other type of drug is used to treat bipolar disorder? What is one possible mechanism by which these drugs achieve their effects?

3. *Seasonal affective disorder*
   a. What is seasonal affective disorder (SAD)? How is it treated?

b. How are the sleep and temperature rhythms of SAD patients different from those of other depressed patients?

Module 15.3 Schizophrenia
1. *Characteristics*
    a. What is the origin of the term schizophrenia?

    b. What are the negative symptoms of schizophrenia? How stable are they?

    c. What are the two clusters of positive symptoms of schizophrenia? How stable are they?

    d. What is the overall incidence of schizophrenia? Of schizoid disorder? Does this incidence vary among ethnic groups, sexes, or economic levels?

e. How does the prevalence of schizophrenia today compare with that of the mid-1900s? Give two reasons why Third World countries might have a lower incidence of schizophrenia than do the developed countries.

2. *Genetics*
    a. What evidence from twin studies suggests a genetic basis for schizophrenia? What are concordance rates?

    b. What other factor may explain the greater concordance for monozygotic over dizygotic twins and for dizygotic twins over non-twin siblings?

    c. What evidence from adoption studies suggests a genetic basis for schizophrenia?

    d. What advantage is there to studying paternal half-siblings? What other factor might account for the higher concordance among paternal half-siblings, compared to the general population?

e. What conclusions can be drawn from studies of children of monozygotic twins that had or did not have schizophrenia?

f. What can we conclude about the role of genetics in schizophrenia?

3. *The neurodevelopmental hypothesis*
    a. What three lines of evidence suggest that schizophrenia may result from abnormalities in the early development of the brain?

    b. What specific prenatal and neonatal conditions have been associated with increased risk for schizophrenia?

    c. In which season of birth is there a slightly greater likelihood of developing schizophrenia? What factor may account for this effect?

d. What are some of the brain abnormalities that have been linked with schizophrenia?

e. Which brain areas have been strongly implicated? What are some psychological functions of those areas? Do schizophrenics show impairment of those functions?

f. Why do researchers believe that these abnormalities resulted from developmental effects, rather than gradual brain damage in adulthood?

g. How might one explain the late onset of schizophrenic symptoms, if the brain damage occurred during early development?

4. *Neurotransmitters and drugs*
   a. What is the dopamine hypothesis of schizophrenia? What are the main lines of evidence favoring it?

b.   What are two chemical families of antipsychotic (neuroleptic) drugs that have been in wide use for many years? What is their major effect on receptors?

c.   Which drugs can induce a state similar to schizophrenia? What are the similarities and differences between drug-induced psychosis and schizophrenia?

d.   How does stress affect schizophrenia? What are the implications for the dopamine hypothesis?

e.   What are two problems with the dopamine hypothesis?

f.   What other neurotransmitter has been hypothesized to be abnormal in schizophrenia? What are three types of interactions between these two neurotransmitters?

g. Why may blockade of dopamine receptors have beneficial effects, if the original problem is deficient glutamate?

h. What is phencyclidine? What are its effects on receptors? What are its psychological effects?

i. What kinds of evidence suggest an abnormality in glutamate release or receptors?

j. Why would it be unwise to administer glutamate to schizophrenic people? What kind of drug has been found to block the behavioral effects of PCP in rats?

k. What is glycine? How does it affect NMDA receptors? What were the clinical findings concerning glycine or a similar drug?

l. On which dopamine system are antipsychotic drugs are thought to exert their beneficial effects? Effects on which system may underlie the unpleasant motor side effects?

m. What is tardive dyskinesia? How rapid is its onset? What drug effect may account for it?

n. What is one atypical antipsychotic drug? What are its effects on receptors? What brain area is most affected?

o. What are two advantages of atypical antipsychotic drugs? Why are they less likely to produce tardive dyskinesia?

POSTTEST

Multiple-Choice Questions

1. Type II alcoholism
   a. has a stronger genetic basis than does Type I.
   b. develops gradually over the years.
   c. affects men and women about equally.
   d. all of the above.

2. Low serotonin turnover is associated with
   a. Type II alcoholism.
   b. impulsivity.
   c. a strong genetic basis.
   d. all of the above.

3. Acetaldehyde dehydrogenase
    a.   is the generic name for Antabuse.
    b.   controls the rate of conversion of acetic acid, a toxic product of alcohol metabolism, into acetaldehyde, a source of energy.
    c.   controls the rate of conversion of acetaldehyde, a toxic product of alcohol metabolism, into acetic acid, a source of energy.
    d.   if present in high levels, would make us feel very ill after drinking alcohol.

4. Which of the following is true?
    a.   Antabuse is effective primarily because it makes people sick when they drink alcohol.
    b.   Antabuse primarily acts as a supplement to the alcoholic's commitment to stop drinking.
    c.   Sons of alcoholics show greater than average intoxication after drinking a small to moderate amount of alcohol.
    d.   Sons of alcoholics experience less than average relief from tension after drinking alcohol; therefore, they have to drink more for the same effect.

5. Which of the following is **not** a common symptom of major depression?
    a.   excessive sleeping
    b.   sadness and helplessness
    c.   lack of energy
    d.   little pleasure from sex or food

6. Which of the following is true of depression?
    a.   A gene on chromosome 11 is now known to be the cause of most cases of depression.
    b.   Hormonal changes before menstruation or after childbirth can cause depression, even in women without a biological predisposition to that disorder.
    c.   Since no specific genetic abnormality has been discovered, it is now commonly agreed that depression does not have any genetic basis.
    d.   It is likely that several genes increase the risk for some sort of disorder, including depression, alcoholism, and anxiety disorder.

7. Depression is frequently associated with
    a.   increased activity in the left prefrontal cortex.
    b.   decreased activity in the left prefrontal cortex.
    c.   increased activity in the right temporal cortex.
    d.   decreased activity in the right temporal cortex.

8. Research on Borna disease suggests that
    a.   a virus causes an autoimmune attack on the brain.
    b.   any illness that causes a fever also causes major depression.
    c.   a virus may be one cause of depression.
    d.   the viruses that infect animals cannot infect humans.

9. Which of the following is **not** a type of antidepressant drug?
    a.   monoamine oxidase inhibitors
    b.   tricyclics
    c.   serotonin reuptake inhibitors
    d.   dopamine receptor blockers

10. Which of the following is true?
    a. The effects of drugs on transmitter systems are immediate, but their effects on depression are delayed for one to two weeks.
    b. The effects of drugs on transmitter systems are delayed for one to two weeks, but their effects on depression are immediate.
    c. Depression results from having too little of all the monoamine transmitters.
    d. The major effect of fluoxetine is to block serotonin receptors.

11. Repeated use of antidepressant drugs
    a. results in decreased sensivity of postsynaptic receptors.
    b. stimulates autoreceptors and thereby decreases further release.
    c. increases production and release of brain-derived neurotrophic factor in parts of the hippocampus and cerebral cortex.
    d. all of the above.

12. Electroconvulsive therapy
    a. is effective because it confuses patients, and they forget their depressing thoughts for several years.
    b. is rarely used anymore because of its bad reputation.
    c. is usually used on patients who do not respond to antidepressant drugs or who are suicidal.
    d. must be administered to the left hemisphere, which produces severe loss of language ability.

13. Depressed people
    a. enter REM sleep more slowly than do normal people.
    b. are sometimes helped by an earlier bedtime, in phase with their declining body temperature.
    c. have their symptoms worsened by exposure to transcranial magnetic stimulation.
    d. all of the above.

14. Bipolar disorder
    a. is characterized by cycles between depression and normal moods.
    b. is characterized by cycles between depression and mania.
    c. is much more common than unipolar depression.
    d. is characterized by higher glucose metabolism in the brain during depression, and lower activity during mania.

15. Lithium
    a. has complex effects on several second messenger systems, which may somehow stabilize fluctuating brain activity.
    b. is extremely safe because it is so simple.
    c. is helpful for depression but not for mania.
    d. all of the above.

16. People with seasonal affective disorder (SAD)
    a. become more depressed during winter because of the cold.
    b. are frequently helped by sitting in hot sauna baths for an hour or more each day.
    c. show phase-advanced sleep and temperature rhythms, similar to other depressed people.
    d. are frequently helped by exposure to bright lights for an hour or more each day.

17. Schizophrenia
   a. refers to multiple personalities.
   b. refers to a split between the emotions and the intellect.
   c. is caused primarily by stress.
   d. is typically first diagnosed in the elderly.

18. Which of the following is true of the positive symptoms of schizophrenia?
   a. They consist primarily of visual hallucinations.
   b. They include deficits in social interactions, emotional expression, and speech.
   c. They include two clusters: a psychotic cluster, consisting of delusions and hallucinations, and a disorganized cluster, consisting of inappropriate emotions, bizarre behaviors, and thought disorder.
   d. They are more stable over time than are the negative symptoms.

19. The prevalence of schizophrenia
   a. is declining, for unknown reasons.
   b. is higher in Third World countries because of increased stress there.
   c. is higher in women than in men.
   d. is fairly easy to study, since schizophrenia is one of the easiest disorders to diagnose.

20 Which of the following appears to support a genetic basis for schizophrenia?
   a. The season-of-birth effect is greater in families in which there is at least one schizophrenic relative.
   b. The concordance rate for schizophrenia is greater for dizygotic than for monozygotic twins.
   c. It is now very clear that when one monozygotic twin has schizophrenia and the other doesn't, the children of the nonschizophrenic twin are hardly ever schizophrenic.
   d. Paternal half-siblings of schizophrenics are more frequently schizophrenic than would be predicted from the overall population frequency.

21. A problem with the evidence for a genetic basis for schizophrenia is that
   a. common prenatal factors may at least partially explain the greater concordance rate of monozygotic over dizygotic twins, and of dizygotic twins over non-twin siblings.
   b. common prenatal factors, such as smoking, drinking, and other poor health habits may at least partially explain the paternal half-sibling effect.
   c. the data from children of monozygotic twins, one of whom does and the other does not have schizophrenia, are based on a small sample size and tend to show a lower incidence of schizophrenia in children of the nonschizophrenic twin.
   d. all of the above.

22. Research on possible causes of schizophrenia has demonstrated that
   a. a prenatal viral infection may cause fever, which results in impaired brain development.
   b. several studies have converged on a single gene as the primary cause of schizophrenia.
   c. conflicting messages from parents are a major cause of schizophrenia.
   d. the season-of-birth effect occurs more often in the tropics, where diseases are harder to control.

23. Studies of the brains of schizophrenics have revealed that
    a. they have shrunken ventricles.
    b. their prefrontal and temporal cortex, hippocampus, and amygdala are smaller, especially in the left hemisphere.
    c. they have more abnormalities in rapidly maturing areas than in slowly maturing areas such as dorsolateral prefrontal cortex.
    d. they have a large proliferation of glia cells, indicating that much of the damage was caused gradually during adulthood.

24. Drug-induced psychosis
    a. is usually permanent and causes a full-blown state of schizophrenia, complete with auditory hallucinations.
    b. is caused by drugs that block dopamine receptors.
    c. is caused by drugs that increase the stimulation of dopamine receptors.
    d. is caused by drugs that stimulate glutamate receptors, especially in young children.

25. Which of the following is not an effective neuroleptic drug?
    a. haloperidol
    b. chlorpromazine
    c. amphetamine
    d. clozapine

26. According to the dopamine hypothesis of schizophrenia, people with schizophrenia have
    a. excessive activity at dopamine synapses.
    b. deficient activity at dopamine synapses.
    c. glutamate in neurons that should release dopamine.
    d. too little dopamine activity in the mesolimbocortical system and too much in the basal ganglia.

27. A problem with the dopamine hypothesis is that
    a. neuroleptic drugs improve schizophrenic symptoms before they have a significant effect on dopamine synapses.
    b. people with schizophrenia usually have approximately normal levels of dopamine and its metabolites.
    c. densities of all types of dopamine receptors are higher in people with schizophrenia, whereas they would be expected to be lower.
    d. amphetamine, cocaine, methamphetamine, and LSD increase activity at dopamine receptors, but are among the best treatments for schizophrenia, suggesting that excess dopamine activity cannot be a cause of that disorder.

28. Which of the following is true?
    a. PCP is an atypical neuroleptic drug that treats schizophrenia by stimulating glutamate receptors.
    b. Since there is too much glutamate in the brains of schizophrenic people, a good way to improve their symptoms is to block glutamate receptors.
    c. Glycine interferes with the binding of glutamate to NMDA receptors, thereby worsening schizophrenic symptoms.
    d. In many brain areas, dopamine inhibits glutamate release, or glutamate stimulates neurons that inhibit dopamine release, or glutamate excites neurons that dopamine inhibits.

29. Tardive dyskinesia
    a. recedes completely once all traces of antipsychotic drugs have left the body.
    b. usually occurs soon after beginning antipsychotic drug treatment.
    c. may result from denervation supersensitivity of dopamine receptors in the basal ganglia.
    d. develops because of decreased numbers of dopamine receptors in the basal ganglia.

30. Atypical antipsychotic drugs
    a. include haloperidol and chlorpromazine.
    b. decrease dopamine activity primarily in the mesolimbocortical system.
    c. decrease dopamine activity primarily in the basal ganglia.
    d. should be avoided because they produce more tardive dyskinesia than do typical neuroleptics.

31. Clozapine
    a. blocks dopamine D_4 receptors more than D_2.
    b. also blocks serotonin 5-HT_2 receptors.
    c. has undesirable side effects, including a decrease in white blood cells.
    d. all of the above

Answers to Multiple-Choice Questions

1. a	6. d	11. d	16. d	21. d	26. a
2. d	7. b	12. c	17. b	22. a	27. b
3. c	8. c	13. b	18. c	23. b	28. d
4. b	9. d	14. b	19. a	24. c	29. c
5. a	10. a	15. a	20. d	25. c	30. b
					31. d

Moods and Psychoses

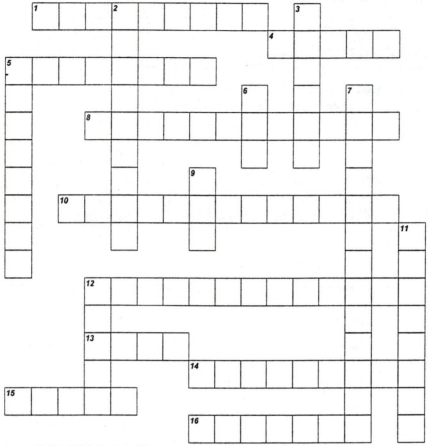

Constructed by Elaine M. Hull using Crossword Weaver

ACROSS

1 Transmitter that may be deficient in schizophrenia

4 A possible cause of schizophrenia

5 Neurotransmitter whose receptors are blocked by antipsychotic drugs

8 Prefrontal cortex area that matures slowly and has deficits in schizophrenia

10 Positive symptom of schizophrenia

12 Type of visual system neuron projecting mostly to right hemisphere and promoting perception of visual motion

13 Drug that inhibits reuptake of serotonin and is used to treat depression (abbr.)

14 Drug that inhibits reuptake of monoamine transmitters and is used to treat depression

15 Man who discovered brain area that promotes fluent speech and use of connectives

16 Disorder in which moods vary between mania and depression

DOWN

2 Planum _____: Cortical area larger in left hemisphere than right

3 Season when schizophrenics are somewhat more likely to be born

5 Reading disorder in otherwise normal people

6 Disorder most common in regions where nights are long in winter (abbr.)

7 Type of visual system neuron projecting mostly to left hemisphere and promoting language

9 Treatment for depression that works more quickly than drugs (abbr.)

11 Man who disocvered brain area that promotes naming and understanding speech

12 Ability that right hemisphere specializes in

326

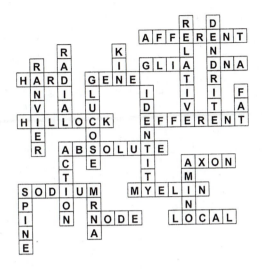

Genes, Neurons and Behavior

Synapses, Drugs, and Hormones

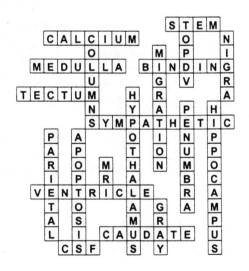

Brain Parts and Development

Sensational Senses

Doing and Dreaming

Heat, Sex, and Gluttony

Emotions and Memories

Moods and Psychoses

328